ARTIFICIAL INTELLIGENCE AND LAW IN THE COMMUNICATION PROFESSIONS

This book analyzes the current attempts to regulate artificial intelligence (AI) and its impact on the communication field.

Examining existing and proposed laws, policies, and regulations of AI in the U.S. and the European Union, this book analyzes how the technological development of AI will be governed in the next decade and how this will impact the communication industry. Chapters explore the influence of laws on key communication issues including free speech, disinformation, intellectual property, privacy, and discrimination, as well as the AI industry's approach to self-regulation. It shows how communication professionals such as public relations practitioners, advertisers, and journalists will be affected by generative AI content production and how communication will ultimately be shaped by the regulations and laws placed on AI.

Providing readers with a working knowledge of the contemporary legal issues surrounding AI and communication, this book will be of interest to scholars and students in the fields of Media and Communication Law, Public Relations, Advertising, and Journalism.

Cayce Myers is a Professor and Director of Graduate Studies in the School of Communication at Virginia Tech, USA, where he teaches Public Relations and Communication Law. He is also the author of *Public Relations History: Theory, Practice and Profession* (Routledge, 2020).

ARTIFICIAL INTELLIGENCE AND LAW IN THE COMMUNICATION PROFESSIONS

Cayce Myers

Routledge
Taylor & Francis Group
NEW YORK AND LONDON

Designed cover image: Getty Images

First published 2025
by Routledge
605 Third Avenue, New York, NY 10158

and by Routledge
4 Park Square, Milton Park, Abingdon, Oxon, OX14 4RN

Routledge is an imprint of the Taylor & Francis Group, an informa business

ISBN: 978-1-032-73078-3 (hbk)
ISBN: 978-1-032-73073-8 (pbk)
ISBN: 978-1-003-42656-1 (ebk)

DOI: 10.4324/9781003426561

Typeset in Sabon
by KnowledgeWorks Global Ltd.

For my wife, Anne Carroll Myers

CONTENTS

INTRODUCTION

For the past decade, the communication industry has been deeply affected by laws and ethics that regulate technology, data, and media. With the growth of digital media and the changes in media consumption, new issues have emerged. Since the mid-2010s, there has been an increasing awareness of the problems associated with this new media landscape with particular attention being paid to mis- and disinformation. The impact on democracy and the erosion of trust within legacy media have created a new social reality. However, in November 2022, these changes in society were amplified by the launch of ChatGPT. The platform exploded overnight with people being unable to access the system because it could not handle demand. It created a new shift in technology and accelerated the issues that were already percolating within society. Soon the rise of artificial intelligence (AI) became a dominant discussion, especially within the communication field. Communicators of all sectors began asking questions about what AI was and how it could be used. There were fears of displacement and also hope for better quality work. As with any new technology, there were skeptics and early adaptors, and more questions than answers.

When writing this book, I remembered the first time I ever heard of the field of AI. It was during graduate school orientation in the early 2000s when one master's student said he studied AI. I remember a professor saying that the program in AI studies interesting things that one day may change the world. That has turned out to be truer than we ever imagined some 20 years ago. In early 2023, I began working on what would become this book. Recognizing that the advertising and public relations industry would be heavily impacted by AI, I wanted to learn more about the technology and its regulations. As a scholar of media law, particularly those laws and regulations that impact public relations, I knew that AI was a legal and ethical game-changer. First, in a truly global practice, I knew that AI posed unique issues around privacy, especially within the jurisdiction of the European Union (E.U.) where privacy laws were robust. Second, I knew that public relations (PR) practitioners and advertising professionals were going to face new opportunities and challenges within content creation. Intellectual property (IP) laws were not designed with an artificial creator in mind, so there would be gaps in the way IP law addressed AI creation. For over a decade, I researched the regulation of social media. Those regulations evolved from focusing on consumer confidence shifting to privacy protections and then shifting again to disinformation. AI presented a new research opportunity and was one that had real application for the industry. So, I set out to learn more about it through executive education and following the development of laws and policies governing this new technology.

As 2023 progressed, I started to give a series of lectures on AI to PR professionals, healthcare communicators, civic organizations, communication associations, and business groups about how AI was evolving and how that evolution required new regulations and guidelines. These invitations continued through the year, and I noticed a trend that people were both fearful and hopeful of AI. Most had no background knowledge of the technology, and only a few used it on a regular basis. However, all of them thought that it was a game-changer for work and that the impact once the power of AI was unleashed would be transformative. There were, of course, fears that AI would displace workers, but there was also the belief that it could help people do their work better. Small businesses and departments within companies thought that AI could help them make-up for the fact they couldn't afford to hire extra help. AI would be their able assistant and help them compete on equal footing with better-financed competitors.

One thing stood out, however. Many people thought that AI regulations would set the boundaries of how the technology would be used. From my research on law and policy of media, I knew that a uniform legal answer to all AI problems was highly unlikely. I also knew that as a global phenomenon, there would be a conflict over the standards of AI regulation. This would only be exacerbated by the fact that there was a large geopolitical dimension to AI. The AI race between the U.S. and China as well as the economic soft power of the E.U. would make it difficult for uniform global standards to exist. As an attorney, I also thought that U.S. law likely would try to force novel AI questions into preexisting paradigms of understanding. How this would take place was something I set out to understand more fully and was the genesis of this book.

While writing this book, I have continued to speak about AI to professional and academic groups and to the media. I have watched with great interest the novel legal questions this new technology presents and have seen a shift within the professional communications industry where professionals are embracing AI platforms. I would describe the current adoption of AI to be still in its early phases, but it is no longer a novelty. Being pro-AI myself I think that the power of this technology can be harnessed for a lot of good, and I encourage my students and professionals I meet to use it and learn its power and limits. My hope for this book is that it explains some of the contours of the technology and how attempts to regulate it may redefine out own concepts of justice, ethics, liability, privacy, and property.

When writing this book, I made a decision to focus on the AI laws and regulations of the U.S. and E.U. because of their global dominance in the marketplace. I also wanted to address issues that represent the contemporary issues facing the industry. That is why the following chapters have topics such as discrimination, liability, and decision-making along with traditional legal categories such as intellectual property. Because mis- and disinformation have become such a major topic within the field of communication and given AI's power to facilitate it through deepfakes, I decided to include a chapter addressing those concerns as well. However, I wanted the book to be more than a list of laws related to AI. I wanted to get to the bigger issue of how to use the technology and how industry self-regulation presented some solutions. I had been part of a group within the Public Relations Society of America (PRSA) called Board of Ethics and Professional Standards that wrote an ethical AI guidance entitled *Promises and Pitfalls: The Ethical Use of AI for Public Relations Practitioners*.[1] That co-authored industry guidance focused on the nuanced ethical issues of the technology and raised some questions professionals should ask themselves when employing it. Because of that experience, I included ethics as part of this book as a means to demonstrate that some of the biggest decisions about AI will not be made by lawmakers but by the communication professionals who decide to use the tool.

Of course, this is a big topic, and this book is meant to be a primer on the current legal and ethical issues of AI within the context of the U.S. and E.U. As the technology evolves, new issues will emerge. New laws will also be written, and novel ethical scenarios will emerge. Most of the writing of this book occurred during 2024 during the administration of President Joseph Biden. Revisions to the book were made during the first months of the administration of President Donald J. Trump. Both presidents present the tension between regulation and market forces that both control and encourage AI development and growth. My hope for this book is that it provides an overview of the legal and ethical landscape of the current status of AI. There are other books that will be written, and these laws certainly will be updated. Perhaps this book can contribute in addressing some of the more novel questions that may emerge and even generate new questions for lawmakers and industry to answer. As with any law book, this one is not meant as advice but as a learning tool for professionals, lawyers, media scholars, students, and AI users. Each chapter concludes with some discussion questions for those who may use this book in a class or just in their own reflection of the reading. There are no right answers to most of these questions. They're a jumping off point to larger discussions and may generate a few questions of their own. If a reader does have a specific AI question, ask an attorney in your jurisdiction. As this book shows, AI laws are developing at a fast pace at the national and local levels. Knowing the specific rules in your jurisdiction is essential in this shifting legal landscape.

Because understanding AI law and ethics necessitates a foundational technological comprehension of AI, Chapter 1 delves into this subject. It provides an overview of the way AI works and some of the technical issues that create legal challenges around concepts like transparency and disclosure. It also provides a history of the development of AI, which shows that the technology has long been anticipated but has ebbed and flowed through the decades since the 1950s. Chapter 2 transitions into the important, yet esoteric, topic of humanness and AI. What does it mean to be "artificial" intelligence and how is that decision-making different than that of a person? This chapter discusses bias and learned experience as well as the larger goals that lawmakers have concerning this technology. Chapter 3 builds on this examining how mis- and disinformation are facilitated by AI. Exploring the role of deepfakes and voice clones the chapter looks at AI's responsibility within the marketplace of ideas and how its speed and power can facilitate the erosion of trust in institutions, news, and democracy.

Chapter 4 examines the concept of intellectual property as it relates to AI creation. Specific attention is paid to the use of AI in the development of copyright and patents, and the potential AI has to create unintentional infringement. It also discusses the larger concept of ownership and how AI potentially can produce content that no one owns and, ironically, reproduce content that someone already owns. Chapter 5 examines how AI makes decisions and how the fear around AI decision-making has prompted responses to discrimination. Specific attention is paid to employment laws and the technology behind AI decision-making that can both prevent and facilitate bias and discrimination. Chapter 6 looks at the broader issue of AI responsibility. Who ultimately bears the obligation of being held accountable for an unjust AI decision or output? How does AI provide a challenge for contemporary understandings of negligence? Is AI a product or a service? These questions get to a larger regulatory issue of how AI serves (or doesn't serve) human needs and how the human oversight of AI may not be enough.

Chapter 7 explores the issue of privacy particularly in context with data. Because the concept of privacy rights is so different between the U.S.

and E.U., the chapter explores the historical underpinnings of these jurisdictions' legal traditions and shows how AI privacy regulation presents a conflict of legal philosophies. Chapter 8 shifts from the discussion of law to industry self-regulation and ethics. Because the law of AI is developing, the role of ethical guidelines seems to be more important than ever. The chapter discusses the current philosophies of AI companies and also how industry norms are developing to provide rules for AI adoption, implementation, and accountability.

Chapter 9 concludes with a discussion of the future of AI. Thinking of the future of AI is difficult because AI presents such a futuristic reality in its current form. However, there will be a point where there is a post-AI world, and thinking about the issues that will emerge in the 2020s, 2030s, and beyond is important. The present is a distillation of the past, and as such the decisions made now about how to regulate the technology will undoubtedly impact the field. Because this is a book that primarily focuses on communicators, each chapter also concludes with a discussion of the communication field.

It is also important to note that the laws and ethics of AI are not confined to the U.S. and E.U. They are discussed at length here because of their power within the global economy. Other countries are part of the growing AI landscape, and they will likely present different forms of regulation. While the book discusses some of these efforts in Chapter 9, specifically about the U.S.-China AI race, this is not a comprehensive guide to all laws affecting AI. Instead, it represents a cross-section of legal and ethical issues with a U.S./E.U. focus. Also, of note, this book was written primarily in 2024, which was a global election year. As politics changes in the last half of the 2020s, these laws and priorities are likely to change alongside the technology.

As with any book, there are many people to thank who made this work possible. I want to thank the Virginia Tech School of Communication for their support during this project and for their encouragement to research this important area. I also want to thank the two editors at Routledge, Alexandra de Brauw and Zoya Gayle, for their support and help during this writing process. I also want to thank my daughter Cayce Anne, who has always been patient when I'm working on a new book, and my wife, Anne Carroll Myers, who has always served as my editor on all of the drafts of my books. Without Anne, this work could not be done, and appropriately it is dedicated to her.

Note

1 Public Relations Society of America, "*Promises and Pitfalls: The Ethical Use of AI for Public Relations Practitioners*," accessed December 1, 2024, https://www.prsa.org/docs/default-source/about/ethics/ethicaluseofai.pdf?sfvrsn=5d02139f_2

1

WHAT IS AI AND HOW IS IT RESHAPING OUR SOCIETY IN THE 2020s?

Chapter Overview

This chapter discusses the basics of artificial intelligence (AI) and its impact on communication, ethics, and law. Specific attention is paid to how AI works technologically, and how these technological aspects of AI impact the way ethical and legal regulations will impact the field. The trends of AI use within contemporary communication and the impact of generative and predictive AI in the communication industry writ large are discussed along with the historical development of AI as a technology. The chapter concludes with an analysis of the future of AI use within communication, and trends communicators should watch for in the coming years, including increased complexity of ethical issues within AI, future regulations on AI, trends of AI use within communication, and the net benefit of AI within the communication industry.

Keywords: Artificial Intelligence, Generative AI, Predictive AI, Large Language Models, AI Law, AI Ethics, Autonomous AI, Narrow AI

The role of artificial intelligence (AI) within communication has been transformative for society. Professional communicators are now leveraging the power of AI technology to do faster, more accurate work, and they are able to place those communications strategically to resonate with readers. The power of AI has great potential to revolutionize the communications industry including advertising, public relations, journalism, marketing, organizational communication, and strategic communications. However, the opportunities that AI presents also create an equal number of risks.

DOI: 10.4324/9781003426561-1

AI is now more accessible than ever, paired with an easy-to-use interface that enhances user experience. As a result, more people have unprecedented access to AI without requiring specialized knowledge to use it effectively. Additionally, the quality of large language model (LLM) generative AI platforms, such as ChatGPT, has increased significantly since its widespread use in the market in late 2022. That means people are now more than ever able to produce high-quality, low-cost AI content without too many specialized skills or training. The net result is opportunity and risk. The opportunities lie within streamlining communication functions, and the ability for communicators to utilize AI to do otherwise time-consuming menial tasks, such as scheduling. There is also the power of AI to provide a feedback loop for idea generation, and its predictive capacity allows for messaging strategy that increases resonance with target audiences. Conversely, like all technology, AI can be used for nefarious ends. Mis- and disinformation have proliferated in no small part thanks to AI. Voice cloning and deepfake video allow for realistic audio-visuals that can impact decision-making in high-stakes aspects of society, such as voting and healthcare decisions.

AI is predicated on data points and algorithms. The output of the system has both the opportunity to eliminate human bias and amplify it based on the underlying construction of the platform. Because of that, AI can produce results that may be subtly or unintentionally biased, which causes great concern when AI is being used as a decision-maker or content producer. That means that the user bears the ultimate responsibility to fact-check the output of the AI, and that ethical responsibility has to be accepted as part of using AI-generated information. While AI can provide helpful insights and data, it is essential for users to ensure the accuracy, relevance, and appropriateness of the content by cross-referencing it with reliable sources. This helps maintain integrity and accountability in how the information is utilized, ensuring that decisions or actions based on AI output are well-informed and ethically sound. On a practical level, that may mean that communicators can do some tasks faster and more accurately than AI, which also means that the decisions around implementing AI have to be deliberate and reflective of the norms and needs of a specific industry.

To fully appreciate the power of AI and its limitations, it is important to know what AI actually is and is not. Much of the representations of AI within the media and in societal conversation conflate aspects of the technology and focus on potential theoretical outcomes. That has caused a significant amount of societal concern over AI, and potentially a reluctance to fully embrace its potential within the workforce. Many people believe that humans fundamentally perform tasks better than AI, and many have a fear of AI creating bad results, specifically around decision-making. Compounding this is a fear that AI will replace jobs and displace workers in the coming years. While it is true that some industries are more affected by AI, e.g. high-income content-producing jobs, much of AI in its current form is an enhancement to current job tasks. Understanding this power and potential of AI is essential for users, communicators, and lawmakers in shaping the use, implementation, and guardrails of the technology.

A Brief History of Artificial Intelligence

The rapid proliferation of AI post-2022 makes the technology appear to be a recent phenomenon that has taken society by surprise. However, AI has a much longer and richer history that many are unaware of. This history illustrates how AI today is an extension of these early developments, and it is only now that computing power and data have reached a significant inflection point that AI, as we now know it, can exist. Theoretically, AI has its genesis in the work of Alan Turing, the famed British mathematician known for his code-breaking work during World War II, first conceptualized of AI in his groundbreaking paper "Computing Machinery and Intelligence" published in 1950.[1] In it, he asked if machines could think and introduced the test of whether machine outputs were indistinguishable for human beings. The answer to this question became known as the Turing Test, in which a human is asked to distinguish between human-created and machine text-based conversations. If the content is indistinguishable, then the machine shows intelligent behavior. Turing also anticipated many of the moral, religious, and philosophical objections to labeling computer behavior as intelligent. He predicted this type of technology would be mainstream by the year 2000 and thought the technology would adapt itself in a way that would make its outputs indistinguishable from humans.[2]

The term artificial intelligence (AI) would become popularized in 1955 with an influential workshop held at Dartmouth University entitled, "A Proposal for the Dartmouth College Research Project on Artificial Intelligence."[3] That conference brought together Dartmouth Professor John McCarthy, Harvard Professor Marvin Minsky, I.B.M. researcher Nathaniel Rochester, and Bell Telephone Labs researcher Claude Shannon. These men were an amalgamation of computer scientists, engineers, and mathematicians, although their academic backgrounds were more theoretical and interdisciplinary compared to the contemporary description of computer science. Their workshop served as the foundation of AI as a concept and called for the interdisciplinary research of AI and its capabilities as a technology. It would set the agenda for AI research for decades, especially in terms of leveraging the technology for problem solving and learning.[4]

Researchers continued to make advances in the theoretical discussion of AI in the 1950s. In 1956 researchers Allen Newell and Herbert A. Simon published their influential article "The Logic Theory Machine: A Complex Information Processing System."[5] In it, they introduced the Logic Theory Machine, a computer program that could solve mathematical theorems. This showed that computers could be used for complex cognitive processes that mimicked human thinking. It would showcase the relationship between AI and cognitive science and demonstrate that computers could engage in reasoning and go beyond simple mathematical calculations. By the 1960s, AI continued to be developed with some programs such as ELIZA, an early AI system created by MIT computer scientist Joseph Weizenbaum. ELIZA was an early iteration of what is now called a Chatbot. It used a sympathetic tone of American psychologist Carl Rogers to engage with users.[6] During that same time, other AI programs DENDRAL and MYCIN were also created that addressed niche fields of chemistry and medical diagnoses.[7]

However, the momentum of AI development slowed in the 1970s through the 1980s, giving way to what has been called the "AI winter" when academic interest, research, and development waned. This was in part because technology did not exist to implement many of the theoretical ambitions articulated by early researchers. Other fields in computer science gained more attention because of the promise of federal funding, and the scale of systems such as MYCIN was so narrow they had limited mass appeal. The industry of tech development shifted their focus to creating the early groundwork for the internet and focused on the development of graphics in gaming systems. AI became a field that was more theoretical than applied, but development of programming language did continue setting the foundation for later development.[8]

By the late 1980s, AI had renewed interest in the academic and business community. Unlike the work done in the 1950s and 1960s, the interest in AI began to be more applied. The interest in neural networks, a type of machine learning (ML) model designed to mimic the structure and function of the human brain, had renewed interest for applied business applications. One area this was implemented was in shipping and finance. The AI program XCON (eXpert CONfigurer) was developed in 1978 at Carnegie Mellon and used by the Digital Equipment Corporation for VAX computer system to configure what parts and connections customers wanted in their custom-built machines.[9]

The innovations in the 1990s and early 2000s saw the proliferation of AI technology and innovation. Part of the reason for this exponential growth was the use of large datasets to train AI. These data sets were available because of the explosive growth of the internet and later by social media. This coincided also with the technological ability to store large amounts of data, which could train AI models. Neural networks, which are computer programs that mimic how the human brain works, were improved by programmers. With the creation of convolutional neural networks (CNNs) that can recognize patterns and images, and recurrent neural networks (RNNs) that can understand sequences, these programs became much more effective. Video game technology also improved the development of AI. Graphics Processing Units (GPUs), computer chips that can process several calculations at the same time, also became more widespread in use facilitating a growth of AI. The late 1990s also saw AI being discussed in mainstream news. In 1997, world chess champion Garry Kasparov was defeated by IBM's Deep Blue, which had been improved after losing in a six-match series the previous year.

Financial backing for research and development from large corporations, such as Google, Meta, Microsoft, and Amazon, spurred AI growth. This generated public interest in the technology, especially when there were high-profile media events related to AI, such as when IBM's Watson won the quiz show *Jeopardy!* in 2011. During this time, AI use of natural language processing (NLP), the ability of AI to understand, interpret, and create human speech, dramatically improved with RNNs and long-short term memory (LSTM). Advances in speech and language technology, as seen in virtual assistants such as Apple's Siri and Amazon's Alexa, provided for better user experiences based on sophisticated understanding of speech patterns and instructions. By the 2010s, the access to AI became more mainstream with the introduction of Google's TensorFlow in 2015 and Facebook's PyTorch in 2016. By 2019, OpenAI introduced Chat-GPT2 and ChatGPT 3 a year later. These models were significant in their commercial appeal to non-programmer audiences. The ease in which these platforms could perform complex tasks, such as code writing and content creation, created a greater interest in AI's capacity to train on smaller sets of data.

Open AI would release its commercially successful ChatGPT 3.5 in November 2022. That model would become instantaneously popular with so much traffic that sometimes users could not log in to the platform because of server overload. In 2023, the company would release Chat-GPT 4, which improved both quality and speed from 3.5. A paid subscription model, called Chat-GPT Plus, was introduced in February that same year, and the next month Chat-GPT plug-ins were available. These plug-ins allowed for enhanced user experience by harnessing the power of Chat-GPT with third-party websites. As a result of Chat-GPT's success, many other tech companies came out with competitors. These included Google's Bard and Microsoft's Copilot for Office 365. Microsoft also partnered with OpenAI to integrate Chat-GPT into its Bing search engine. Meanwhile, other AI platforms have emerged such as Google's Notebook LM, which has a unique feature of taking complex content and repackaging it into understandable material including making podcasts through its Audio Overview feature. Apple also launched Apple Intelligence, a play on the acronym AI, in 2024. Elon Musk, who cofounded OpenAI in 2015 but left in 2018, has launched Grok, an AI system associated with the social media platform X. Unlike other AI systems, Grok has fewer guardrails and more freedom for users creating content. Musk argues his platform is transformative and has gone as far as to encourage users to enter personal medical data, including medical scans, into the AI system for analysis.[10] As of this writing, AI systems have emerged as a multibillion-dollar industry with a value of $200 billion in 2023 and estimated value of over $1 trillion by 2030.[11] In 2024, ChatGPT and DALL-E, both owned by OpenAI, remain dominant platforms for business use. However, other platforms are gaining traction in specialized areas and niche uses such as Qualifier.ai (Marketing), Drift (Customer Service), Leena AI (Human Resources), and Fireflies (Business Meetings).[12]

How Does AI Work? The Basics

As AI has proliferated, there are many terms that are used within the AI and tech industry that directly impact the understanding, development, and regulation of AI technologies. These terms shape the way professionals, policymakers, and the general public perceive and engage with AI systems. Understanding these concepts is essential for comprehending AI's current capabilities, limitations, and implications. However, these terms are hyper-technical, and oftentimes they are imprecisely used in a way that conflates many of the aspects of AI technology. This technical aspect of AI also presents unique challenges for lawmakers who may be unfamiliar with AI development. This lack of awareness creates obstacles in precise regulation of the platforms, which has led the government, both U.S. and abroad, to lean on industry to self-regulate to prevent the technology's power to create unintended and harmful consequences.

Artificial intelligence is an umbrella term that encompasses many different types of functions from content generation to predictive analysis to driving. The Oxford English Dictionary (OED) defines AI as, "the capacity of computers or other machines to exhibit or simulate intelligent behaviour."[13] The OED provides a contemporary update of the term stating that it is "software used to perform tasks or produce output previously thought to require human intelligence, esp. by using machine learning to extrapolate from large collections of data."[14] IBM provides this more general definition:

> Artificial intelligence (AI) is technology that enables computers and machines to simulate human learning, comprehension, problem solving, decision making, creativity and autonomy.[15]

Common discussion of AI frequently conflates the work of different types of AI with many of the larger media discussions of the technology discussing general AI as opposed to narrow AI. Artificial General Intelligence (AGI) is a hypothetical form of AI that can theoretically mimic the thought process of a human being. It is, in effect, no different than a human in terms of intelligence and cognitive ability. This type of AI presents a host of possibilities and is related to the concept of artificial superintelligence (ASI), which surpasses human intelligence. While a sensational topic for discussion, it does not yet exist, and while discussions about its use and excesses are important, the more immediate issue within AI is narrow AI. Current platforms of AI, such as ChatGPT, are examples of narrow AI, which perform specific tasks with prompt writing. They are designed to perform well as specified tasks such as writing, designing, or playing games with clearly defined rules, such as chess. Narrow AI, unlike theoretical AGI, does not have consciousness or the ability to have feelings and experiences. Its task-specific design means its outputs sometimes lack the type of consciousness and experience that human beings bring to a situation. Narrow AI is highly dependent on the data and algorithms that underpin its design. Because of that, its results can be truthful according to its data and algorithm, but not accurate in its reflection of the larger reality that its data is contextualized within. This is because narrow AI may have data, algorithmic, or contextual limitations that skew outputs. For example, narrow AI used in real-time stock predictions may be truthful in their outputs on market trends, but it can lack real-time contextual knowledge about what is actually going on within the moment that affects stock prices. Its data dependency and algorithmic constraints make it less accurate and more limited in its analysis of a specific scenario.

Machine Learning (ML) is a major component of how contemporary AI works, serving as the foundation for natural language processing (NLP). The key aspect of ML is that it provides guidance on AI outputs by examining data. In effect, ML provides the mechanism to learn from data. Neural networks also make use of what is termed supervised and unsupervised learning (although this type of learning occurs in non-neural network algorithms). Supervised learning is when the AI is trained on a specific data set, whereas unsupervised learning is when AI is trained on an unlabeled data set. The unsupervised learning process tries to find hidden patterns within the data such as previously unknown associations and relationships between data. An example of supervised learning are spam detectors, image recognition, or systems that would provide estimates on housing prices. Unsupervised learning would result in processes that would identify customers for certain products that the customer may be interested in purchasing based on prior purchases, fraud detection based on unusual purchases compared to prior purchasing behavior, or identifying themes within an aggregate group of documents. This type of learning is particularly useful to those involved in areas like reputation management or crisis communication where sentiment analysis is essential in uncovering trends within social media and the internet. It also has the ability to streamline decision-making processes to provide for quicker outcomes in areas of complex decision-making such as mortgage underwriting, document review during discovery in a lawsuit, or prior authorization for medicines. However, the issue with such use is the potential overreliance of the platform at the expense of human decision-making. Such concerns have prompted a call for there to be outlets for appeals to human decision-makers when such decisions are adverse.[16]

Neural networks are a subset of ML that are specialized models which allow for complex analysis, such as non-linear relationships and high dimensional data, that metaphorically mimic the way a human mind works. Neural networks are different than more simplistic models of processing, like decision trees. These networks have interconnected neurons that process data. Multiple neural networks facilitate what is called deep learning within AI. This deep learning can provide even more in-depth analysis and understanding such as speech recognition, image recognition, and NLP.[17] NLP is also a part of AI that focuses on human language and allows platforms to understand and generate human language in a way that is understandable to users through the use of computational linguistics. This technology allows for the existence of AI, such as chatbots, that provide for an understandable human interaction between users and computers. They are frequently used in search engines and voice-operated global positioning system (GPS). NLP can break down human language into understandable parts through the use of algorithms and neural networks.[18]

Within communication, the two largest areas of AI are generative AI and predictive AI. Though distinct, the two have a synergistic relationship with each other in outputs. Generative AI creates new content, such as reports, articles, music, or images, from prompts that generate responses from existing data. Its ability to do this relies heavily on NLP and natural language generation (NLG), which make these outputs more like a human creation. In contrast, predictive AI uses predictive models to provide potential solutions and strategies using supervised learning to understand potential outcomes. Both of these tools operate in a way that enhances the speed and potentially the quality of content and strategy. For example, a generative AI platform can create new communication content, such as a logo, press release, or journal article, from prompts written by users. Predictive AI, in comparison, could take that content and design a strategy for implementation of a brand campaign, publication strategy, or customer recommendations. Compare this with autonomous AI, such as self-driving cars and drone technology. It makes use of both predictive and generative AI to perform its specific tasks. The predictive AI allows autonomous AI to anticipate potential actions, such as other drivers on the road, while generative AI allows it to provide real-time communication and even new approaches to the underlying task.

These types of AI make use of NLPs, NLGs, and LLMs to facilitate the AI output. Generative AI uses these to create human-like responses and content based on prompts from users. Predictive AI uses more of the NLPs to create its predictions and suggestions and then may use NLGs and LLMs to produce human-like responses to questions. Autonomous AI uses all three in its decision-making and then in its communication with humans. All of these aspects of the technical side of AI, which is more complex than what is detailed in this section, illustrate the issue lawmakers and regulators face when dealing with regulating this technology. Types of AI also lend themselves to different regulatory issues. For example, generative AI has issues with intellectual property protection, dis- and misinformation, and issues of defamation, whereas predictive AI has more issues with privacy, bias, and inaccurate content. Autonomous AI presents issues with liability, specifically in decision-making that results in unsafe actions. Understanding this aspect poses a challenge for regulators trying to create specific governance over these issues.

From an ethical perspective, generative AI and LLMs present a unique issue of mis- and disinformation because of their capacity to create deepfakes and voice cloning. Deepfakes are digitally altered content in which video and audio are altered to create lifelike audio-visuals of a person. It has been used for election disinformation and even in bullying within schools. Its lifelike features are convincing, especially as the quality of such content improves with technological innovation. Predictive AI, with its power to process large amounts of data, also provides unique issues of discrimination. Because the data and algorithms that are used produce results quickly, it is sometimes easy for users to blindly follow suggestions and outputs of the data without considering potential inherent biases.

Understanding these dimensions to the mechanics of AI allows regulators and lawmakers to create regulations that have both control and flexibility over a fast-paced and innovative technology.

How AI Is Utilized for Communication

Within the diverse field of communication AI is used in various capacities both as an enhancement to work product and to streamline operations. However, within the larger communication industry, there are concerns over the use of the technology and its impact on both work quality and displacement of professionals. Within regulated industries, such as health-care, education, and finance, there is the added concern over the privacy compliance of AI systems. Because of that, many in those areas have sought out proprietary platforms that conform to legal requirements as well as industry expectations of ethics. Despite the advances within AI, many Americans fear the technology and have a high level of distrust of it.[19] Within the broader communications industry, there is also the concern of how AI can undermine the core values and purpose of information dissemination. Mis- and disinformation have existed before the advent of mass communication, but AI provides both an ease of creating high-quality disinformation content and also a targeted strategy for promotion. The concern is amplified by changes in information consumption that encourage fast-paced scrolling of shallow content without verification of source. This is compounded by the increased number of users who turn to non-professional, personal accounts, including influencers, for information about substantive, high-impact issues, such as law, politics, and healthcare. The lack of vetting of these sites, coupled with their unverified, content, allows for a less informed public that may be more easily duped by AI-generated disinformation.

Within the field of communication there is also a concern over AI's role in job displacement, which has caused a resistance, or at the least a cautious reluctance, to fully embrace the technology. In fact, workers who use AI are even more fearful that the technology will replace them, according to one study.[20] AI presents unique challenges to those fields that are content driven, pattern-oriented professions. Fields like accounting, clerical roles, customer service, logistics, and administration are exposed to job displacement by AI. Even highly specialized fields, such as diagnostic radiology, are potentially going to be heavily augmented, if not displaced, by the growth of AI. Communicators are positioned in a unique space where AI provides clear enhancements for work quality, while also presenting potential job displacement for roles that are more menial in task.

The use of AI in communication varies by sector, but some uses stand out. Content generation using generative AI is one of the biggest uses of AI for communicators. Being able to create new content easily and within a fast pace allows communications, whether it be journalists, advertising creative, or public relations practitioners, the time and ability to focus on other activities. The editing function within generative AI is particularly useful because it allows for both quality and logic assessments of content. There is particular usefulness in image generation and photo editing within generative AI that allows communicators the ability to create higher-level content without having to incur the cost of more staff or expensive technology. For communicators engaged in customer service, chatbots, which utilizes both generative and predictive AI technology, provides for greater interaction and high-quality information. It can provide better customer experiences and save time and talent for higher-level inquiries. There is anticipation that this technology can streamline operations for organizations that deal with routine and rudimentary inquiries, such as general health questions, that take up a great deal of human time. This technology has been heavily developed in the customer service industry and remains one of the most cost-effective tools within AI for business.

Within strategic communications the ability to predict and monitor public opinion and crisis is important. AI technology allows for real-time sentiment analysis which assists communicators in engaging in proactive communications concerning issues and crises. There is also the ability for communicators to use this analysis to formulate predictive strategies for campaigns, leveraging AI for targeted communications such as email and social media campaigns. Moreover, the language barriers that previously required expensive translations can be done without much cost using AI, although it is probably wise to have it proofread by a human speaker fluent in the language. Within social media, content moderation has become an essential task for all communicators, but AI can use NLP for text analysis to identify offensive or untrue comments for removal. This moderation is not limited to written text but also includes audiovisual content that can be flagged as inappropriate or offensive. Adaptive learning through ML and training allows for this moderation to improve with time to be more focused and vigilant in its implementation freeing communicators up to perform other important tasks.

Ethical Challenges to AI Regulation

With the power and ubiquity of AI use in communication, there are ethical concerns that arise. Perhaps one of the most pressing issues of AI ethics is disclosure of when AI is used. This ethical issue has evolved with the ubiquity of AI within operating systems and technology. Other issues include how to provide consent for those who may be providing information to the AI platform, such as when interfacing with a chatbot. Having human oversight of the AI platforms also raises questions about accountability and control. A human alternative, especially when dealing with high-stakes decisions, is something that many have called for in the industry. But for communication, the biggest ethical dilemma in the 2020s is the role of AI in mis- and disinformation. While AI provides a technology that improves both the quality and proliferation of mis- and disinformation, it is also perhaps the greatest tool to combat it. While legal regulations around the topic involve complex dynamics, especially in the U.S. where disinformation can potentially be protected under the First Amendment, ethical guidance on the use of AI and its content generation positions communicators in a unique space to have an outsized impact on its role within society.

Ethical guidance on AI presents other unique challenges, however. Frequently, ethics attempts to provide guidance based on longstanding ethical codes that do not anticipate unique technological changes. The sheer speed of AI development means that ethical guides have to be written with a degree of elasticity to anticipate unique situations, and those codes seeking to be more durable should focus on more overarching principles of the field, such as transparency, and less on specific technological situations. This is also compounded by the opaque nature of many AI platforms, particularly deep learning algorithms, which complicate efforts to create clear cut guidelines for practice. Compounding this issue with the difficulty in the explainability and traceability of such outputs that contribute to mis- and disinformation.[21]

Other constraints on ethical guidance is found in the ambiguity of what is meant by truth and accuracy in outcomes, and who or what is going to be the final arbiter of AI decisions. As the mechanics of AI demonstrate, the algorithmic and data-driven decision-making can create "truthful" content or predictions that are internally consistent within the platform but lack an external accuracy. One of the major ethical dilemmas this presents determining what accountability individual users will have. Specifically, in decision-making, will there be human alternatives to address AI outcomes that seem unfair, inaccurate or biased? Moreover, how does the potential for bias within AI get identified and combatted by AI or human beings? How much responsibility does an organization that unwittingly uses biased outcomes or content have when relying on the platforms? Is there a point where an organization has an ethical duty to test the AI systems regularly to ensure unintended consequences of bias do not occur? At what point is that responsibility met? Complicating this issue is the paradox of providing both security of content and data but also showing transparency in the AI process itself. Striking that balance requires understanding privacy and transparency are common ethical and practical issues that requires a delicate balance between two equally important competing interests.

At the core of the ethical dilemma of AI use is the issue of moral agency of technology. Does AI have morality rooted in ethical reasoning, and should users even expect that level of work? Given the technological limitations of current AI platforms is it even possible or reasonable to expect that level of capability? Moral agency is simply the autonomous ability to act independently based on moral understanding and philosophy. It is the ability to recognize right and wrong, and act upon those instincts like a human being. Within humanity this moral underpinning comes from life experience, identity, and beliefs that are embedded in the character of a person. This may be the byproduct of personal philosophy or religion, and it shapes the core of personal decision-making and sense making within the world. However, within AI, moral agency is not instinctive and is not based on personal experiences. Weak moral agency can exist where programmers use data and algorithms to create ethical decisions but do not make those decisions independently or deep understanding of ethical issues. The morality of these decisions are simulated through the AI designers. A strong moral agency for AI would exist when the AI had consciousness and self-awareness that provided for independence in thought. This raises both a philosophical and technological question as to whether this could ever exist within these platforms. Current AI platforms do not technologically have the capacity for consciousness, so their moral or ethical decision-making is rooted in the designer's inputs that result in deterministic behavior. There is no moral feedback loop for AI like that found in humanity, and emotions like guilt, shame, empathy, remorse, joy, sympathy, and love are currently not part of an AI platform's capacity.

The practical implications of this are that AI platform's ethical and moral compass are a byproduct of programming. That means that there has to be questioning of whose morality and ethics are being imposed when using an AI platform. This is an area that directly impacts discrimination, but it also brings into account a broader question of cultural standards. Using preselected standards of morality into AI decision-making comes at the expense of creating ethical hegemony for users and outputs. The design also has implications for complex ethical dilemmas that require nuanced decision-making that oftentimes requires contextual knowledge and introspection on the part of the user. In short, what does AI do when it is asked to make a decision that requires tradeoffs? What if the tradeoffs are high stakes, like determining when to have a medical procedure? Can AI accurately process the nuance of these issues and appreciate the complexity of the decision-making? Or is the AI platform performing a shallow analysis resulting in a deterministic outcome without considering the larger implications of the decision? Human factors, emotions, morals, ethics, and appreciation of right and wrong are perhaps lost, or at the very best only considered at a surface level.

Philosophically to act deterministically means that there is no free will. Because of that, AI currently lacks moral agency, failing the Turing Test because it only mimics human behavior and moral understanding. This means that the content and decisions made by AI are simulations of the real processes that humans use. This places an ethical responsibility on the programmers, designers, and users, e.g., communication professionals, of AI. It also mandates that users carefully consider the ethics and morality of both their and the technology's actions. Concerns about discrimination and unfair results are byproducts of deeper questions about programming and design. Determining whose values and ethics are being used within the platform and how those values and ethics evolve over time within AI learning processes are important. It requires thoughtful conversations, but also a heightened awareness and level of responsibility for communicators who use AI for sensitive and nuanced communications to diverse audiences. This requires the development of thoughtful ethical guidance and regulatory guardrails around the technology to ensure it operates in a manner that is beneficial to society.

Legal Challenges for Regulating AI

Ethical guidance on AI presents an aspirational approach to utilizing the technology. Ethics are frequently described as the high-water mark of action within an industry, and they represent principles that communicators strive to achieve. Laws, however, represent a baseline of compliance. Adherence to them is mandatory under threat of money damages or even loss of freedom. Currently, many communicators are looking to lawmakers to control the manner in which AI will impact society. However, there are challenges on what to focus on and how to create regulations that do not stifle the innovations in the AI technology. To date, regulation of AI has centered around three areas, privacy, intellectual property, and discrimination.

However, the challenge of regulation is one of focus. As with all technologies, the pace of innovation is much faster than the law. Moreover, the regulatory environment of AI is akin to the internet in the mid-1990s. Lawmakers, particularly in the U.S., want the technology to thrive and make the U.S. a world leader in this area. Overregulation or poorly written laws serve as an impediment to technological growth potentially making the U.S. a country hostile to the new technology. However, as the following chapters illustrate, there is a concerted effort to address the new issues of AI within the existing framework of law. That also presents certain challenges as the technology has made lawmakers rethink and reconsider basic aspects of laws themselves, such as what does it mean to be a human, what can a machine own, if anything, and how can law ensure that human alternatives exist in decision making. Compounding this issue is the role of non-U.S. laws, particularly from the European Union, that take a more proactive approach to regulation, particularly in an effort to minimize manipulation, discrimination, and social scoring.

There are other more nuanced AI concerns within lawmaking that go beyond privacy, intellectual property, and discrimination. For example, laws crafted today need to consider long-term goals of human beings, particularly if autonomous AI were to be achieved. Economic issues, such as job displacement by AI, also warrant considerations by lawmakers who should consider the long-term impact of AI on workers and their rights. Could AI ever achieve legal personhood, similar to a corporation? Achieving that status would create a new legal reality in which AI would enjoy freedoms such as freedom of speech, owning property, or entering into contracts. Should lawmakers demand that AI systems have standardized data portability, which is the ability to transfer personal data from system to system, so consumers and businesses are not locked into fragmented AI ecosystems? This is a longstanding issue with all technology, and with the growth of AI use within business, there is the question of whether a user leaving a provider means all of their data and outputs are lost as well (similarly to losing one's phone number when changing providers).

Governments have also demanded guardrails of transparency for AI providers, but those requirements also present unique challenges. For instance, there are calls for transparency within AI data and algorithms, yet some AI platforms utilize "black box" technology, which is opaque in its decision-making practices. Lawmakers should consider how and even if these types of systems can be used in high-stakes decision-making such as healthcare, finance, mortgage underwriting, or university and college admissions. Explainability of systems presents a similar issue, especially as AI becomes more complex both algorithmically and within the data itself. For example, trade secret data held within AI present unique challenges for AI transparency when the property right itself is rooted in its lack of disclosure. Liability of AI also presents unique legal issues when the transgression occurs with the AI platform and then is amplified by the user. For example, if an AI platform provides defamatory information that a user believes is true and then republishes, is both the user and platform at fault? If this jurisdiction allows for joint and several liability, also known as proportionate liability, how does the percentage of the judgment get assigned between the user and the AI? Making this even more complicated are issues when highly sophisticated autonomous AI engages in outputs or behavior that causes harm. What is the standard of care required of that autonomous AI within the legal standard of negligence, or lack of ordinary care? This is even more nuanced of a discussion when the AI has adaptive learning, where the AI changes its behavior over time generating unforeseen actions and consequences that may result in a lawsuit.

If these questions were not complicated enough, a larger, and more pressing, issue is the cross-jurisdictional challenges of AI litigation. The U.S. federal government is slow to create comprehensive federal statutes on the issues of AI. Federal agencies also have other issues of creating rules and regulations that are specific to segments of AI, and, in all likelihood, early efforts to regulate the technology will have cross-agency regulations that could be contradictory or difficult to discern when the topics overlap. Because of political gridlock and the protracted rulemaking process of federal agencies, some states have stepped in create more comprehensive AI regulations, particularly around privacy and disclosure.[22] The pace of regulation seems purposefully slow at times, particularly in the United States. In December 2024, the U.S. House of Representatives released their long-awaited AI Report, which acknowledged some level of regulation was necessary but that there could not be a static set of laws for a fast-evolving technology like AI.[23] It encourages an incremental, sector-specific approach to regulating AI in the coming years.

However, the more challenging legal situation is when non-U.S. laws impact U.S.-based AI practices. As communication has grown into a global practice, there is the inevitable issue of so-called foreign law impacting U.S.-based companies. Chief among these non-U.S. jurisdictions is the European Union which has passed several AI-specific laws including the 2024 AI Act. The so-called Brussels Effect, which is when E.U. law becomes the de facto legal norm because of the requirements the E.U. places on foreign businesses attempting to do business within the E.U. or with E.U. customers. Because the E.U. has a history of robust regulations on privacy, as evidenced by the AI Act and the General Data Protection Regulation (GDPR), the Brussels effect may be amplified the era of AI.[24]

The Future of AI: Considerations for Law, Ethics, and Communications

The opportunities and challenges of AI are manifold. No technology has the potential to make life and work easier and at a higher quality than AI. However, no technology to date has presented the practical and existential threats to society either. As AI becomes more ubiquitous in the communication industry and society, there are several likely outcomes that professionals, lawmakers, programmers, and society will have to consider. These considerations will have to go beyond mere questions about implementation but must address hard-to-assess truths about bias, morality, humanness, and power. This is why AI has created both so much anticipation and fear within the global community. It at once has the ability to enhance and destroy society as we know it.

Within the communication field more practical issues abound. First, is implementation. The use of AI within work requires communicators of all stripes to make deliberate decisions up-front. Are we going to disclose use? If so, under what circumstances? How do we fact check the AI? How do we choose a platform? At what point do we stop using a platform? What are our obligations to our readers, publics, or audiences within the context of AI use? How do we educate our various constituency groups about AI (including clients, readers, and society writ large)? When will we use AI, and for what specific tasks? These are important questions that involve an ongoing discussion. It may require there to be a policy about the technology, and, should an organization endeavor to create one they should be sure to consider all aspects of how AI will impact their workplace and work product. It is important in drafting those rules to bring in a diverse set of voices from different aspects of the organization to fully consider the impact of the technology. And this is not going to be a single conversation, but an ongoing dialogue that will change with the technology.

There is also an ongoing conversation legally and ethically about who is in control of AI and who is responsible for its outputs. Currently, there are two approaches to AI liability. One side argues that the human user is responsible for the output of AI, and in most cases, they should be held accountable for any bad action on the part of the technology. On the other side, there is the view that AI is not a service, but a product that should be held strictly accountable for its work. This presents a complex situation for communicators who are leveraging the technology as part of their work as professionals. For them, AI is a tool that does not have autonomous features. However, as chatbots and anthropomorphic AI become refined and as AI becomes autonomous, there are scenarios where the discussion of who is responsible becomes more nuanced. This requires communicators to have important conversations up-front with clients, peers, and within the industry about the responsible and legally sound use.

Ethics and legal issues of AI will no doubt evolve as well. In the early days of widespread use of AI, such as ChatGPT, there was a collective sense that AI needed to be disclosed at all times. Yet as the technology grew in use and as it was part of many other platforms, such as Meta and Google, the answer to disclosure changed. This is an example of the evolving norms and expectations of the technology, and no doubt this will continue to evolve as the technology improves. Lawmakers now are concerned with privacy, intellectual property, and disinformation. In the 2030s, those concerns may give way to issues of AI's legal personhood and liability for autonomous AI decisions. By the 2050s, the issues may be more complex than that and sound more like a question posed in a science fiction movie than in a courtroom or legislature. Consider, the sovereignty of an AI system and whether it receives political rights and governmental recognition.[25] However, the more immediate concern for those using AI is how will the law grapple with ongoing concerns over privacy and liability in an era where governments are reluctant to regulate a new technology for fear of stifling innovation. What is likely to occur is an outsized importance of professional norms and ethics as a stopgap measure to regulate a fast-growing, largely ungovernable technology.

Discussion Questions

1 Why are the morals of an AI system so important? How should communicators and programmers work together to establish the morality of an AI platform? Can there even be a universally agreed upon algorithmic and data morality?
2 What technological aspect of AI presents the most important legal and ethical challenge? How can ethical codes and lawmakers best deal with this issue?
3 Suppose you are tasked with creating an AI policy for a communication organization. What groups of people should be represented in the working group for the policy? What are the top 5 issues the AI policy should address?
4 What is the biggest ethical issue concerning AI-facing communicators? Is there a comprehensive ethical rule that can best address it? Why are why not?
5 Scenario: You are working as a corporate communication officer in a large company. Your team has started to use generative AI to edit content for grammar, clarity, and logic. The content is written by a human and then edited in the AI platform. After the editing the team reviews the content and decides which suggestions to keep or discard. Should you disclose this AI use to your readers? Suppose the content was created entirely by AI and the human team edited the content after it was generated. Would that change your answer?

Notes

1 Alan M. Turing, "Computing Machinery and Intelligence," *Mind* 59, no. 236 (1950): 433–60, https://doi.org/10.1093/mind/LIX.236.433.
2 Ibid.

3 John McCarthy, Marvin Minsky, Nathaniel Rochester, and Claude Shannon, *A Proposal for the Dartmouth Summer Research Project on Artificial Intelligence* (Hanover, NH, 1955), http://jmc.stanford.edu/articles/dartmouth/dartmouth.pdf.
4 McCarthy, Minsky, Rochester, and Shannon, *A Proposal for the Dartmouth Summer Research Project on Artificial Intelligence*.
5 A. Newell and H. Simon, "The Logic Theory Machine: A Complex Information Processing System," *IRE Transactions on Information Theory* 2, no. 3 (September 1956): 61–79, https://doi.org/10.1109/TIT.1956.1056797.
6 Joseph Weizenbaum, "ELIZA—A Computer Program for the Study of Natural Language Communication Between Man and Machine," *Communications of the ACM* 9, no. 1 (1966): 36–45.
7 Bruce G. Buchanan and Edward H. Shortliffe, eds., *Rule-Based Expert Systems: The MYCIN Experiments of the Stanford Heuristic Programming Project* (Reading, MA: Addison-Wesley, 1984).
8 Nils J. Nilsson, *The Quest for Artificial Intelligence: A History of Ideas and Achievements* (Cambridge: Cambridge University Press, 2009).
9 John McDermott, "R1 a Rule Based Configurer of Computer Systems," *Artificial Intelligence* 19, no. 2 (1982): 39–88, 7; David E. Rumelhart, Geoffrey E. Hinton, and Ronald J. Williams, "Learning Representations by Back-Propagating Errors," *Nature* 323, (1986): 533–36, https://doi.org/10.1038/323533a0.
10 Melissa Rudy, "Elon Musk Wants People to Submit Medical Scans to His Grok AI Chatbot," *Fox News*, October 2024, https://www.foxnews.com/health/elon-musk-wants-people-submit-medical-scans-grok-ai-chatbot.
11 Statista, "Artificial Intelligence – Worldwide," accessed November 12, 2024, https://www.statista.com/outlook/tmo/artificial-intelligence/worldwide.
12 "Forbes Advisor Business Team, "Best AI Tools Of 2024," *Forbes*, accessed November 12, 2024, https://www.forbes.com/advisor/business/ai-tools/.
13 Oxford English Dictionary, "Artificial Intelligence," accessed November 12, 2024, https://www.oed.com/dictionary/artificial-intelligence_n?tab=meaning_and_use#38531565.
14 Ibid.
15 IBM Cloud Education. "What Is Artificial Intelligence (AI)?" IBM, accessed November 12, 2024. https://www.ibm.com/cloud/learn/what-is-artificial-intelligence.
16 The White House, "Blueprint for an AI Bill of Rights," accessed November 14, 2024, https://bidenwhitehouse.archives.gov/ostp/ai-bill-of-rights/
17 IBM, "Deep Learning," IBM, accessed November 14, 2024, https://www.ibm.com/topics/deep-learning.
18 IBM, "Natural Language Processing (NLP)," IBM, accessed November 14, 2024, https://www.ibm.com/topics/natural-language-processing.
19 Pew Research Center, "What the Data Says about Americans' Views of Artificial Intelligence," November 21, 2023, https://www.pewresearch.org/short-reads/2023/11/21/what-the-data-says-about-americans-views-of-artificial-intelligence/.
20 Jack Kelly, "Workers Who Use Artificial Intelligence Are More Likely to Fear That AI May Replace Them," *Forbes*, January 8, 2024, https://www.forbes.com/sites/jackkelly/2024/01/08/workers-who-use-artificial-intelligence-are-more-likely-to-fear-that-ai-may-replace-them/.
21 Public Relations Society of America, "The Ethical Use of Artificial Intelligence," accessed November 18, 2024, https://www.prsa.org/docs/default-source/about/ethics/ethicaluseofai.pdf?sfvrsn=5d02139f_2.

22 National Conference of State Legislatures, "Artificial Intelligence 2024 Legislation," last modified September 9, 2024, accessed November 18, 2024, https://www.ncsl.org/technology-and-communication/artificial-intelligence-2024-legislation.

23 U.S. House of Representatives, "Artificial Intelligence Task Force Report," December 2024, https://www.speaker.gov/wp-content/uploads/2024/12/AI-Task-Force-Report-FINAL.pdf.

24 European Union, General Data Protection Regulation (GDPR), Regulation (EU) 2016/679 of the European Parliament and of the Council of 27 April 2016 on the Protection of Natural Persons with Regard to the Processing of Personal Data and on the Free Movement of Such Data and Repealing Directive 95/46/EC (General Data Protection Regulation, Official Journal of the European Union, L 119 (4 May 2016): 1–88, https://eur-lex.europa.eu/legal-content/EN/TXT/PDF/?uri=CELEX:32016R0679. European Union, Regulation (EU) 2024/1689 of the European Parliament and of the Council of 13 June 2024 Laying Down Harmonised Rules on Artificial Intelligence and Amending Certain Union Legislative Acts (Artificial Intelligence Act), Official Journal of the European Union, L'2024/1689 (12 July 2024), https://eur-lex.europa.eu/legal-content/EN/TXT/PDF/?uri=OJ:L_202401689

25 While this sounds extremely far-fetched it is akin to the issue of micronation development in international waters.

2

AI AND THE LAW

Human vs. Machine Decision-Making

Chapter Overview

This chapter provides an overview of how artificial intelligence (AI) decision-making is regulated. Specific concerns about AI are discussed with a focus on how AI systems can provide both inaccurate results and an echo chamber of decision points that replicate inaccurate or unfair consequences. The chapter also discusses what aspects of human thought are important within decision-making, and how those aspects of humanity should be preserved within AI regulation and law. Regulations within the European Union and the United States are discussed along with an analysis of how these regulations fail to comprehensively address AI decision-making. Particular attention is paid to the call for human-AI oversight and limits that oversight plays within regulating inaccurate or biased AI. The chapter concludes with discussion points about the nuances of AI decision-making, and how over reliance on the technology erodes trust.

Keywords: AI Decisions, Bias, Human Oversight, Transparency, and Trust

AI presents many opportunities for automated tasks and predictive analysis. This has the ability to free humans from time-consuming tasks so they can work and contribute to higher-level work that have greater resonance. However, the concern over the power of AI to make decisions that have lasting impact and significance to human lives remains a concern for many lawmakers and society in general. For instance, could an AI platform provide the type of analysis that could set bail for a person accused of a felony through a statistical analysis of recidivism through analyzing their criminal record? Could AI determine who gets what medical treatment based

DOI: 10.4324/9781003426561-2

on the analysis of medical scans? Will there be a point where mortgages and loans are decided not by loan officers and underwriters, but an AI system that can determine financial risk within seconds? All of this presents a paradoxical issue of how to counterbalance the speed and accuracy of AI with the ethics and reasoning of a human. To date, it seems that society is more comfortable with humans, flaws and all, making the final decision about high-stakes issues.

Legal frameworks are currently under development to address these issues of AI decision-making. Those laws follow certain themes such as explainability of the system, guardrails for bias, accountability of the platform, human oversight, and ethical governance. They also examine the limits of AI's technology and decision-making capacity. Humans and machines "think" differently and understanding that core difference is important to how this technology can be regulated and controlled. The common theme in much of the legal discussion about AI decision-making is that AI should never be the last word on any decision, no matter how small. This means that human oversight is essential to the AI decision-making process, and that users must resist the temptation of allowing AI to make decisions at their expense and without considering the technology's limitations of thought. There is also an awareness and sentiment within society that decisions are complex. The core concept of decision-making is not choosing a path forward, but also leaving other alternatives behind. In fact, the root of the word decision, Latin's *decider* means to cut off or leave behind. Within AI that philosophical underpinning is profound because it means that within the decision-making process, AI may be the arbiter of options, but it is ultimately the human, the one who is affected, who has the definitive final say. When AI is the sole arbiter of decision-making, it is making the decision to cut off options, and by extension takes away human agency and value in the process. AI also poses another problem, which is that its convenience is so alluring that many users may willingly give up self-autonomy in exchange for fast, definitive decisions. Reflective action requires time and an understanding of context – two things AI does not do especially well.

That leaves lawmakers and regulators with a question of how to regulate decision-making. While later chapters will delve into the discriminatory risks and ethical uses of AI, this chapter examines the legal measures put in place to ensure human oversight in AI with a focus on how legal frameworks are evolving to prevent AI from being the sole decision-maker in high-stakes scenarios. The chapter explores the mechanisms designed to maintain accountability, such as requiring transparency in AI processes, mandating explainability in algorithmic decision-making, and instituting safeguards like the right to appeal AI-driven outcomes. By focusing on key areas such as employment, healthcare, criminal justice, and financial services, this chapter highlights how laws are being tailored to preserve human judgment and provide avenues for recourse, ensuring that AI supports rather than undermines fundamental rights and ethical principles. However, the ultimate decision, and probably the most consequential, is not how does AI make a choice, but who is in charge? AI or human beings?

General Overview of AI and Decision-Making

The word artificial intelligence (AI) evokes the idea that somehow the artificial mind can replicate the human one. The truth is that it cannot, despite the level of sophistication of algorithms and datasets. AI has no consciousness and subjective experience. It has no emotive behavior. It cannot make decisions on intuition or past lived experience like many humans do. It also has no moral and ethical reasoning that uses complex dilemmas and empathy or cultural understanding to know the "right" thing to do. Its ethical guidance, if it can be called that, is predicated on pre-programmed patterns. It does not appreciate the moral weight of the decisions it makes, and it cannot adapt its thinking within truly novel scenarios. Perhaps most significantly, it has no emotional intelligence. While it can simulate emotion in its responses, it does not truly understand them. The human mind is unpredictable, and that level of unpredictability allows it to think in paradoxical ways. It can act irrationally and meaningfully at the same time as it is driven by subconscious, gut feelings. AI's algorithmic programming ensures predictability in outcome, which can be useful. However, current AI will not provide the type of innovation and creativity that a human mind does through its non-defined pathways of inspiration. Perhaps most important for communicators is the human mind provides for narrative creation. It uses the lived experiences of the narrator and emotion to craft meaning and identity. AI can only mimic this type of output and only do that if its data and programming allow for it.[1]

The prior chapter noted the technical side of how AI systems differ. Their ability to make decisions is largely predicated on algorithms and datasets. The input from that data and the processes by which they are analyzed provide the output. These outputs can be highly accurate and can even find trends and issues that might be overlooked by a human. However, these systems can also come to conclusions that are highly inaccurate. This is why human verification of AI outputs is so essential to maintaining integrity. Overuse and overreliance on AI can create biased and discriminatory results. However, this issue of overreliance and overestimation of technology is part of the problem with AI. This so-called "technochauvinism" has led many to think technology has a superior place within the world, and that machines, including AI, automatically perform tasks better than humans.[2] Core parts of that assumption are underpinned by the belief that math is more objective and fairer than human considerations. This is compounded when insular groups that are like minded make decisions that only reiterate and reaffirm preexisting beliefs. However, if users think that AI can provide solutions to nuanced human problems better than human beings own thought processes, then there is a higher risk of bad AI outputs impacting society.

Part of the reason many may think AI is superior to human beings in decision-making is speed. Well-built AI platforms can provide answers and outputs in seconds compared to humans. But accuracy and task matters. In structured and repetitive tasks, AI excels because it can process datasets faster than humans. This is illustrated in how early AI systems excelled in games like chess, which have pre-defined highly structured rules. Ambiguity is not something AI does well with because those types of decisions require nuanced understanding and perhaps creative decision-making. Moreover, nuanced decisions require a contextual awareness that is rooted in experience, another thing AI does not have. Current models of AI work on predefined data. It does have adaptability through machine learning (discussed in Chapter 1), but it cannot fully understand the broader context or implications of certain decisions. This is seen in direct marketing of items. AI can predict what a consumer may want to purchase, but it cannot predict purchase behavior from an emotional or social context. Contrast that with a human who understands the cultural, ethical, and emotional frameworks of society. Using the example of the purchase decision, an AI platform may suggest a flower bouquet to a customer who has bought flowers during the same time last year, but it would not know that such a suggestion could be sensitive if the flowers were purchased for a funeral. Similarly in predictive decision-making an AI platform could recommend termination of an employee based on performance metrics. However, a human may choose not to fire the employee because they are aware of certain external circumstances that are impacting work performance, such as health concerns, grief over a loss, or personal issues. Contextual sensitivity is at the root of the human concept of mercy. In fact, the act of mercy is tied to biased decision-making, yet the outcome of merciful decisions is frequently thought of as more just. Justice and bias are not at the polar ends of a spectrum, they can be complimentary. For example, using AI to determine if a person's work productivity warrants termination may provide an objective analysis, but if that person is a caretaker for a relative dying of cancer, then that contextual situation requires an empathetic consideration. The just result is not termination, but support. That paradoxical conclusion is rooted in humanity, and is ultimately something an AI system would not process in the same way as a human being.

This issue of decision-making gets to a larger emotive issue of AI. Human beings are emotional and make decisions through emotional paradigms. One of those paradigms is ethics. This application of ethics uses the paradigms of emotion, which include a range of perspectives of empathy, guilt, compassion, or indignation. It is thought that unemotional decisions are better, especially in the realm of ethics. However, non-emotional decision-making ignores the context-sensitive choices people have to make that are laden with emotional issues. Cold rationality is thought to be dehumanizing and morally bankrupt by many. Emotional considerations serve as a counterbalance to this decision-making. In using emotion, human beings are frequently able to achieve a higher level of ethical adherence that provide justice, fairness, care, and empathy for the human condition. Emotions are also a driver of ethical decision-making and compliance. The emotion of shame or the concept of personal accountability may serve as a trigger for people to compel ethical decisions. AI cannot and does not have the ability to provide for that type of cognitively complex and idiosyncratic decision-making that ultimately provides for a better, i.e., ethical or just, result.

It is important to note that the concept of artificial intelligence is rooted in the artificiality of its thought. It mimics the human mind in the way that creates outputs but is not a replacement for it. Ethical decision-making is a mimicked act, which is predicated on programming not personal values. This presents ethical dilemmas in which AI would only be able to use cold rationality to provide an answer. For example, an AI system used to prioritize healthcare for patients based on odds of survival may give preference to older patients than a young child while not considering the child's likelihood of having a longer life and the impact of the child's parents and family. This scenario also demonstrates the issue of rigidity and flexibility within humans and AI. Even deep learning AI is limited by its data and algorithms. Situations that fall outside of that data or training cannot be processed and solutions cannot be improvised. Human beings have the ability to engage with and handle truly novel situations even if they don't have a background or experience with the situation. A classic example is communicating with someone who speaks a different language when neither of the parties is bilingual. Even with that verbal communication barrier, humans can "understand" each other in a way that AI would not be able to do.

As AI use becomes more mainstream, it is up to the law and users to make sure these differences are acknowledged and considered in implementation. Lawmakers are right to think that human decision-making is superior to that of AI, and current law struggles to create a regulatory system that enshrines that. This superiority is not because human thinking is faster or more logical. AI has proven that it excels and exceeds human capacity in those areas. Human thinking is superior because of its own imperfection. It is those imperfections that allow for results that resonate with humanity. Empathy, learning from mistakes, and seeing meaning within chaos are hallmarks of humanity. That allows for changing understandings of the world, development of ethics, and the creation of truly novel ideas and interpretations. It is through this process that human beings identify the problems to be solved, and AI is a tool to achieve that purpose. The ultimate decider of the solution should always be humankind as those solutions will reflect the values, interest, aspirations, and beliefs of humanity. The challenge is how to enshrine that core philosophy of abstract thought into legal and regulatory codes. It is a matter of identifying what parts of humanity should be protected.

Legal and Regulatory Responses to AI Decision-Making

The current approach to regulation of AI in decision-making is a mix of legal and ethical considerations. On the ethical side, there is an increased awareness that human verification is necessary to provide protection for inaccurate decisions by AI. This oversight by people presents logistical problems. For example, in highly complex decisions where there are many data points there could be just too much information for a human to make a complete verification of the process. For example, suppose a company uses AI to screen job applicants in which thousands of applicants are analyzed. A human is not going to be able to double check those decisions on all of the applicants. In fact, such an approach would undermine the process altogether, and make it not worth using AI since a human being is, in effect, doing the work of the AI. This is a classic case of scalability, which prevents complete oversight because of resource limitations. Moreover, AI decision-making can occur in real time, which further complicates human oversight because real-time monitoring may be too resource intensive.

Other challenges also prevent true human oversight. Many AI systems operate within a black box, which is an opaque system that prevents humans from fully understanding the way the AI system works. This issue is compounded by humans lacking the technological knowledge of AI where they can fully understand how the systems work. There is also an issue of what objectives the AI is trying to provide. What are the human priorities versus the AI priorities? While speed, accuracy, and fairness may be the priority these priorities are independent of each other. The AI and human may bring different strengths in the decision-making process. Even with a highly aware and educated human to oversee AI output, there are logistical impediments to full human supervision. Moreover, even if a human could fully oversee AI's outputs, there is the logistical issue of this becoming a self-defeating endeavor as AI is meant to provide humans greater flexibility and freedom within their time because of AI's tremendous workload capacity.

Within regulation of AI, there are certain themes that emerge. They are transparency of platform, risk management, ethical AI development, vigilance in data privacy, and human oversight. Transparency is the most prominent of these approaches. Laws, including the E.U.'s AI Act, mandate that there is clear traceability for high-risk AI systems. Because many AI systems act as so-called "black boxes" explainability regulations attempt to provide a deep understanding of how inputs influence outputs. This includes the concept of traceability, which is the ability to track AI systems' lifecycles and how they develop with data over time. This requires informing users of how data is used, and how decisions are made. The E.U. AI Act requires high-risk, black box systems to provide transparency and explanations of its process and risk management. This is particularly important to systems that use medical information, serve as medical devices, or provide biometric identification. Of particular concern within the AI Act is the ability of AI to be leveraged for social scoring, a system that evaluates and ranks individuals based on their actions or characteristics. AI has great potential for this type of use because it can evaluate high amounts of aggregate data including social metrics such as finances, social media use, health decisions (e.g., vaccination status), and surveillance. This type of system is rife with privacy concerns, discrimination, and social control, which the AI Act attempts to eliminate as a potential use.[3] However, the issue with the E.U. AI Act and others like it that try to rein in the decision-making power of AI is that they do not account well for real-time use. That is, these laws focus on the developmental stage of AI and do not focus as much on the phase of creation that develops with contemporary use of the platform.

At the core of the AI Act is the requirement that interaction between humans and AI is fully disclosed, and that humans know when they are interfacing with AI technology. The concern is rooted in the fact that AI has become so sophisticated as a technology that it is frequently difficult to determine when an individual is dealing with an AI system or another human.[4] There are also a list of prohibited uses of AI that are rooted in manipulation or non-disclosed interactions with humans including use of AI for "subliminal techniques," AI that exploits users based on immutable traits, i.e., age, AI social scoring, AI risk assessment for criminal profiling, use of AI to create facial recognition systems through "untargeted scraping" of facial data, and the use of AI for various issues within biometric categorization.[5] However, at the core of AI control within the AI Act is human oversight of the technology, especially within decision-making. Article 14 section 2 of the Act states:

> Human oversight shall aim at preventing or minimising the risks to health, safety or fundamental rights that may emerge when a high-risk AI system is used in accordance with its intended purpose or under conditions of reasonably foreseeable misuse ....[6]

This oversight requires human understanding in the systems and gives individuals who are in administrative roles the ability to override high-risk AI decisions. Those high-risk decisions are focused on decisions that impact human rights, safety, health, or income. The Act goes further stating that no decision can be made based on the results of a high-risk AI system, unless the result is verified by two humans who are knowledgeable and trained in this area of expertise.[7] However, this oversight provides practical and technological limitations. The knowledge and training of the two human verifiers is not operationalized, and the verified decision-making seems to assume that there is a decision-making process that is long enough to allow for human involvement. Real-time decisions made by AI pose a distinct challenge in these scenarios since it is unlikely that a two-human verification process would practically work. Still other considerations need to be considered, chief among them being automation bias, which is the process in which humans, even those tasked with AI oversight, can become too reliant on technology outputs as final decision-makers.

These high-risk AI systems have led to a movement called explainable AI (XAI), which mandates that complex AI models can be broken down into explainable components to assist users in understanding the technology. There are some techniques that assist with this, called SHapley Additive exPlanations (SHAP values) or Local Interpretable Model-Agnostic Explanations (LIME), that provide understandable descriptions of AI. Each of those techniques has its own benefits and risks, but the overarching goal of each is to assist in human decision-making and comfort when using AI systems. SHAP values explain how much each part of a model contributes to a prediction by dividing the credit of the result, similar to a co-authored paper. LIME provides a simplified model behavior by creating a small, easy-to-understand version of the AI model. The end product of both is the same. Each system wants to make AI more understandable for the user and build transparency. AI platforms that use reinforcement learning or online learning can update their process of decision-making using new data that is contemporary to the use itself. This means the process by which the platform is making decisions is not a pre-set system, but a dynamic system that makes safeguards very difficult to pre-apply. To be more robust in the area of monitoring transparency within AI there should be regulations that look at dynamic, post-deployment transparency to monitor how platforms will develop on their own. Naturally, the AI Act focuses on high-risk use, but low-risk AI is not without some level of risk, especially if the system uses reinforcement learning.

The U.S. approach to transparency in AI decision-making can be best described as a patchwork of federal and state laws mixed with federal agency rules and guidelines. Currently, the U.S. has not led the world in AI regulation, perhaps because it seeks to lead the world in AI development. These geopolitical considerations make for a highly complex political discussion in which politicians are conflicted over the priority given to innovation versus regulation. One of the first attempts at creating an overarching guidepost for AI was the introduction of the Blueprint for An AI Bill of Rights (Blueprint) in October 2022, which was later rescinded by President Donald Trump's Executive Order Removing Barriers to American Leadership in Artificial Intelligence signed on January 23, 2025.[8] In the Blueprint, AI decision-making was a primary concern, specifically how decisions can lead to discrimination, but also how the finality of these decisions can have a major long-term impact on individuals. While no longer in effect, the Blueprint is illustrative of the concerns of AI. In the Blueprint, there is a call for human alternatives to decision-making:

> You should be able to opt out, where appropriate, and have access to a person who can quickly consider and remedy problems you encounter. You should be able to opt out from automated systems in favor of a human alternative, where appropriate. Appropriateness should be determined based on reasonable expectations in a given context and with a focus on ensuring broad accessibility and protecting the public from especially harmful impacts. In some cases, a human or other alternative may be required by law.[9]

The Blueprint also addresses issues of transparency within AI systems, and the protection against data privacy breaches and algorithmic discrimination. However, its biggest takeaway is the incorporation of the human in the decision-making process. This human alternative is the "fallback" to decisions made by AI that are adverse. However, the limitations of the Blueprint were self-evident as it is non-binding, lacks clear implementation, contains non-operationalized terms, has little mention of systemic risks within AI, and does not address technological feasibility for implementation. It also has a structure that encourages power sharing between the government, corporations, and developers about resolving some of the bigger conflicts within AI.[10]

One of the major attempts to address AI decision-making going beyond the aspirational Blueprint for an AI Bill of Rights was 2023 Executive Order on AI Development issued by President Joe Biden, which was also rescinded by President Donald Trump's Executive Order. While the Blueprint was a high-level framework for AI development, the Executive Order took these points and made them have more enforceable mechanisms within the federal government, especially in agencies. In the Order, Biden directed federal agencies to create guidelines to ensure AI transparency. There is specific discussion of post-deployment analysis. The Biden Executive Order said:

> Testing and evaluations, including post-deployment performance monitoring, will help ensure that AI systems function as intended, are resilient against misuse or dangerous modifications, are ethically developed and operated in a secure manner, and are compliant with applicable Federal laws and policies.[11]

The Executive Order attempted to address some of the growing issues of AI and establishes Chief AI Officers within federal agencies to monitor and implement the order. Additionally, it tasked the Department of Homeland Security (DHS) with establishing AI security protocols and working with private AI companies to assess AI threats. It also directed the National Institute of Standards and Technology (NIST) to supplement the AI Risk Management Framework (AI RMF), which was created in 2023 as a voluntary guide to help organizations manage AI. The AI RMF was an interesting attempt to create a voluntary structure of governance around AI that is industry agnostic. It is focused on four core areas: increasing trustworthiness of the AI, risk mitigation, long-term elastic guidance for industries, and as is a theme in U.S. regulation, encouraging AI development. Within the guidance is a concern that AI monocultures, that is AI use that uses a single AI to make decisions, lead to high levels of risk because they operate as an echo-chamber of ideas. For example, in market forecasting, monocultural AI can lead to financial shock because risk is not seen because of what AI groupthink is essentially. This also can lead to creation of systemic bias, which can result in discriminatory outputs that are replicated by multiple AI systems. The AI Executive Order stated that the AI RMF can be improved by "conducting public consultation; assessing data quality; assessing and mitigating disparate impacts and algorithmic discrimination; providing notice of the use of AI; continuously monitoring and evaluating deployed AI; and granting human consideration and remedies for adverse decisions made using AI."[12]

The Biden Executive Order also was concerned with the promotion of AI technology but also feared the misuse of AI to create civil rights violations. Specifically, President Biden noted that AI has the ability to discriminate in its decision-making. President Biden noted in the order:

> My Administration cannot – and will not – tolerate the use of AI to disadvantage those who are already too often denied equal opportunity and justice. From hiring to housing to healthcare, we have seen what happens when AI use deepens discrimination and bias, rather than improving quality of life. Artificial Intelligence systems deployed irresponsibly have reproduced and intensified existing inequities, caused new types of harmful discrimination, and exacerbated online and physical harms.[13]

President Donald Trump's Executive Order, Removing Barrier to American Leadership in Artificial Intelligence, is illustrative of the tension in regulation. Where the Biden Executive Order addressed many of the concerns around AI use, President Trump's Executive Order highlighted that establishing the U.S. as a pro-AI environment requires a regulatory environment that encourages innovation and development. Whether that can be achieved through mechanisms to curb the technology's excesses is a matter of political debate. Regulating the transparency of AI within the U.S. frequently involves a discussion of how much transparency is needed in relation to consumers and their choices within the marketplace that could be manipulated by AI. Big data has been part of consumer decision-making for over a decade, and the Federal Trade Commission (FTC) has been part of the discussion of the manipulative factors of big data manipulation.[14] In light of the growth of AI, the FTC has now focused on AI manipulation. The agency states that the AI systems must be used in a way that does not create deception for users.[15] Of particular concern is how AI can be used to gain "unearned human trust," which erodes consumer confidence and the ability to make informed decisions. Leveraging this AI to gain trust by steering people to make "harmful decisions in areas such as finances, health, education, housing, and employment" is the basis of many of the false advertising claims investigated by the FTC.[16] The agency's focus on transparency also advocates for clear disclosure that AI is being used, such as with customer bots, and that independent evaluation of the platforms through regular audits is essential to maintain platform integrity.[17] However, these rules have a problem with mandatory compliance, enforcement, and the rapid evolution of technology of AI.

Other agencies have focused on AI decision-making and risk. The DHS issued guidance on how AI works within infrastructure. An issue for DHS is how AI can be used or misused in automated decision-making processes. Among their suggestions is fine-tuning models to create protections of private data, creating "critical infrastructure entities" that provide data integrity, creating a system that prioritizes and elevates AI risks, creating development that provides "system hygiene," and measuring impact of AI within system health.[18] The DHS also points out that stewardship and role of "civil society" and the public sector plays within the development of AI standards and protocols. This group represents a cross-section of industry including non-governmental organizations (NGOs), unions, charities, professional associations, foundations, and universities which are tasked with creating the "standards, frameworks, and solutions that can help measure and communicate the impact of technology on individuals and communities."[19] As with many of the U.S.-based protocols on AI decision-making this DHS guidance leaves many open ended suggestions and places the responsibility of the technology back onto industry and society to make the necessary changes.

The current U.S. regulations on AI demonstrate a lack of cohesion and the challenges that a fragmented governance structure has within AI regulations. In many situations, the philosophic underpinning of U.S. law on AI is reactive to contemporary scenarios as opposed to creating a comprehensive AI regulation on issues like transparency. Compounding this issue is the one of oversight. Accountability challenges persist particularly when there are non-operationalized terms, such as transparency, that appear to be more like legal slogans than terms of enforcement. The technology of AI also provides barriers to this approach to comprehensive law because there are significant explainability gaps within AI. The opaque decision-making process found in "black box" systems coupled with the inconsistent mandates for operationalized transparency makes it difficult to know how AI should work. There are some instances where there are also laws that specifically discuss transparency and privacy, such as the California Consumer Privacy Act (CCPA), which was passed prior to the proliferation of generative AI programs. It grants many of the rights articulated in the E.U.'s GDPR, including the right to know how data is collected and used. However, it does not anticipate or address the issues of high-risk AI, and it also contains loopholes for certain businesses that make certain organizations exempt based on revenue thresholds.[20] What laws like this show is that there must be a rethinking statutes and rules that deal with accountability and decisions in light of the prolific use of AI. This may require both a retooling of existing law as well as an effort to create new comprehensive legislation on the subject. The problem with all of these efforts is the backdrop of technological innovation, and the need to create a regulatory environment that does not stifle innovation. That balance is delicate, and increasingly more complex as the stakes of AI become more consequential for the economy and geopolitical power. This theme of power within AI leadership is the basis of the U.S. approach to the regulation of the technology. The U.S. House of Representatives Report on the Current Status of AI, issued in December 2024, reiterated this stating:

> The United States is the global leader in Artificial Intelligence, a transformative technology that also comes with risks that must be addressed responsibly. To ensure the economic and national security benefits accrue in the United States and the technology is developed and deployed

responsibly here and across the world, the United States must take active steps to safeguard our current leadership position.[21]

AI Decision-Making and Communicators

Within communication the issue of AI decision-making is complex because of the lack of comprehensive laws on the matter. While the E.U. AI Act provides the most comprehensive approach to the subject, its jurisdictional boundaries limit its enforceability. Within the U.S., there are concerns around AI and transparency, but the common theme of all U.S. regulations is human oversight and self-monitoring. There are also more industry-focused regulations that task AI systems to create AI guardrails to prevent bad decisions and outcomes. Moreover, most of the legal and regulatory concerns focus on high-risk AI and do not provide the same level of restrictions on medium or low-risk AI. These forms of AI include basic inquiry chatbots, personalized marketing, and customer support chatbots, which are tools that many communicators use on a daily basis.

What does this mean for communicators? Practically it means that communicators have a higher degree of flexibility in how and when they use AI. It also places communicators in a unique role of thought leaders because they can create ethical AI boundaries and practices without the constraints of restrictive laws. As such, communicators also have the opportunity to be educators and advocates of AI use, especially given the general lack of knowledge of AI by society. In fact, the larger societal conversation about AI transparency and disclosure are subjects that are familiar to any communicator. Moreover, stakeholder interests and public good are part of the core ethical philosophy within good communications. This positions communicators as highly credible speakers on the issue of AI decision-makering as they are cultural translators well equipped to bring in the ethical and emotional intelligence into the discussion of AI development and use. Communicators also serve as stewards of public trust that shape the larger conversations around technological innovation and use. This includes conversations around AI inclusivity and divergent voices, which positions communication as a field that can combat the larger technological ecosystems that can lead to AI echo chambers. In a world where the larger issue is the displacement of humanity's role within individual agency, communication can serve as a mechanism to dismantle the biases that may result in so-called "intelligent" systems. After all, AI is a tool for humans, not a technology to dictate their lives.

However, regulations around AI decision-making present unique issues. In many ways, the regulatory environment is one of competing cultural values. U.S. lawmakers seem to focus heavily on innovation at the expense of preemptive regulation where the E.U. prioritizes ethical oversight to preserve cultural values, specifically privacy (another area where the U.S. and E.U. significantly differ). Which values actually prevail will likely be one of messaging, which again gives communicators an outsized voice in this arena. Communication professionals, particularly those in strategic communication and public relations, are used to the ubiquitous and ill-defined term of transparency. Their insight on what is actually transparent in AI decision-making could prove helpful. While transparency is frequently mentioned as an essential part of AI communication there is a balance between complete openness about AI and complete opaque use. There is a problem too with complete transparency in that the technical explanation of the systems is overwhelming for a non-technical audience. Sometimes the transparency of a message actually garbles it, creating more confusion and concern that it would have otherwise been.

There is another deeper human problem with this type of oversight. It is a core essentialism within law and ethics that bias is bad. However, there can be biases that ultimately yield better results. As mentioned earlier in this chapter, suppose a person is evaluated annually by AI, but the AI does not consider the personal challenges the person has faced in the past year. Maybe they are dealing with illness, caring for a loved one, or overcoming an obstacle that has impacted their otherwise good work performance. AI may provide a clear-cut analysis of utility of that worker, but the human dimension is lost. A human's bias, i.e., empathy or mercy, may create a better result. Taking into those non-objectified considerations presents a just decision even though it may not be a totally un-biased one.

So, can AI decision-making effectively be regulated? Most likely the answer is yes, but a comprehensive AI law is unlikely to work. Because of the nuances within decision-making of AI, it is more likely and practical that AI is regulated in an incremental, sector-specific way. For example, healthcare, finance, and other high-level sectors will have tailored rules for explainability and predictive fairness (similar to what the E.U. mandates in the AI Act). Global norms set by the United Nations (U.N.), World Trade Organization (WTO), and the Organization for Economic Co-operation and Development (OECD) may also establish broad standards within ethical AI decision-making. This coupled with co-regulation with private partnerships will allow the government to leverage industry knowledge of technology to craft appropriate regulations that allow for well-structured and workable solutions. However, technological complexity, divergent global standards, and industry reluctance may present obvious obstacles. Regulation is achievable, but it is important to expect imperfections. But these imperfections are better than the alternatives where AI becomes out of control creating and perpetuating unequal results that erode privacy, autonomy, and fairness within democratic society.

However, human beings have to make more concrete decisions on what they expect from AI. The technology is not a system that is imposed upon people or systems. Instead, it is a technology that can be leveraged by humankind in a manner that they wish. When analyzing decision-making within AI, it is important to remember that the ultimate decision, and responsibility, falls to the user, not the technology. As legal liability and ethical guides are developed for AI, it is likely they will emphasize the human responsibility and accountability. The net result of this could be a prioritization of proactive decision-making and the establishment of industry-wide AI principles that determine best practices. This may result in an anticipatory decision-making culture that requires not just legal compliance but ethical vigilance.

Discussion Questions

1 Can there be a limit on what type of decisions AI makes? What categories of decisions should only be made by humans?
2 Are humans inherently better than machines in decision-making? What flaws do both decision-makers have?
3 What does transparency mean? How is it a liability and an asset in AI communication?
4 How should AI be used in decision-making? Why do people think humans are the best failsafe for poor AI decisions?
5 **Scenario:** Suppose you are a communicator who is using AI to provide market analysis of the best potential consumers for a new product. The AI provides analysis of not only who the best consumers are but also provides a geographic location of where to find these potential customers. It suggests that your company provide a targeted media campaign in that area and also provide the customers a trial of the product that includes a company credit card offer. Any problems with this type of decision-making? What biases could AI provide in that analysis? Are there any legal concerns that arise with this type of offer?

Notes

1 R. Keith Sawyer, *Explaining Creativity: The Science of Human Innovation* (Oxford: Oxford University Press, 2012); Brené Brown, *The Gifts of Imperfection: Let Go of Who You Think You're Supposed to Be and Embrace Who You Are* (Center City: Hazelden Publishing, 2010); Carl Folke et al., "Resilience Thinking: Integrating Resilience, Adaptability, and Transformability," *Ecology and Society* 15, no. 4 (2010), http://www.ecologyandsociety.org/vol15/iss4/art20/.
2 Meredith Broussard, *Artificial Unintelligence: How Computers Misunderstand the World* (Cambridge, MA: MIT Press, 2018), 156.

3 European Union, Regulation (EU) 2024/1689 of the European Parliament and of the Council of 13 June 2024 Laying Down Harmonised Rules on Artificial Intelligence and Amending Certain Union Legislative Acts (Artificial Intelligence Act), Official Journal of the European Union, L'2024/1689 (12 July 2024), https://eur-lex.europa.eu/legal-content/EN/TXT/PDF/?uri=OJ:L_202401689
4 Regulation (EU) 2024/1689 of the European Parliament and of the Council of 20 June 2024 on Artificial Intelligence (AI Act), 1.
5 Ibid.
6 Ibid.
7 Ibid.
8 White House Office of Science and Technology Policy, *Blueprint for an AI Bill of Rights*, accessed November 29, 2024, https://bidenwhitehouse.archives.gov/ostp/ai-bill-of-rights/; Donald J. Trump, "Removing Barrier to American Leadership in Artificial Intelligence," Executive Order 14179, January 23, 2025, https://www.whitehouse.gov/presidential-actions/2025/01/removing-barriers-to-american-leadership-in-artificial-intelligence/.
9 White House Office of Science and Technology Policy, *Blueprint for an AI Bill of Rights.*
10 White House Office of Science and Technology Policy, *Blueprint for an AI Bill of Rights.*
11 Joseph R. Biden Jr., "*Executive Order on the Safe, Secure, and Trustworthy Development and Use of Artificial Intelligence,*" Executive Order 14110 October 30, 2023, https://www.federalregister.gov/documents/2023/11/01/2023-24283/safe-secure-and-trustworthy-development-and-use-of-artificial-intelligence.
12 Biden, "*Executive Order on the Safe, Secure, and Trustworthy Development.*"
13 Ibid.
14 Federal Trade Commission, *Big Data: A Tool for Inclusion or Exclusion? Understanding the Issues* (Washington, DC: Federal Trade Commission, January 2016), https://www.ftc.gov/system/files/documents/reports/big-data-tool-inclusion-or-exclusion-understanding-issues/160106big-data-rpt.pdf.
15 Federal Trade Commission, "Keep Your AI Claims in Check," *FTC Business Blog*, February 27, 2023, https://www.ftc.gov/business-guidance/blog/2023/02/keep-your-ai-claims-check.
16 Federal Trade Commission, "Luring the Test of AI and Engineering Consumer Trust," *FTC Consumer Alerts*, May 3, 2023, https://www.ftc.gov/consumer-alerts/2023/05/luring-test-ai-and-engineering-consumer-trust.
17 Federal Trade Commission, "Using Artificial Intelligence and Algorithms," *Business Blog*, April 8, 2020, https://www.ftc.gov/business-guidance/blog/2020/04/using-artificial-intelligence-algorithms; Federal Trade Commission, "Aiming for Truth, Fairness, and Equity in Your Company's Use of AI," *Business Blog*, April 19, 2021, https://www.ftc.gov/business-guidance/blog/2021/04/aiming-truth-fairness-equity-your-companys-use-ai.
18 Department of Homeland Security, *Artificial Intelligence Roles and Responsibilities Framework in Critical Infrastructure*, November 14, 2024, https://www.dhs.gov/sites/default/files/2024-11/24_1114_dhs_ai-roles-and-responsibilities-framework-508.pdf.
19 Ibid 24.
20 California Consumer Privacy Act of 2018, Cal. Civ. Code §§ 1798.100–1798.199 (2020).
21 U.S. House of Representatives, "Artificial Intelligence Task Force Report," December 2024, https://www.speaker.gov/wp-content/uploads/2024/12/AI-Task-Force-Report-FINAL.pdf, v.

3

AI AND DISINFORMATION

Combatting Fake News

Chapter Overview

This chapter discusses how laws and regulations are attempting to combat disinformation created by artificial intelligence (AI). Specific attention is paid to how AI can be leveraged to create and amplify dis- and misinformation with a specific focus on disinformation content during elections. The chapter discusses the issues of regulation of disinformation under the U.S. First Amendment, application of defamation laws, and potential liability of AI platforms under U.S. federal law, specifically the Communication Decency Act section 230. The chapter concludes with a discussion on how combatting dis- and misinformation through AI ultimately falls to user verification of content as regulations in this area present complex legal questions and issues with enforcement.

Keywords: Misinformation, Disinformation, Defamation, First Amendment, Election Communications

Mis- and disinformation are some of the most concerning issues of the 2020s. Part of the concern is rooted in the idea that this type of communication has an insidious quality that undermines the legitimacy in many of the institutions and values that underpin society. Misinformation and disinformation are distinct, yet interrelated, forms of communication that have existed throughout communication's history. Misinformation is broadly defined as dissemination of false or inaccurate information without the intent to deceive, while disinformation is the deliberate creation and distribution of misleading, false, or malicious content with the intention of deception. Their distinction is one of intent, but they work together in a

DOI: 10.4324/9781003426561-3

synergistic way. For example, disinformation may utilize people's propensity to not verify information to lead to its sharing and distribution. This is amplified by the scrolling consumption patterns of social media, which facilitates a passive consumption of content. The motive of this type of content is rooted in strategic advantage of the sender, but those advantages vary. For instance, disinformation has been used for centuries for military advantage to make an opponent prepare for conflict that puts them at a strategic disadvantage. In modern times, the strategic advantage is manifold and can include political power, financial gain, promotion of ideology, revenge, and social disruption. Disinformation also plays a large role within the troll culture of the internet. Trolling, the deliberate act of posting offensive, false, or disruptive messaging online to generate emotional responses or to detail internet conversations, has been around since the 1990s. It is a form of baiting other users to engage in conflict. The troll culture of the internet has also facilitated the rise of disinformation as well as some users derive social enjoyment and amusement from creating chaos.[1] The spread of disinformation by these types of users helps to normalize falsehoods and manipulate public opinion. While their strategic motive ranges from personal gratification to a larger political agenda, the insidious quality of their content creates a social problem that has major implications for democracy, information integrity, and public health.

Artificial intelligence (AI) plays an important role in both the production and combatting of disinformation. The creation of this content using deepfake technology (discussed in Chapter 1) allows for realistic creation of synthetic content. Compounding the problem is that deepfakes can be amplified with AI technology by leveraging the predictive analysis to target social media in a manner that increases the chance of the content going viral. The nature of social media content consumption, with its emphasis of passive scrolling, provides a format where content then can be shared and liked further amplifying the message. Lawmakers have raised concerns that this type of ease of disinformation production provides a perfect opportunity for the proliferation of disinformation. However, despite AI's role in producing high-quality deepfakes and other disinformation content, it also has the ability to combat it through its algorithmic detection. Language processing, pattern recognition, and deep learning provide tool to create a mechanism for detection. So, in effect, AI has the ability to combat a problem it is largely contributing to. However, that detection is not absolute, and many regulators and lawmakers point to the AI industry to self-regulate platforms' ability to create this type of content. In this chapter, the issue of dis- and misinformation as it relates to AI is discussed, and the legal mechanisms for regulating this type of issue are examined with an eye toward what communicators can do proactively to engage and discredit this type of content.

The Role of AI in Disinformation

On May 22, 2023, a deepfake photo of the Pentagon engulfed with dark clouds went viral on Twitter (now X), prompting a dip in the U.S. Stock Market with the Dow Jones Industrial Average losing 80 points before rebounding. The impact of this disinformation campaign illustrated both the speed at which deepfakes can spread and the vulnerability institutions, like the stock market, have in responding to this type of content.[2] Similarly, in 2024 in the aftermath of Hurricane Helene, deepfakes of victims in North Carolina spread throughout social media depicting displaced children and pets, and even showed politicians, including President Donald Trump and Vice President Kamala Harris, helping them.[3] These deepfakes were frequently tied to scams asking for money for victims. The content sometimes contained factual disinformation about government services, prompting the U.S. government through FEMA, to create a "Hurricane Rumor Response" strategy to debunk disinformation that was going viral.[4] The impact of this disinformation ranged in content and included allegations that the agency was confiscating donations made to hurricane victims. The nature of both of these incidents demonstrates the high-stakes impact of AI-generated disinformation, and the ease in which it is created and spread. The growing access of AI and the ease in which users can create deepfake content makes this only the beginning of a long-term and escalating problem.

The mechanics of deepfakes are found in technology of AI. Generative adversarial networks (GANs) allow neural networks to compete to create highly realistic synthetic images and audio. Machine learning algorithms provide the ability for AI to mimic facial expressions and voices from a dataset of real audio and video. This allows for facial mapping and voice cloning. The amount of data needed for this is also very small. Base voice cloning, which is lower quality, only requires approximately 5–30 seconds of audio where higher quality needs perhaps up to 5 minutes. AI's ability to create lip synching and synchronization that aligns this manipulated audio with video creates an expression of real-life content. Audio-visual manipulation has been around for decades. Notably the HBO series, *The Sopranos*, used computer-generated imagery (CGI) in 2000 to create a lifelike scene when actress Nancy Marchand who played Livia Soprano. Marchand passed away, but her image and voice were recreated by CGI to create a minute-long scene that cost approximately $250,000. Today, AI technology could produce that scene with higher quality and subtle facial expressions at a fraction of the cost and in a much faster time.

It is thought that deepfakes first appeared on Reddit in 2017 when a user began manipulating celebrity photos. From that point, awareness of deepfake technology grew with well-known uses of deepfake technology going mainstream, such as comedian Jordan Peele's creation of a manipulated image of former President Barack Obama.[5] Deepfake technology also began to become more available with programs DeepFaceLab and FaceSwap allowing for recreational deepfake content. By the 2020s, the technology improved with the sophistication of GANs and algorithms. Today users with little to no coding ability or even sophisticated knowledge of prompt writing can easily create deepfake content using free generative AI accounts. This content ranges from humor to politics but has serious implications.

Today deepfake technology is used not only for political disinformation but scams. Some of these include replicating a relative's voice and then calling victims asking for money for high-stakes requests such as bail or ransom. The voice clone calls' realistic sound of the voice proves effective, especially given the fact that many of the victims are in a heightened state of panic and are not vetting the caller's request or content. These so-called "family emergency scams" illustrate the personal nature of deepfakes and the pervasiveness of them given so much personal data is available about people.[6] Deepfakes have also proliferated in other harmful ways including school bullying and other forms of retaliation. In 2024, a Maryland principal was placed on leave for making racist and antisemitic comments. The recorded statements went viral on social media, creating public backlash against the principal and school. However, the content was a deepfake created by the school's athletic director who was reprimanded by the principal over his work. The data for the clone likely came from an authentic voicemail that was then used to create the new content. The result was a public relations crisis for the school and reputational harm for the principal.[7]

These cases present a unique issue for lawmakers who are concerned about the spread and impact of disinformation on society. Do there need to be new laws put in place to combat this proliferation of untrue content, or do existing laws provide enough of a solution? The answer lies in how the government wants to combat the problem. If it is at the source, which is with the platforms themselves, then there have to be regulations that address disinformation creation in the form of platform guardrails. If the law seeks to combat the problem by addressing it when it impacts society, then that presents a unique challenge because the source of the disinformation is frequently unidentifiable. Moreover, the disinformation, once viral, has so much resonance within society that combatting it with litigation has a minimal impact beyond money damages.

Legal Implications of AI-Generated Disinformation

Dis- and misinformation within AI create novel legal issues that bring into question existing frameworks of laws and regulations. Deepfakes' status under the First Amendment, defamation, and immunity of section 230 of the Communications Decency Act are areas that current laws and lawmakers are struggling with. While current legal frameworks may not have a direct application to AI, they do anticipate some of the broader issues of the technology. In dealing with these novel AI issues, lawmakers will likely struggle to keep up with the fast changes AI is presenting as they apply established legal norms to novel legal issues.

First Amendment Protection of Dis- and Misinformation

The specter of mis- and disinformation is viewed as a mechanism to upend democratic institutions and faith in the bedrock of truth within society. Because of that, many lawmakers and politicians have called for enhanced regulation of dis- and misinformation and have argued that prohibiting this type of speech is required to preserve the democratic system. However, such efforts are thwarted when using the existing legal framework of free speech. European countries and the E.U. have a legal system that lacks an absolute free speech doctrine, which allows for greater regulations on mis- and disinformation such as the Digital Services Act (DSA), General Data Protection Regulation (GDPR), and AI Act.[8] The E.U. Code of Practice on Disinformation also created a voluntary framework for digital platforms to combat disinformation in the wake of the Cambridge Analytica scandal in 2016.[9] These laws and regulations place the E.U. at the forefront of combatting mis- and disinformation, but they also come with criticism from free speech advocates who say they are a threat to free speech. Other critics from the tech industry argue these types of regulations place too high a burden on tech companies for compliance, especially since enforcement of these standards is difficult to effectuate and costly.

The regulation of mis- and disinformation presents unique challenges within the U.S. legal framework of the First Amendment. Unlike the E.U., the U.S. approach to speech rights encourages minimal government interference. This is rooted in the historical experiences of the Founders with British seditious libel laws during the colonial era, and the Enlightenment philosophy of John Locke that influenced many of the Drafters of the U.S. Constitution. This foundational approach to the First Amendment meant that U.S. speech law developed in a specific way that prioritizes broad protections for individual expression, tolerating even false or offensive speech to avoid government overreach, and emphasizing the "marketplace of ideas" as the mechanism for resolving disputes and uncovering truth. Rooted in the philosophical traditions of John Milton's 1644 book *Areopagitica* and later in John Stuart Mill's *On Liberty*, the marketplace of ideas influenced jurists in the development and interpretation of case law concerning the First Amendment.[10] Milton was writing in a historical era in Britain where censorship was legally instituted through government licensing. His premise in *Areopagitica* was that government licensing was censorship, and the fears associated with subversive ideas were unfounded since the marketplace of ideas served as a natural self-corrective measure. His philosophy was rooted in an anti-authoritarian view of government, and the belief that self-discovery led to human intellectual growth. Mill argued that only through public debate could good ideas gain traction within society, and allowed them to fully understand and appreciate the truth. Similar to the economic marketplace, it was in the marketplace of societal discourse in which the best ideas rose to the top gaining traction within society, according to Milton. Commenting on the role that good and bad information plays within societal discourse Mill wrote:

> The peculiar evil of silencing the expression of an opinion is, that it is robbing the human race; posterity as well as the existing generation; those who dissent from the opinion, still more than those who hold it. If the opinion is right, they are deprived of the opportunity of exchanging error for truth; if wrong, they lose, what is almost as great a benefit, the clearer perception and livelier impression of truth, produced by its collision with error.[11]

Chief among these devotees of the marketplace philosophy was influential U.S. Supreme Court Justice Oliver Wendall Holmes, who was arguably the most impactful figure in shaping First Amendment jurisprudence in American history. Holmes's views on the power of the marketplace as a regulator of "bad" speech is seen in his influential dissent in *Abrams v. U.S.* In that case, Justice Holmes criticized the majority's opinion in upholding the Espionage Act of 1917, which allowed for the prosecution of anti-war protestor anarchist for his views, writing:

> But when men have realized that time has upset many fighting faiths, they may come to believe even more than they believe the very foundations of their own conduct that the ultimate good desired is better reached by free trade in ideas – that the best test of truth is the power

of the thought to get itself accepted in the competition of the market, and that truth is the only ground upon which their wishes safely can be carried out.[12]

Even though Holmes dissented in that case, his philosophy of the marketplace of ideas gained traction with later courts. The concept of marketplace of ideas has become a major philosophical thread in many U.S. Supreme Court and lower court decisions.[13] It undergirds democratic values, discussion of ideas, seeking of truth, serves as a bulwark against censorship, and encourages self-regulation of speech. However, there are critics of marketplace of ideas who cite that power dynamics and an overemphasis on the rationality of speakers and listeners provide a false reality that truth will prevail. Those critics argue the market systems of communication actually create an environment where there is a communication ecosystem that manipulates public opinion that drives individuals to echo chambers where the best-packaged content becomes accepted as objective "truth." Many argue that it is this faith in the marketplace of ideas that actually allows mis- and disinformation to proliferate within society, and, as a result of the adherence to this philosophy, there are institutional obstacles barring meaningful reform and regulation of this content.[14]

In the U.S., false information and content is largely protected under the First Amendment so long as it is not unprotected speech, e.g., defamation, obscenity, or fighting words.[15] This means that absent those three categories of speech, which generally can be called unprotected speech, mis- and disinformation are fully protected under the First Amendment. The role of disinformation and false claims have actually been found to have value within free discourse in society, according to the U.S. Supreme Court. For example, in *New York Times v. Sullivan*, the case that established the actual malice standard for defamation of public officials, the court suggested that false statements about public officials had some level of protection (though the statements in that case were mild inaccuracies).[16] Later, the court held that non-intentional political misstatements of fact in a political campaign were not unprotected under the First Amendment. In the watershed case *Hustler Magazine v. Falwell*, the Court unanimously held that parodies and exaggerated claims not claiming to be purported fact are protected under the First Amendment.[17] Notably the court in 2012 struck down the Stolen Valor Act, a federal law that criminalized false statements about receiving military decorations with enhanced penalties for false claims of winning the Medal of Honor, because it violated the First Amendment. In the court's analysis, they held that some false statements are not without First Amendment protection. Writing for the majority, Justice Kennedy explained that "falsity alone may not suffice to bring the speech outside the First Amendment. The statement must be a knowing or reckless falsehood."[18]

Of course, these discussions of the marketplace of ideas and government censorship pre-date AI-generated content. Milton, Mill, and Holmes did not anticipate deepfake technology and voice cloning that coupled with social media led to the proliferation of mis- and disinformation in society. Moreover, their issue was largely with government censorship that was meant to suppress so-called subversive activities that undermined governmental authority and control. Today, AI-generated mis- and disinformation serve a purpose to undermine the underpinnings of democratic society, and the subversiveness of the content is not to question authority but to challenge the reality of members in society. Disinformation also has insidious qualities that are meant to defraud, defame, harass, and intimidate others. The consequences are severe, such as the stock market reaction to the fake Pentagon explosion image that went viral in 2023. Election disinformation proliferated in 2024, which was a major election year globally. In the U.S. presidential election, a deepfake voice clone of President Joe Biden's voice was used to robocall voters in the New Hampshire Primary encouraging them not to vote in the election.[19] The Democratic operative behind the stunt was fined $6 million by the Federal Communications Commission (FCC) as the content violated rules on inaccurate caller ID information.[20] The campaign Florida Governor Ron DeSantis, who sought the Republican nomination for President, allegedly used deepfake technology to spread messages of President Donald Trump embracing the controversial Dr. Anthony Fauci and then spread the information on X. The pro-DeSantis PAC, Never Back Down, also issued an ad with non-contextualized clips of Trump firing people on his show *The Apprentice* with voice over of Trump explaining why did not fire Fauci. Images within those segments of Trump embracing Fauci and kissing him were said to be deepfake according to Agence-France Press (AFP) fact checkers.[21] The same PAC has also used an ad with DeSantis with altered AI video showing fighter jets in the background.[22]

However, the issue with deepfakes is not necessarily when companies or campaigns use the technology in a transparent way. The big concern with disinformation and AI is when the deepfake technology is used to deliberately deceive by passing itself off as authentic content. That did not appear to be the case in 2024 (at least on a large scale). Rather, deepfake content worked as a form of political satire that when coupled with meme culture allowed for greater divisions within society.[23] This was particularly worrisome for some because platforms, such as X, provide lower guardrails on content. Elon Musk, the owner of X, posted an AI-generated fake audio clip of Vice President and Democratic nominee Kamala Harris praising

President Joe Biden for dropping out of the race and hailing herself as a diversity hire calling Biden the "ultimate deep state puppet."[24] It concluded with Harris in her voice saying, "You think the country went to shit over the last four years? You ain't seen nothin' yet."[25] There were also many AI-generated images of African American supporters of Donald Trump, Trump dressed in a Nazi uniform, and Harris wearing sexually suggestive outfits.[26]

Advocates of altered deepfake ads state that this is no different than any other graphics tools that can be used for communication. In 2024, Coca-Cola introduced an AI-generated holiday ad that used traditional holiday seasonal imagery. The company faced criticism over this, but Coca-Cola stood by the ad saying that it represented the tradition of the product and represented a consistency of high-level work product. In addition to the manipulation of the content through AI, the criticism also centers around the displacement of artists and producers of ad content (something that has been a universal fear of AI dominance).[27] Celebrity culture is also affected by AI deepfakes such as the highly publicized deepfakes of Katy Perry, Rhianna, and Dua Lipa at the famed Met Gala in May 2024. Perry's own mother was said to be duped by a realistic image of her daughter at the Gala wearing a flowing gown with flowers.[28] Even Pope Francis has been the subject of deepfake AI photos with him wearing a white puffer jacket. Those photos went viral in 2023 with many thinking the image was authentic.[29]

The central issue with celebrity deepfakes lies in understanding the actual harm they may cause. Are these digital creations merely harmless entertainment, or do they pose significant risks to privacy, public trust, and reputations? Proponents of deepfakes like these say they are a harmless means of expression. What is the real harm in thinking the Pope wore a jacket that he didn't? Others within political circles will say deepfake content did not change the outcomes in 2024. Rather, they served as a form of political expression that allowed social media users to voice their opinions of the candidates in unique and expressive formats. Musk's AI platform Grok, known for its limited guardrails on content creation, produced many deepfake videos that were so outlandish that no one would take them seriously as the truth. Yet, concerns over disinformation are not without merit. Grok has been accused of pushing election disinformation about ballot integrity.[30] AI-generated photos of victims of Hurricane Milton were the basis of much of the disinformation campaigns and scams that followed the storm.[31] The disinformation from that event that was fueled by AI led to the U.S. government putting out its own debunking campaign against the viral online content.[32]

There is no federal law that directly deals with AI disinformation and its mandatory disclosure. Also, no federal law exists that comprehensively deals with mis- and disinformation and its dissemination. States, however, have become increasingly involved in addressing AI deepfakes and disinformation. While traditional legal outlets, such as false light and defamation laws, remain outlets for holding content producers responsible, there have been novel approaches by states to address the problem of deepfake and AI disinformation. California has the boldest plan to address the problem of disinformation generally, but the legality of its recent laws has been called into question by a federal court. In 2024, Governor Gavin Newsome signed three bills into law that directly addressed disinformation and its spread. The first, AB 2655, requires large online platforms to remove or label deceptive, digitally altered, or AI-generated content related to elections during specified periods. It also requires these platforms to provide a feedback mechanism for reporting deceptive content and authorizes legal action against platforms that are non-compliant.[33] Another law, AB 2839, prohibits the distribution of deceptive content within 120 before and 60 days after an election. It also provides an expansive list of individuals who have standing to bring suit that includes politicians, election officials, and recipients of the content.[34] The third law, AB 2355, required that election advertisements that use AI-generated or substantially altered content disclose that the material has been altered or used AI technology. The law provides for enforcement through the Fair Political Practices Commission.[35] However, these laws have been challenged under the First Amendment, and AB 2655 and AB 2839 as of this writing being challenged in the U.S. District Court for the Eastern District of California. The judge in the case, John Mendez, issued a preliminary injunction against AB 2839 citing First Amendment concerns for fully protected speech. In his order, Judge Mendez wrote:

> Supreme Court precedent illuminates that while a well-founded fear of a digitally manipulated media landscape may be justified, this fear does not give legislators unbridled license to bulldoze over the longstanding tradition of critique, parody, and satire protected by the First Amendment. YouTube videos, Facebook posts, and X tweets are the newspaper advertisements and political cartoons of today, and the First Amendment protects an individual's right to speak regardless of the new medium these critiques may take.[36]

The court notes that other remedies are available to those affected by deepfakes from AI including copyright infringement, privacy torts, and defamation.

Despite California's legal challenges, other states have moved forward with more targeted regulations. Many of these regulations have centered on disclosure of AI for political advertisements. As of September 2024, there were at least 19 states that had laws specifically addressing AI use in election communications. These states are Arizona, California, Colorado, Delaware, Florida, Hawaii, Idaho, Indiana, Michigan, Minnesota, Mississippi, New Mexico, New Hampshire, New York, Oregon, Texas, Utah, Washington, and Wisconsin.[37] These laws grapple with definitions and processes, however. Many of the states' attempt to define AI and struggle with enforcement mechanisms, especially what constitutes disclosure. Many are concerned with the deception of AI itself and use the term "materially deceptive media" to define the type of communication they are seeking to ban or regulate.[38] In total in 2024, 45 states introduced AI bills on various issues, and 31 states along with Puerto Rico and the Virgin Islands enacted legislation.[39]

Federally there have been laws introduced that address AI disclosure, but as of this writing there are no comprehensive federal disclosure laws. In the 118th Congress, there have been several laws introduced to mandate disclosure of AI use within elections. The Protected Elections from Deceptive AI Act sought to prohibit AI-created content from being used in federal elections.[40] Another bill, AI Transparency in Elections Act of 2024, mandates disclosure of when AI is used in election-related content and activities.[41] The Candidate Voice Fraud Prohibition Act criminalizes the use of AI in election communication that contains deceptive audio that misleads voters.[42] Other bills focus on aspects of political use of AI in similar ways. The Federal Artificial Intelligence Risk Management Act of 2024 focuses on managing AI risks through standardized protocols, regular audits, and transparency measures, requiring federal agencies to report AI usage and compliance to Congress.[43] The Securing Elections From AI Deception Act prohibits the use of AI-generated content to mislead voters or deprive them of voting rights, mandating disclosure of AI usage in political campaigns and oversight by the Federal Election Commission (FEC).[44] Similarly, the AI Transparency in Elections Act of 2024 attempted to amend the Federal Election Campaign Act of 1971 to require disclaimers on AI-generated political advertisements and compel campaigns to disclose AI tools and usage to the FEC.[45] These laws promote transparency, focusing on preventing election disinformation, and attempt to provide guardrails for AI use in elections. They also share one other similarity – none have been enacted into law underscoring the political difficulty in passing AI-related legislation in an increasingly polarized U.S. Congress.

Despite these political challenges, there is a recognition that disinformation through AI in elections poses a significant risk. The Cybersecurity and Infrastructure Security Agency, a federal agency under the control of the Department of Homeland Security (DHS), cites the use of deepfake and voice clones as a major problem for election integrity citing deepfake videos, altered images, voice clones, and LLM conversions of non-English manipulated content to English. This last category is particularly applicable to non-U.S. actors who seek to disrupt U.S. elections through orchestrated disinformation campaigns. The agency is concerned that this AI-generated disinformation goes beyond political advertising and has the potential to manipulate election stations, early voting, and basic information about the election process. Rather than suggest legislation, they suggest that individuals take a more proactive stance on verifying information. This includes making social media accounts private, using two-factor analysis for access to accounts, requesting the removal of personal information from public websites, and regular reporting of suspicious activity.[46]

Federal agencies, such as the Federal Communication Commission (FCC), FEC, and Federal Trade Commission (FTC), have also proposed measures to combat disinformation in political ads. In 2024 the FCC proposed rules to clearly disclose deepfake and AI-generated content in political ads.[47] The FEC adopted an interpretation of a preexisting rule on deceptive political content that included AI deception. They interpret the existing prohibition of fraudulent misrepresentation to include AI as the statute is not technology specific.[48] The FTC has also issued some guidance on determining fraud within AI, and about how users ultimately bear the responsibility of verifying information from these platforms.[49] Ultimately, it is the self-awareness that is likely the best approach at uncovering mis- and disinformation as regulations may have mixed success in enforcement. The 2024 Bipartisan House Task Force Report on Artificial Intelligence specifically mentions job training as part of the mission to combat disinformation stating:

> Because parts of the internet contain large amounts of disinformation, bias, and hate speech, without intervention, these systems are prone to mimic toxic content. This kind of human feedback requires workers to have appropriate skills and training to interpret the content correctly. As companies seek to improve AI systems on complex topics, there will need to be a commensurate increase in the skills required for humans to provide relevant feedback in RLHF [Reinforcement Learning from Human Feedback] or similar AI training paradigms.[50]

Defamation and Trade Libel Within AI

While combatting dis- and misinformation presents novel issues for courts and lawmakers, there are existing laws that can combat the issue. Chief among them are existing defamation laws. In the U.S. defamation is governed by state law, and it typically requires a plaintiff, person bringing the lawsuit, to show the following elements: (1) statement is made, (2) identifying the plaintiff, (3) published to at least one other person, (4) causing reputational harm with (5) the required degree of fault. The U.S. Supreme Court has held that defamation of certain types of plaintiffs, including public figures, limited purpose public figures, and public officials, requires actual malice which is either knowing falsity or reckless disregard for the truth.[51] In many defamation cases, the defendant, i.e., the entity being sued, is a media outlet. Given the difficulty of the actual malice standard proving reckless disregard for the truth is a much easier standard to prove in court. Part of the reason is that reckless disregard of the truth is rooted in behavior at the time the defamatory statement was published. This behavior demonstrates that the speaker had serious doubts about the statement's truth or acted in a way that disregarded obvious indicators that suggested the statement was false. This falls into two broad categories: subjective awareness of the speaker or failure to do proper investigation. This could be shown by not following standard journalistic practice with source verification or flawed research.[52] Knowing falsity is rooted in the mindset of the speaker at the time the defamation was made. It shows that a speaker knew what he or she said was untrue by showing conscious knowledge or intent. While challenging, it can be proven in court through evidence that the speaker had prior knowledge of the falsity of the statement.[53]

What does all of this have to do with AI? Well, it makes defamation a lot more complex. Suppose a journalist uses AI to craft a news story about a person and uses factually inaccurate information that causes reputational harm. That is textbook defamation, but who is to blame? Within the actual malice standard, there is the principle that the speaker has intention either through reckless behavior or intentional falsity. The problem is that AI lacks intentionality and knowledge, which means the accountability of the AI is difficult to assign, as it operates without the conscious intent to harm or awareness of truth and falsity, making it challenging to pinpoint responsibility either to the AI itself or to its creators, users, or the platforms distributing its content.

Within defamation if the plaintiff is a private citizen, then they must show that the defendant made the comments with negligence. If the plaintiff is a public figure, public official, or limited-purpose public figure, then the standard of fault is the much higher level of actual malice.[54] In the scenario above the journalist is the publisher, but the use of AI complicates the matter. Suppose the AI platform is producing generative content that is defamatory that is seen by users. In that scenario, the AI is the publisher and is potentially liable for the defamatory content. However, because of the lack of intentionality and the difficulty in proving high-level fault standards like actual malice, could the liability fall to other people such as the AI developers or the AI platforms themselves? These questions present unique problems when considering deepfake technology, which can produce highly defamatory content that ruins reputations by creating outlandish images and statements that are then pushed through social media. The audience size for such content is enormous, and the reputational damage is long-term. Can there be liability for a platform that would even produce such content, and does this potential liability create a situation where AI platforms are incentivized to avoid generating harmful material, or is it too difficult to attribute responsibility effectively?

These types of legal issues are not theoretical. In January 2024, a conservative radio host sued OpenAI for defamation when the platform generated fabricated content that alleged he had embezzled money from a gun rights advocacy group.[55] The defamatory statement was found incidentally while another gun advocate was researching a lawsuit using a chatbot. The case has been challenged by OpenAI based on the fact that actual malice cannot be proven.[56] This type of lawsuits demonstrate the issue of culpability of someone who relies on AI to their detriment. Platforms, such as ChatGPT, do provide disclaimers that users need to verify the information they receive is accurate. Hallucinations, which are false or fabricated content created by generative AI, pose unique risks for defamation and can cause situations where a user may find themselves liable for spreading false information, even if they did not intentionally create the defamatory content, complicating issues of accountability and legal responsibility in cases involving AI-generated outputs.

The issue of actual malice within AI is one that has gotten attention within recent cases, but there is another issue within defamation fault analysis. Suppose a private person is defamed by AI, could they have a successful defamation case under the negligence standard of defamation? In all likelihood, the answer is yes, and because negligence is a much lower legal standard than actual malice, the chances of them being successful in such a lawsuit are higher than if they were a public person. Negligence is legally defined as a lack of ordinary care, and that standard of fault can be proven by the AI designers failing to provide reasonable safeguard for the technology to prevent this type of output. However, there is a complex technological problem with generative AI and defamation by negligence. What if the defamatory content that the AI trains on is provided by a user rather than by the developer? Could the AI platform then be held liable under negligence? The answer is not certain. Plaintiffs would argue that the platform has a responsibility to vet information and provide a standard of care that filters out this type of content through platform guardrails and rules. Defendant AI companies would argue that individual users were the primary purveyors of the defamatory content, and at the most the AI platform would constitute a secondary publisher. It is important to note that the standard of fault whether it be negligence or actual malice is a standard the plaintiff must bear the burden of proving in court. The U.S. Supreme Court has held that no defamation case, regardless of plaintiff status, can hold speakers accountable under the standard of strict liability.[57] The lack of strict liability in defamation law is good for AI because it ensures accountability is based on fault, fostering innovation and responsible use without unduly penalizing developers for unintended errors. In effect, it allows AI to grow and innovate without the fear of being hamstringed by defamation litigation.

What if the defamation does not involve a person, but instead is product or business? In years past, there has been a concerted effort by organizations to engage in reputation management by using data analytics to conduct trend analysis of content being written about their organization online. There has also been a deliberate attempt by communicators to maximize their placement within internet searches through search engine optimization (SEO). However, AI presents a new challenge in that what an AI platform says about a product, service, or company is now part of the reputation management strategy. How those platforms construct that content is important, and there are potential issues if the AI description is inaccurate or defamatory. Inaccurate and harmful information about a company, service, or product falls into the category of trade libel, sometimes called commercial disparagement, which is similar to defamation. It requires plaintiffs to show the defendant made a false statement, published it, caused financial harm, and did so with a required degree of fault (typically negligence). This is especially true because of AI-powered chatbots that provide for both amplification and scalability of messages creating an echo-chamber effect. Moreover, personalization, which is a hallmark of predictive AI, provides for greater message resonance. Like defamation, the issue becomes one of whether AI has the ability to be held legally accountable for negligent behavior or, even more legally challenging, of actual malice. The answer to this will come in the lawsuits that are in all likelihood going to appear in federal and state courts over the next several years.

Communication Decency Act Section 230 and AI

A bigger question for AI platforms in this context is whether they hold federal immunity for any type of defamatory content under section 230 of the Communications Decency Act (CDA 230).[58] The CDA 230 immunizes "interactive computer services" from liability for third-party content published on their platforms. It was created to protect ISPs, online companies, and social media platforms from facing a flurry of lawsuits based upon users' content. For example, if a Facebook user writes a defamatory post, the user, not Facebook, is held legally responsible for the defamation. There have been many criticisms of this federal law, chief of which is that large multi-billion-dollar companies are largely not held legally accountable for the content their platforms host. However, in 2023 the U.S. Supreme Court has largely sidestepped the question of whether CDA 230 is constitutional, and any attempt to strike the law down will need to come from Congress, not the courts.[59] CDA has been controversial for decades in part because it provides such widespread immunity for wealthy online companies. However, those who challenge its immunity have lost. Courts have consistently provided that CDA 230 provides blanket immunity for interactive computer services.[60]

The new question is whether AI companies enjoy the same type of immunity under CDA 230. That is a complex question without a clear-cut answer. Broadly speaking the answer seems to be no because AI is not an "interactive computer service" merely hosting content. Rather AI is materially contributing to the production of content, which means that it would be ineligible for CDA 230 protection. Although the U.S. Supreme Court has not examined what it means to materially contribute to content, many other courts have developed a "material contribution" test for when the platform actively creates content.[61] However, the integration of AI presents new issues. For example, AI is now part of search engine results. Those results, which would normally not permit a search engine to be sued because of CDA 230, now present a new issue because the results generated by AI are not simply reproductions of third-party content but often constitute newly created or synthesized content. This raises the question of whether such outputs should be considered the product of the search engine itself, rather than merely hosted or distributed third-party content. If AI-generated content includes defamatory statements, courts may need to determine whether Section 230 immunity applies, as the content may not clearly fall within the protections for "information provided by another information content provider."[62] Instead, the search engine could be deemed the creator or co-creator of the content, potentially exposing it to liability.

This scenario has already been the subject of a lawsuit in the U.S. District Court of Maryland. Though not expressly dealing with CDA section 230, the plaintiff in the lawsuit was an aerospace professor and engineer whose name is similar to a convicted terrorist.[63] Microsoft's search engine Bing in conjunction with Bing Chat provided a search result of the plaintiff in which his description and biographer were conflated with the terrorist. The result provides a brief bio acknowledging his credentials and professional background then concludes with a statement that the plaintiff was sentenced to 18 years in federal prison for pleading guilty to seditious conspiracy and war against the U.S. That last portion about the conviction is false. The plaintiff sought $25 million in damages, and, at the time of this writing, the case is ongoing.[64] This represents a unique issue, and one that is likely to present itself in other lawsuits. The integration of content moderation, algorithmic outputs, and product disparagement by generative AI requires a deeper analysis of CDA 230, as it pushes the statute into areas it was not designed to address when originally enacted in 1996.

AI, Disinformation, and Communications: Navigating a Difficult Terrain

The challenges of regulating disinformation, misinformation, and AI lie in balancing the need for transparency and accountability with protecting free speech. What contemporary U.S. efforts show is that the First Amendment provides structure to speech laws in a way that makes it difficult to create a disinformation ban that can pass Constitutional scrutiny. Additionally, the fact that the enforcement of these laws requires active monitoring and screening shows the underlying practical challenges lawmakers face. Compounding this issue is that compliance with mis- and disinformation laws would largely come from institutions and individuals that are predisposed to comply with the law and not create disinformation anyway. Many of the disinformation efforts in the U.S. and globally come from bad actors who by their very existence are not predisposed to comply with laws or regulations. Additionally, these actions may reside outside the boundaries of U.S. jurisprudential reach, which makes holding them accountable logistically and legally impossible.

Perhaps the best way to combat these issues of disinformation through AI is to create a higher awareness among users. Having an awareness of vetting content and understanding the due diligence required of consuming information in the age of AI may mute the impact of this type of content. However, that also presents logistical difficulties as AI becomes better at deepfakes and voice clones. The maxim that “seeing is believing” no longer provides the same truth as it did in the pre-AI world. As the 2024 election showed, AI’s disinformation may also have ancillary issues of polarization, which is a more nuanced problem than pure disinformation. Structurally U.S. law has limitations on how it can regulate disinformation. Creating comprehensive and impact laws that effectively regulate dis- and misinformation that passes First Amendment scrutiny will require thoughtful and careful balancing of competing interests. This process will demand extensive collaboration among legal experts, policymakers, and technology experts to ensure that any regulatory measures are narrowly tailored, evidence-based, and flexible enough to adapt to evolving communication technologies. It will also require an investment in educational programs that teach media literacy among citizens, enabling them to identify credible information from falsehoods in an increasingly nuanced media landscape.

Discussion Questions

1 Should disinformation receive some First Amendment protection? Why or why not?
2 CDA section 230 likely does not immunize artificial intelligence platforms from liability for defamation. What are the practical implications for these businesses? Does this lack of immunity impact their growth?
3 What responsibilities do users have to verify that the information they receive from AI is correct? Is there a potential to use AI to fact-check AI content?
4 Should AI platforms provide guardrails for the content they produce, or should the user be able to use AI for generative and predictive uses as they see fit?
5 Hypothetical: Suppose you create a video in English to provide important information about a social services program. You use AI to create a voice clone of your voice to create a new video of you delivering the same message in Spanish. The translation is accurate, and a native speaker of Spanish would not be able to tell this is an altered audiovisual. What are the legal and ethical issues with this? What are your responsibilities to disclose? Does this constitute disinformation? Why or why not?

Notes

1 Whitney Phillips, *This Is Why We Can't Have Nice Things: Mapping the Relationship Between Online Trolling and Mainstream Culture* (Cambridge, MA: MIT Press, 2015).
2 Shannon Bond "Fake, Viral Images of an Explosion at the Pentagon Were Probably Created by AI," *NPR*, May 22, 2023, https://www.npr.org/2023/05/22/1177590231/fake-viral-images-of-an-explosion-at-the-pentagon-were-probably-created-by-ai.
3 Lars Daniel, "Hurricane Helena Deepfakes Flooding Social Media, Hurt Real People," *Forbes*, October 4, 2024, https://www.forbes.com/sites/larsdaniel/2024/10/04/hurricane-helena-deepfakes-flooding-social-media-hurt-real-people/.

4 Federal Emergency Management Agency (FEMA), "Hurricane Rumor Response," U.S. Department of Homeland Security, accessed November 19, 2024, https://www.fema.gov/disaster/recover/rumor/hurricane-rumor-response.
5 Jordan Peele, Deep Fake of Barak Obama, AggieVideo, February 22, 2021, https://video.ucdavis.edu/media/Deep+Fake+of+Barack+Obama/1_6zmvebuf
6 Aahsa Saeidi, "Voice Cloning Scams are a Growing Threat. Here's How You Can Protect Yourself," CBS News, May 17, 2024, https://www.cbsnews.com/newyork/news/ai-voice-clone-scam/.
7 Ben Finley, Deepfake of Principle's Voice Is the Latest Case of AI Being Used for Harassment, Associated Press, April 30, 2024, https://apnews.com/article/ai-maryland-principal-voice-recording-663d5bc0714a3af221392c-c6f1af985e.
8 European Union, *General Data Protection Regulation (GDPR)*, Regulation (EU) 2016/679, *Official Journal of the European Union*, April 27, 2016; *Proposal for a Regulation on Artificial Intelligence (AI Act)*, COM(2021) 206 final, April 21, 2021; *Digital Services Act (DSA)*, Regulation (EU) 2022/2065, *Official Journal of the European Union*, October 19, 2022.
9 European Commission, "The 2022 Code of Practice on Disinformation," Digital Strategy, last modified June 2022, https://digital-strategy.ec.europa.eu/en/policies/code-practice-disinformation
10 John Milton, *Areopagitica: A Speech for the Liberty of Unlicensed Printing* (London, 1644); John Stuart Mill, *On Liberty* (London: John W. Parker and Son, 1859).
11 "Marketplace of Ideas," in *Oxford Reference*, 5th ed., accessed November 21, 2024, https://www.oxfordreference.com/display/10.1093/acref/9780191843730.001.0001/q-oro-ed5-00007298. This quote comes from Mill's *on Liberty*.
12 Abrams v. United States, 250 U.S. 616 (1919).
13 McCreary County v. American Civil Liberties Union, 545 U.S. 844 (2005) (striking down a Ten Commandments display in front of a courthouse); Randall v. Sorrell, 548 U.S. 230 (2006) (invalidating expenditure limits for candidates for political office); Reno v. American Civil Liberties Union, 521 U.S. 844 (1997) (barring enforcement of the Communications Decency Act's provisions on censoring internet content); Matal v. Tam, 582 U.S. 218 (2017) (invoking the marketplace of ideas in holding that the disparagement clause of the Lanham Act violates the First Amendment).
14 Hannah Arendt, *The Origins of Totalitarianism* (New York: Harcourt, Brace, 1951); Timothy Wu, *The Attention Merchants: The Epic Scramble to Get Inside Our Heads* (New York: Knopf, 2016).
15 Roth v. United States, 354 U.S. 476 (1957) (holding that obscenity is not protected by the First Amendment); Chaplinsky v. New Hampshire, 315 U.S. 568 (1942) (establishing that fighting words are unprotected speech); Gertz v. Robert Welch, Inc., 418 U.S. 323 (1974) (clarifying that defamation is not protected by the First Amendment when it involves a false statement of fact causing harm).
16 New York Times Co. v. Sullivan, 376 U.S. 254 (1964) (holding that false statements about public officials are protected under the First Amendment unless made with "actual malice"); see also Curtis Publishing Co. v. Butts, 388 U.S. 130 (1967) (extending the "actual malice" standard to public figures, emphasizing the importance of the plaintiff's status in justifying protections for untruthful speech).
17 Hustler Magazine, Inc. v. Falwell, 485 U.S. 46 (1988).
18 United States v. Alvarez, 567 U.S. 709, (2012).

19 Ali Swenson and Will Weissert, *New Hampshire Officials Investigate AI-Generated Robocall Claiming to Be Biden, Meant to Suppress Voter Turnout*, *Associated Press*, January 22, 2024, https://apnews.com/article/new-hampshire-primary-biden-ai-deepfake-robocall-f3469ceb6dd613079092287994663db5.

20 David Shepardson, "FCC Finalizes $6 Million Fine Over AI-Generated Biden Robocalls," *Reuters*, September 26, 2024, https://www.reuters.com/world/us/fcc-finalizes-6-million-fine-over-ai-generated-biden-robocalls-2024-09-26/.

21 Yevgeny Kuklychev, "DeSantis War Room Deepfake Attack on Trump Lays Bare AI Threat to Elections," *Newsweek*, June 8, 2023, https://www.newsweek.com/desantis-war-room-deepfake-attack-trump-lays-bare-ai-threat-elections-1805303.

22 Ana Faguy, "New DeSantis Ad Superimposes Fighter Jets in AI-Altered Video of Speech," *Forbes*, May 25, 2023, https://www.forbes.com/sites/anafaguy/2023/05/25/new-desantis-ad-superimposes-fighter-jets-in-ai-altered-video-of-speech/.

23 Pranshu Verma, Will Oremus, and Cat Zakrzewski, "AI didn't sway the election, but it deepened the partisan divide" *Washington Post*, November 9, 2024, https://www.washingtonpost.com/technology/2024/11/09/ai-deepfakes-us-election/.

24 Elon Musk (@elonmusk), "Excited to Announce Our New Project!," *X*, November 22, 2024.

25 Ibid.

26 Verma, Oremus, and Zakrzewski, "AI didn't sway the election."

27 Alex Vadukul, "Coca-Cola's Holiday Ads Were Created with A.I.," *New York Times*, November 20, 2024, https://www.nytimes.com/2024/11/20/style/coca-cola-holiday-ads-ai.html.

28 Rachel Treisman Katy Perry's own mom feel for her Met Gala AI photo. Do you know what to look for? *NPR*, May 7, 2024, https://www.npr.org/2024/05/07/1249570785/katy-perry-met-gala-deepfake.

29 Simon Ellery, "Fake Photos of Pope Francis in a Puffer Jacket Go Viral, Highlighting the Power and Peril of AI," *CBS News*, March 28, 2023, https://www.cbsnews.com/news/pope-francis-puffer-jacket-fake-photos-deepfake-power-peril-of-ai/.

30 David Ingram, "Elon Musk's X Boosts Election Conspiracy Theories as AI Trends Accelerate," *NBC News*, October 26, 2024, https://www.nbcnews.com/tech/misinformation/elon-musk-x-boosts-election-conspiracy-theories-ai-trends-twitter-rcna176941.

31 Erielle Delzer, "Bogus Videos from the Hurricanes Are Going Viral. Here's How to Spot Old and Fabricated Footage Online," *CBS News*, October 15, 2024, https://www.cbsnews.com/news/hurricane-viral-video-how-to-spot-old-fabricated-ai-footage/.

32 "Hurricane Rumor Response," *FEMA*, accessed November 22, 2024, https://www.fema.gov/disaster/recover/rumor/hurricane-rumor-response.

33 California Legislature, "AB 2655: An Act to Amend Sections Related to Online Platforms and Deceptive Content," September 17, 2024, https://leginfo.legislature.ca.gov/faces/billTextClient.xhtml?bill_id=202320240AB2655.

34 California Legislature, "AB 2839: An Act to Prohibit Materially Deceptive Media in Political Advertisements," September 17, 2024, https://leginfo.legislature.ca.gov/faces/billNavClient.xhtml?bill_id=202320240AB2839.

35 Governor's Office, "Governor Newsom Signs Bills to Combat Deepfake Election Content," September 17, 2024, https://www.gov.ca.gov/2024/09/17/governor-newsom-signs-bills-to-combat-deepfake-election-content/.

36 Kohls v. Bonta, No. 2:24-cv-02527 JAM-CKD, Order Granting Plaintiff's Motion for Preliminary Injunction, 752 F.Supp. 3d 1187 (E.D. Cal., October 2, 2024), 1195.
37 "Artificial Intelligence (AI) in Elections and Campaigns," *National Conference of State Legislatures*, accessed November 22, 2024, https://www.ncsl.org/elections-and-campaigns/artificial-intelligence-ai-in-elections-and-campaigns.
38 "Artificial Intelligence (AI) in Elections and Campaigns."
39 National Conference of State Legislatures. "Artificial Intelligence 2024 Legislation." Last modified September 9, 2024. https://www.ncsl.org/technology-and-communication/artificial-intelligence-2024-legislation.
40 U.S. Congress, *Protect Elections from Deceptive AI Act*, S. 2770, 118th Cong., 1st sess., introduced September 12, 2023; and H.R. 8384, 118th Cong., 2nd sess., introduced May 14, 2024, https://www.congress.gov/bill/118th-congress/senate-bill/2770.
41 U.S. Congress, *AI Transparency in Elections Act of 2024*, S. 3875, 118th Cong., 2nd sess., introduced March 6, 2024, https://www.congress.gov/bill/118th-congress/senate-bill/3875; and Amy Klobuchar, "Klobuchar, Murkowski Introduce Bipartisan Legislation to Require Transparency in Political Ads with AI-Generated Content," March 6, 2024, https://www.klobuchar.senate.gov/public/index.cfm/2024/3/klobuchar-murkowski-introduce-bipartisan-legislation-to-require-transparency-in-political-ads-with-ai-generated-content.
42 U.S. Congress, *Candidate Voice Fraud Prohibition Act*, H.R. 4611, 118th Cong., 1st sess., introduced June 12, 2024, https://www.congress.gov/bill/118th-congress/house-bill/4611.
43 U.S. Congress, *Federal Artificial Intelligence Risk Management Act of 2024*, H.R. 6936, 118th Cong., 2nd sess., introduced February 14, 2024, https://www.congress.gov/bill/118th-congress/house-bill/6936.
44 U.S. Congress, *Securing Elections From AI Deception Act*, H.R. 8858, 118th Cong., 2nd sess., introduced March 22, 2024, https://www.congress.gov/bill/118th-congress/house-bill/8858.
45 U.S. Congress, *AI Transparency in Elections Act of 2024*, H.R. 8668, 118th Cong., 2nd sess., introduced April 10, 2024, https://www.congress.gov/bill/118th-congress/house-bill/8668.
46 Cybersecurity and Infrastructure Security Agency. *Consolidated Risk in Focus: Generative AI and Elections*. May 2024. https://www.cisa.gov/sites/default/files/2024-05/Consolidated_Risk_in_Focus_Gen_AI_ElectionsV2_508c.pdf.
47 Federal Communications Commission, *FCC Proposes Disclosure of AI-Generated Content in Political Ads*, October 19, 2023, https://www.fcc.gov/document/fcc-proposes-disclosure-ai-generated-content-political-ads.
48 Federal Election Commission, *Commission Approves Notification of Disposition of Interpretive Rule on Artificial Intelligence in Campaign Ads*, September 2024, https://www.fec.gov/updates/commission-approves-notification-of-disposition-interpretive-rule-on-artificial-intelligence-in-campaign-ads/. The statute and CFR that are affected as 52 U.S.C. § 30124 and 11 CFR 110.16.
49 Federal Trade Commission, *Operation AI Comply: Detecting AI-Infused Frauds and Deceptions*, September 2024, https://consumer.ftc.gov/consumer-alerts/2024/09/operation-ai-comply-detecting-ai-infused-frauds-and-deceptions.
50 U.S. House of Representatives, "Artificial Intelligence Task Force Report," December 2024, https://www.speaker.gov/wp-content/uploads/2024/12/AI-Task-Force-Report-FINAL.pdf, 93.

51 Sullivan, 376 U.S. at 254; Curtis Publishing Co., 388 U.S. at 130; Gertz v. Robert Welch, Inc., 418 U.S. 323 (1974); Falwell, 485 U.S. at 46; Milkovich v. Lorain Journal Co., 497 U.S. 1 (1990).
52 St. Amant v. Thompson, 390 U.S. 727 (1968).
53 Goldwater v. Ginzburg, 414 F.2d 324 (2d Cir. 1969).
54 Sullivan, 376 U.S. at 254.
55 Isiah Poritz, "OpenAI Fails to Escape First Defamation Suit from Radio Host," *Bloomberg Law*, November 19, 2024, https://news.bloomberglaw.com/ip-law/openai-fails-to-escape-first-defamation-suit-from-radio-host.
56 Ibid.
57 Gertz, 418 U.S. at 323.
58 U.S. Code, 47 U.S.C. § 230, "Protection for private blocking and screening of offensive material," accessed November 21, 2024, https://www.law.cornell.edu/uscode/text/47/230.
59 Gonzalez v. Google LLC, 598 U.S. 617 (2023); Twitter, Inc. v. Taamneh, 598 U.S. 471 (2023).
60 Zeran v. America Online, Inc., 129 F.3d 327 (4th Cir. 1997); Blumenthal v. Drudge, 992 F. Supp. 44 (D.D.C. 1998); Doe v. MySpace, Inc., 528 F.3d 413 (5th Cir. 2008); Fair Housing Council of San Fernando Valley v. Roommates.com, LLC, 521 F.3d 1157 (9th Cir. 2008) (en banc); Jones v. Dirty World Entertainment Recordings LLC, 755 F.3d 398 (6th Cir. 2014); Force v. Facebook, Inc., 934 F.3d 53 (2d Cir. 2019); Kimzey v. Yelp, Inc., 836 F.3d 1263 (9th Cir. 2016); Henderson v. Source for Public Data, L.P., 53 F.4th 110 (4th Cir. 2022).
61 Fair Housing Council of San Fernando Valley v. Roommates.com, LLC, 521 F.3d 1157 (9th Cir. 2008).
62 Section 230(c)(1) of the Communications Decency Act, codified at 47 U.S.C. § 230.
63 Battle v. Microsoft Corporation, 2024 WL 4555687 (D. Md. July 7, 2023).
64 Ibid.

4

AI AND INTELLECTUAL PROPERTY

Human or Machine Creation?

Chapter Overview

This chapter examines artificial intelligence (AI) by looking at its impact in the areas of copyright, trademark, patent, and trade secret. AI has caused legal experts and courts in the field intellectual property to reevaluate basic aspects of IP law, specifically the level of humanness required to create IP. There are also underlying issues with AI content production, which arguably infringes on existing IP in the process of creation. This chapter analyses the laws around these issues focusing on the U.S. federal government and courts' response to novel IP questions raised by AI. The chapter concludes with predictions about the future of AI and IP and how legal standards may have to consider new technological realities of generative AI production of outputs.

Keywords: Intellectual Property, Copyright, Trademark, Patent, Trade Secret, Infringement, Human Creation

The proliferation of artificial intelligence (AI) in the 2020s created new questions about how AI will impact society's conceptualization of humanity. There are larger philosophical questions that have been discussed within society, such as can AI have rights, can AI own property, and can AI get to the developmental status where its autonomy can equal that of human beings? Those questions are rooted in concerns over the future of AI and its place within society. However, within the law some of these questions about humanity and AI have already started to be asked. The answers to those questions have considerable impact for communicators and content creators because one area of law that is perhaps the most impacted by humanness and AI is intellectual property (IP). Copyright,

DOI: 10.4324/9781003426561-4

trademark, and patents are similarly positioned to deal with some novel issues brought about by widespread AI use within multiple industries. These issues range in scope. How much AI is too much to constitute a valid copyright or patent? Does the output of AI inadvertently cause infringement of existing IP? Is the training of AI on existing data that has IP protection constitute infringement? How can users verify that their content is not inadvertently infringing existing IP, and what is the level of legal liability for users when innocent infringement occurs?

Currently lawmakers, agencies, and courts are grappling with these questions. While interrelated, each type of IP faces its own unique challenges with AI. U.S. copyright is primarily concerned with whether AI used to create new content can constitute enough originality to pass the threshold to earn copyright status. There is also the concern that training on data that is copyrightable constitutes infringement, or whether that training can constitute fair use. Patents have similar issues, specifically about the novelty of the patent itself when AI uses existing data to create a new patent. There is also the growing question of whether AI can be the inventor of new patents and whether the platform can argue for some level of ownership over the new property. Trademarks present different issues with AI. Specifically, AI-generated logos could constitute infringement of existing trademarks, and existing marks should be concerned that their trademarks can be diluted if included in the training datasets of AI platforms. There is also the complex issue of trademark status in multiple global jurisdictions when created with AI and whether a global brand created with AI can receive recognition in all jurisdictions. Trade secrets also present unique issues as they relate to AI algorithms that inadvertently provide proprietary information, such as trade secrets, in their outputs to users. This relates to privacy protections of the systems, and whether the system is open or closed. Additionally, users working with trade secrets must be trained to use AI platforms to protect information.

The complexity of AI and its fast-paced development is presenting novel issues to protection of IP. While many aspects of this area of law are still under development, there are more concrete rules in the area of IP than in other areas of AI law, such as disinformation or privacy. As this chapter will illustrate, the central issues of AI and IP are the unintended consequences of use and the humanness of AI content.

Copyright Protection of AI Content

Copyright is a form of IP that protects original works that are also fixed in a tangible medium. Originality means that the work has a basic level of individual creativity. That threshold is legally and creatively very low, but there are minimum standards. For example, the U.S. Supreme Court has held that a phonebook is not original enough to obtain copyright protection because the underlying content is facts organized alphabetically.[1] Moreover, the U.S. Code specifically prohibits copyright for certain items such as an:

> idea, procedure, process, system, method of operation, concept, principle, or discovery, regardless of the form in which it is described, explained, illustrated, or embodied in such work.[2]

The case law surrounding originality along with the U.S. Code has been interpreted to not provide originality to *scenes à faire*, which are stock elements, themes, or situations that are so commonplace in a genre that they are expected or necessary to its expression, e.g. wicked stepsister, fairy godmother.[3] The U.S. Code also provides an explicit list of what can be copyrighted:

1 Literary works: novels, poetry, computer programs
2 Musical works (and accompanying words): sheet music, songs, hymns
3 Dramatic works (including music): plays, musicals, screenplays
4 Pantomimes and choreographic works: ballet, choreographs, silent skits
5 Pictorial, graphic, and sculptural works: paintings, sculptures, logos
6 Motion pictures and other audiovisual works: movies, TV shows, online videos
7 Sound recordings: podcasts, recorded performances, audiobooks
8 Architectural works: the structure itself, blueprints of a design[4]

The second requirement of a copyright is fixation in a tangible medium. This requires the work to be fixed in some type of permanent medium for it to be perceived, reproduced, or communicated. This includes physical fixation, e.g. paper, canvas, blueprints, or digital where it can be perceptible by others.[5]

For AI, the issue of copyrightability introduces another element of human contribution. For over a century, the creation of copyright has only focused on originality and fixation. Those are the two foundational elements of copyrightability, and the idea that a human had to be part of the process was implied within the creation itself. Of course, humans use tools to create, but that was not a barrier to creation. The human was driving the creation through the use of the tool whether it be a paintbrush, pencil, typewriter, or software package. However, AI changes the nature of humanness. The AI itself can create through its own algorithm and dataset. The more sophisticated AI becomes, the more it can create. For example, Open AI's Sora, which is a text-to-video creation AI platform, allows for high-quality AI-generated video with very shallow prompts. This presents a legal conundrum of how much human involvement is required to pass the threshold of originality. Some countries have already provided some brightline rules on the subject.[6] These countries include the UK, Hong Kong, Ireland, New Zealand, and India, but a comprehensive framework for copyright originality in the context of human authorship does not exist.[7]

In the U.S., the U.S. Copyright Office (USCO) attempted to address some of the underlying problems of human authorship and the use of AI to create new content. There has been a longstanding tradition in U.S. law that requires a human element to copyright creation. The U.S. Court of Appeals for the Ninth Circuit held that a work must have some element of human creation in order for it to receive copyright protection.[8] In another case, the same appellate court noted that non-humans, in that case a monkey, could not be the holder of a copyright because of their non-human status.[9] The 2021 Copyright Compendium also noted the requirement of human authorship when granting a copyright stating "To qualify as a work of "authorship" a work must be created by a human being."[10] It went on to list examples of works that the USCO will not register because of their lack of human involvement:

> The U.S. Copyright Office will not register works produced by nature, animals, or plants. Likewise, the Office cannot register a work purportedly created by divine or supernatural beings, although the Office may register a work where the application or the deposit copy(ies) state that the work was inspired by a divine spirit. Examples:
>
> - A photograph taken by a monkey.
> - A mural painted by an elephant.
> - A claim based on the appearance of actual animal skin.
> - A claim based on driftwood that has been shaped and smoothed by the ocean.
> - A claim based on cut marks, defects, and other qualities found in natural stone.
> - An application for a song naming the Holy Spirit as the author of the work.[11]

The USCO goes on to note that machines also do not receive authorship of copyright, and that when a machine is used to substantially create a work it cannot receive copyright ownership, nor can the work receive copyright status. The USCO Compendium notes:

> The [USCO] Office will not register works produced by a machine or mere mechanical process that operates randomly or automatically without any creative input or intervention from a human author. The crucial question is "whether the 'work' is basically one of human authorship, with the computer [or other device] merely being an assisting instrument, or whether the traditional elements of authorship in the work (literary, artistic, or musical expression or elements of selection, arrangement, etc.) were actually conceived and executed not by man but by a machine."[12]

Examples of this include various scenarios of machine input in the creation process, which either produces a shallow copyright or a substantially non-human creation:

- Reducing or enlarging the size of a preexisting work of authorship.
- Making changes to a preexisting work of authorship that are dictated by manufacturing or materials requirements.
- Converting a work from analog to digital formats, such as transferring a motion picture from VHS to DVD.
- Declicking or reducing the noise in a preexisting sound recording or converting a sound recording from monaural to stereo sound.
- Transposing a song from B major to C major.
- Medical imaging produced by x-rays, ultrasounds, magnetic resonance imaging, or other diagnostic equipment.
- A claim based on a mechanical weaving process that randomly produces irregular shapes in the fabric without any discernible pattern.[13]

Registration of copyright is not required in order for the copyright to exist. However, a valuable copyright benefits from registration because it establishes a rebuttable presumption of ownership. In addition, the denial registration of a copyright demonstrates that the work will not receive protection under copyright law. While a denied applicant could theoretically argue that copyright still exists even though registration was not granted, it is likely that the work does not constitute a copyright if the USCO does not find the work meets the threshold originality required. The USCO currently requires a disclosure of AI involvement in any submission of copyrightable work with an explanation of the human contributions that provide a clear demonstration of what part of the work can receive protection. Non-disclosure potentially means that a work will not receive copyright registration.[14] The USCO's 2023 guidance on whether originality exists with AI-generated content focuses on the role of the human in the creation process. Specifically, the USCO said when the AI platform determines "expressive elements of its output," then it is not sufficient to receive copyright protection. However, there is also the possibility of an AI platform producing content that is then edited by a human. In that context, the human components are copyrightable while the AI components are not. For the USCO, prompt writing is not a substitute for creation. Rather it is analogous to a patron commissioning art from a painter. The patron tells the painter their preferences, and the painter paints the portrait. The USCO gives the following example:

> For example, if a user instructs a text-generating technology to "write a poem about copyright law in the style of William Shakespeare," she can expect the system to generate text that is recognizable as a poem, mentions copyright, and resembles Shakespeare's style. But the technology will decide the rhyming pattern, the words in each line, and the structure of the text. When an AI technology determines the expressive elements of its output, the generated material is not the product of human authorship. As a result, that material is not protected by copyright and must be disclaimed in a registration application.[15]

This guidance has been the basis of much discussion as the USCO, and courts figure out the contours of originality within copyright. While there is a sense of what the underlying philosophy of AI and copyright is, there is no brightline rule established to know when human contributions are enough to warrant protection. Lawsuits have shown this is a growing issue. The U.S. District Court for the District of Columbia upheld a denial of copyright registration for an AI-generated painting entitled, "A Recent Entrance to Paradise" by digital artist Stephen Thaler.[16] Another graphic artist, Kris Kashtanova, failed to secure copyright for "Zarya of the Dawn," which was an AI illustration for a graphic novel. In their denial of registration, the USCO cited that the AI platform used, Midjourney, had no control from the artist in its selection of the content. The USCO wrote:

> Rather than a tool that Ms. Kashtanova controlled and guided to reach her desired image, Midjourney generates images in an unpredictable way. Accordingly, Midjourney users are not the "authors" for copyright purposes of the images the technology generates."[17]

The USCO also rejected the idea that prompt writing was part of the authorship of the image. They argued:

> Because Midjourney starts with randomly generated noise that evolves into a final image, there is no guarantee that a particular prompt will

generate any particular visual output. Instead, prompts function closer to suggestions than orders, similar to the situation of a client who hires an artist to create an image with general directions as to its contents.[18]

So, what does it mean for copyright rights if a work does not receive protection? The reality is originality is in a state of flux. The use of AI does not prohibit the ability to receive copyright protection, but its use is analyzed on individually. The U.S. Copyright Office issued a report in January 2025, Copyright and Artificial Intelligence Part 2: Copyrightability, which discusses the ability of content creators to receive copyright. The report's conclusion is that there is no need for new copyright laws on the subject of copyrightability using AI, but that the use of AI raises unique questions around how much human control is required for copyright to exist remains an ongoing discussion and one that is likely going to be sorted out by courts and the USCO on a case-by-case basis.[19] Copyright law in the U.S. gives specific rights to copyright holders. The owner of a valid copyright has the right to:

1 to reproduce the copyrighted work in copies or phonorecords;
2 to prepare derivative works based upon the copyrighted work;
3 to distribute copies or phonorecords of the copyrighted work to the public by sale or other transfer of ownership, or by rental, lease, or lending;
4 in the case of literary, musical, dramatic, and choreographic works, pantomimes, and motion pictures and other audiovisual works, to perform the copyrighted work publicly;
5 in the case of literary, musical, dramatic, and choreographic works, pantomimes, and pictorial, graphic, or sculptural works, including the individual images of a motion picture or other audiovisual work, to display the copyrighted work publicly; and
6 in the case of sound recordings, to perform the copyrighted work publicly by means of a digital audio transmission.[20]

The net effect of these rights is the right to control the copyright. The owner has the ability to manage and license the copyright as they see fit and have the exclusive right to do this for a set duration of time. Practically this means that a communicator has control over their message, and also has control over who else can use it.

Within copyright there is also a point where the property ceases to have protection. Usually, this occurs with the expiration of a set duration of time. Post-1978 the duration of new copyrights is life of the author plus 70 years, and for works for hire the duration is 95 years from publication or 120 years from creation, whichever is shorter.[21] For works published prior to 1978, the duration of copyright depends on compliance with formalities required under the Copyright Act of 1909, such as registration and renewal. These works were initially protected for 28 years, with an optional renewal for 28 years, later extended to a total of 95 years under the Sonny Bono Copyright Term Extension Act. Once this duration expires, the work enters the public domain, allowing anyone to use it freely without restrictions under the six rights enumerated in 17 U.S.C. § 106. For example, *The Great Gatsby*, published in 1925, entered the public domain in 2021, meaning F. Scott Fitzgerald's heirs no longer receive royalties or control its use. For works that do not receive copyright protection, such as some works created by AI with substantial human involvement, they too are part of public domain meaning anyone can use them for whatever purpose. This creates a logistical problem for communicators who may use AI to create content they want to control. If that content does not rise to the level of originality needed to create a copyright, then the work never becomes property. It is free for anyone to use, and, as a result, there is no control over the content for the communicator or their organization.

However, this is not to imply that AI does not provide a competitive edge for organizations and communicators. But they should be aware that a great AI generated work may not be "property" at all, and instead is public domain for anyone to use. There is a higher level of creativity in using AI platforms to create content, and the final output may be more innovative given that it has a sort of crowdsourced innovation. But communicators need to be wary too of the homogeneity of output through platforms. Algorithmic and data similarity can create content that is so similar that it saturates the market (and perhaps creating infringement). Additionally, there could be other forms of IP that do provide protection for AI-generated content (such as trade secrets). The handling of protections of AI-generated content signals that human-centered creativity has value, and perhaps the lack of protection under copyright law signals that the concerns of AI replacing professionals will be muted (at least in the content industry).

Copyright Infringement and AI

One of the biggest issues facing AI is the potential of copyright infringement from generated content. This happens in two major ways. First is when the AI platforms generate content that infringes on another protected work. For example, suppose a user asks an AI platform to create a photo of a home. That generated image pulls from existing images under copyright to create the new content. Does that new image infringe on the existing ones? How would a user know that this is infringement if they don't know what data is being used to generate the new content? Is the new image transformative enough to constitute something totally new, and, if so, can that new image be copyrighted even though it has elements from existing copyrights? These questions demonstrate the challenges AI users face when using the technology.

The second way copyright infringement occurs is when the copyright of existing content is used as a dataset for a platform. The platform trains on that data to create new content. While the output of the content may not be infringement, is the training from the data infringement? This calls into question many of the types of data that are used to build an AI platform, which may include famous works of authors and artists that are not paid royalties nor given their permission for the content that is embedded into the system. This poses several questions for users and platforms, namely, whether the platforms themselves are infringing on the copyright of others merely by having a dataset that is made up of copyrighted material.

The prima facie elements, i.e., the basic elements of a lawsuit, of copyright infringement are essentially ownership and copying. The plaintiff must prove they own the copyright. This means the work must be original and fixed in a tangible medium. Though not required to have copyrightable content, registration with the USCO is required to bring an infringement suit in federal court. For those holders without registration, they must first go through the USCO registration process to bring the lawsuit.[22]

The plaintiff also has to show that the defendant infringer had access to the copyrighted works and created a copy of the plaintiff's work that was substantially similar to the protected elements of the original work.[23] Access can be shown through direct access or by the fact the work is well-known and distributed enough that it is reasonable to assume the defendant had access.[24] Substantial similarity is evaluated through an intrinsic/extrinsic test, which looks at the obvious similarities and the subjective intrinsic similarities of the two works.[25] This can go beyond mere visual but can also include the feel of a work, such as in music composition.[26]

Within an infringement suit there are affirmative defenses the defendant can raise to combat the plaintiff's case. They are license or permission, independent creation, de minimis use, statute of limitations, and perhaps most complex, fair use. License and permission means the defendant actually held a license or permission to use the work. Independent creation is another narrow exception to infringement. Merely being similar is not enough to be infringement.[27] De minimis use is another defense where a defendant can show that the portion of the copyrighted work was so small that it is minimal and not rising to the level of infringement.[28] Federal copyright law also requires a plaintiff to bring an infringement claim within three years of when the plaintiff knew or should have known of the infringement.[29]

Fair use is perhaps the largest and best known and least understood affirmative defense to copyright infringement. Its elements are articulated in the U.S. Code and the court looks to four non-dispositive factors:

1. the purpose and character of the use, including whether such use is of a commercial nature or is for nonprofit educational purposes;
2. the nature of the copyrighted work;
3. the amount and substantiality of the portion used in relation to the copyrighted work as a whole; and
4. the effect of the use upon the potential market for or value of the copyrighted work.[30]

The first element of fair use looks at the transformative nature of the new content. If the work is highly transformative, like a parody, then that leans toward fair use.[31] In addition, if the use is more non-commercial, such as an educational purpose, then that also leans toward fair use.[32] The second element of the nature of the copyrighted work. The more creative the work then the stronger the copyright is. So, if the copyright is more factual, then the weaker the copyright. Moreover, courts are less likely to grant strong copyright protection to unpublished copyrighted works. However, this analysis is not just about quantity. The U.S. Supreme Court has ruled that fair use does not apply if the disputed content utilizes the most significant or essential aspect of the copyrighted work.[33] This also goes to the third element of fair use, which analyses the amount of work that was used. Typically, the less of the copyright used, then the stronger the case for fair use. However, it is important to note there is interplay between this third element and the first and second elements. For example, the U.S. Supreme Court held that recording an entire program for personal use was still fair use even though it was the entirety of the copyrighted work because the user was making that recording for personal use.[34] Finally, the last element looks at the impact of the use on the marketplace for the original work. In effect, this element looks at how much the use deprives the copyright owner of making money from their copyrighted work.

The final element of fair use has undergone some recent analysis by the U.S. Supreme Court that makes it arguably the most important of the fair use analysis. If the potentially infringing content replaces the original content within the marketplace, then it is likely not fair use. The U.S. Supreme Court has emphasized this in the recent case *Andy Warhol Foundation for the Visual Arts, Inc. v. Goldsmith*.[35] In that case, the U.S. Supreme Court held that even when there is a transformative use of a copyrighted work that does not allow for fair use when the economic impact of the new content is significant. This is important because the ruling shifts the burden to the potential infringer to prove the extent of the economic impact their content may have on the market.[36]

Within AI there is the question of does AI content actually infringe on existing copyrights? The answer is potentially yes depending on the content created, and the way it is used. If a generative AI platform creates new content, say a picture, that substantially uses an existing copyrighted work as the basis for the new work, then it is likely infringement. A fair use defense might be possible in this situation, but a communicator will have a problem arguing for fair use when the purpose behind the new content is commercial and impacts the market value of the original. This scenario is highly likely in the case of deepfake videos and voice clones where original content is used to create the new content, and the new content relies heavily on existing copyrighted material to create the new video. In light of the U.S. Supreme Court in *Andy Warhol Foundation for the Visual Arts, Inc. v. Goldsmith*, the commercial use of these deepfakes makes it highly unlikely (maybe nearly impossible) for a user to successfully defend infringement under fair use. Ironically, this creates a unique scenario where an AI user can potentially infringe on existing copyrights through their use of new content, while simultaneously lacking copyright protection for the content they create, as the USCO has ruled that AI-generated content without significant human involvement is not eligible for copyright. This was the case in October 2024, when Elon Musk, Tesla, and Warner Brothers were sued Alcon Entertainment, a production company, that owns Blade Runner 2049 for infringement when an AI image generator created promotional artwork for, We, Robot event.[37] Communicators using AI need to be hypervigilant in their use of platforms understanding both copyright law and the technology behind the platform they are using. Frequently there will be new AI-generated content that may be infringement but does not present an obvious infringement to the user unless they are already aware of the content/data that the platform uses. This means that communicators have to engage in a dialogue with developers about AI platform use to better calculate infringement risks.

However, the bigger infringement issue with AI is not the output of the generated content, but the actual training of the platform on existing copyrighted material. Multiple lawsuits have occurred on this specific issue focusing on how AI platforms populate datasets with existing copyrighted content and then use that content to train the AI. Several AI platforms have been sued under copyright infringement because of the training of data from copyrighted work.[38] While these cases are ongoing and at various stages of litigation, they represent an ongoing discussion of AI's use of copyrighted material to train data. There is some suggestion that the issue of using copyrighted material to train AI may not be infringement. In one case, a U.S. District Court judge expressed skepticism that there is infringement because the users are not asking the platform explicitly to use existing work to produce new content.[39] The overarching issue here is one of fair use and whether the use of copyrighted material constitutes transformative use of existing copyright (fair use factor 1). While there is no definitive case on whether AI training constitutes fair use, the decision in *Author's Guild v. Google Inc.* decided in 2015 by the U.S. Court of Appeals for the Second Circuit may be instructive.[40] In that case, the court held that Google's digitalization of copyrighted books constituted fair use. The digitalization project was part of a larger database Google was creating that provided small sections of the books for the public. However, it is important to note that there is limited precedent because it is a case from the U.S. Court of Appeals for the Second Circuit, and also it is a decision made prior to the landmark fair use analysis in the *Andy Warhol Foundation for the Visual Arts, Inc. v. Goldsmith*, which heavily scrutinizes fair use under the fourth factor of economic impact.[41] As the decade of the 2020s progresses, AI training as infringement may become a bigger issue as it works its way through courts. At the time of this writing there is an ongoing issue about the policies AI platforms have regarding use of copyrighted works within a platform. The Trump administration's White Office of Science and Technology ask asked for request for information (RFI) regarding the use of AI from a variety of stakeholders for the Artificial Intelligence Action Plan. OpenAI and Google have asked for the ability to train on copyrighted material in order to maintain U.S. dominance in AI. Over 400 Hollywood actors and other industry figures have countered this with an open letter to President Trump asking for the protection of copyrighted work. At issue is the ability to use otherwise copyrighted work without paying royalties and also the specter of AI taking Hollywood jobs (something that was at the core of the 2023 Hollywood writer's strike). If there are circuit splits in the decisions the issue of data training and fair use may end up at the U.S. Supreme Court. Practically speaking, there is the underlying issue of cost of litigation versus the cost of royalties. Proprietary platforms as well as commercial AI sites may end up reaching copyright agreements with owners of data to create a system that does not potentially infringe. Moreover, there is the possibility of AI-generated content being watermarked or cited in some manner to denote its AI status and the level of copyrightability. However, the implementation of these AI approaches currently remains unresolved.

Trademark

Trademarks are another form of IP that potentially presents novel issues within the widespread use of AI. Unlike copyright, trademarks have the potential to last indefinitely so long as they are protected by the owner.

Trademark registration is not required but is part of the process typically used for major brands as it creates a presumption of ownership. Under federal law, trademarks are defined as a "word, name, symbol, or device" used to identify and distinguish goods or services.[42] Unlike copyright where there is a threshold for creativity that leads to originality, trademarks operate on a spectrum of strength. They are classified in the following ways:

- Fanciful: Made-up words (e.g., "Kodak").
- Arbitrary: Existing words with no relation to the product (e.g., "Apple" for computers).
- Suggestive: Suggest characteristics of the product (e.g., "Netflix").
- Descriptive: Must acquire secondary meaning to be registrable (e.g., "Best Buy").
- Generic: Cannot be trademarked (e.g., "Computer" for computers).[43]

Additionally, trademarks have to be used in a commercial way to have their protection. Their IP status is not based solely on creation. For example, a diary would still receive copyright protection even though it was tucked under a mattress, but a trademarked logo design would not have any IP status if it remained in a computer file on a laptop and was never used.[44] In fact, non-use of a trademark can actually make the mark lose its protected status. This is a process known as abandonment, and it occurs when a trademark owner ceases to use or maintain their trademark. In fact, the U.S. Code states that three years of non-use is presumptive abandonment.[45] Temporary non-use is not abandonment, and there are certain conditions where long-term non-use is still not abandonment such as when a company goes through bankruptcy, supply chain issues, or other business interruptions.[46] Additionally, abandonment does not occur if there is a clear intent to resume use and can serve as a legal rebuttal to abandonment claims.[47]

Another way a trademark can lose its protection is through genericity. This is sometimes referred to as genericide, which is when a trademark loses its distinctiveness because of overuse in a way where the mark no longer identifies a specific product or service. Generic trademarks are by definition not protectable under federal law, so when a mark becomes generic it loses its protection.[48] Famous examples of a trademark becoming generic include aspirin, escalator, thermos, cellophane, yo-yo, zipper, linoleum, and trampoline.[49]

Infringement of trademark is similar to that of copyright. It requires a plaintiff to show they own the trademark (either through registration with the U.S. Patent and Trademark Office (USPTO) or through common law ownership), use of the mark by the defendant, and likelihood of confusion.[50] It's the last part of infringement that looks to factors, sometimes called the Polaroid factors, which include the strength of the mark at issue, the similarity between the alleged infringing mark and the established mark, evidence of actual confusion, consumer sophistication, intent, the proximity of the goods or services within in the marketplace, and marketing.[51] Similar to copyright, trademark also has a set of affirmative defenses which include: first sale (selling a trademarked work after purchase), non-commercial use (such as criticism or commentary), abandonment, genericity, statute of limitations, parody, or the equitable remedy of laches (i.e., waiting too long to bring suit).[52] Trademark also has a fair use doctrine that is either descriptive fair use or nominative fair use. Descriptive fair use, as the name implies, occurs when the trademark name is used, but not to refer to the specific product. For example, selling apples as in the fruit and not the computer brand. Nominative fair use occurs when someone uses a trademark to describe their own work, such as an Apple computer repair shop.[53]

AI creates new problems in these basics of trademark law. First, AI is a technology that increases the possibility of genericide because its outputs can create content that fuels genericity. For example, an AI platform that is trained on data can begin providing outlets that use words like Coke to mean any type of cola beverage. Those working in branding need to be sure that genericity is not being fueled by the way AI algorithms and data speak about products. Conversely, if an AI program is not speaking about a brand when discussing a major product, this could lead to abandonment claims. Both issues require vigilant content monitoring by brands.

Perhaps the biggest issue with AI and trademarks is the use of AI in creating logos and branding. If the trademark uses AI to create the logo, then who owns the logo? Currently, the user owns the content, but because platforms sometimes create similar outputs on a regular basis there is the risk that there is not the uniqueness required of creating a strong mark. Furthermore, there is a risk of trademark dilution or blurred marks due to the repetitive nature of AI outputs, which may either associate trademarks with unrelated items or generate new marks that resemble existing designs. Owners of marks have to be consistent in protecting their existing marks within such an environment. For example, an AI meme could dilute the mark of a famous trademark, like the golden arches of McDonalds, by consistently using that mark in generative visuals. Ultimately the mark could lose its own distinctiveness by this AI-generated.[54]

The biggest concern about AI and trademarks is infringement, specifically unintentional infringement. Content creators may use AI to create new logos for brands, and in the process adopt a mark that is actually an existing trademark that may be registered. Because the number of trademarks in the U.S. are voluminous and AI trains on existing data, there is a possibility a new logo can be created that is a direct infringement. Unless the user knows the original mark, then they may hold this new AI-generated mark out into commerce committing unintentional infringement. Intention is not required for infringement, so the liability of a user in this scenario remains. This calls for mitigation strategies by those using AI to create trademarks including using AI platforms with trademark filters, human oversight and verification of outputs, or engaging in licensing agreements with trademark owners when building proprietary platforms.

The USPTO has addressed these concerns, emphasizing the need for human verification and accountability on infringement and non-permitted use. However, unlike copyright, trademarks do not have the same analysis of human creation. That means that trademarks can be AI generated and still registered by the USPTO This is because creativity is not part of trademark analysis. The creative nature of the mark only applies to the level of strength it receives, and so long as it is not generic or infringing it can qualify for protection. It is important to note that creation of a mark does not mean it receives trademark status, there is still the use in commerce requirement that is mandatory under the U.S. Code.[55]

Patents and Trade Secrets

Patents and trade secrets are less likely an issue for communicators, but because they play a large role within IP litigation, they are important to include in any comprehensive analysis of AI and IP law. Patents are granted exclusively by the USPTO with formal registration. Once registered the owner of patent has exclusive use of that patent for 20 years.[56] A patent can only be granted when there is patentable subject matter, novelty, and non-obviousness. The U.S. Code describes this as "process, machine, manufacture, or composition of matter, or any new and useful improvement thereof."[57] Excluded from this are natural laws, ideas, or natural phenomena. Novelty requires that the patent is new and has never been publicly shared, used, or described before applying for the patent.[58] Non-obviousness means that the work would not be obvious to a person working in the field, i.e., no combining two existing ideas to create a new patent.[59] If the patent meets these criteria then it must be able to be disclosed and enabled to the USPTO in an application.[60] Like trademarks and copyrights, patents can also be infringed when someone uses them without authorization. This is proven when a plaintiff shows they have both a valid patent and the defendant has engaged in unauthorized activity as defined by 35 U.S.C. § 271(a). This unauthorized activity includes making, selling, using, offering to sell, or importing the patent. This infringement can occur either literally or by the doctrine of equivalents. The latter is a legal standard in patent law that indirect infringement occurs when the item performs "substantially the same function, in substantially the same way, to achieve substantially the same result."[61]

AI presents a new dimension in patent law because it serves as both a tool to infringe and catch infringement. Similar to trademark or copyright, the data and algorithm of an AI platform can create a new output that infringes on existing patent. Within patents, AI seems particularly suited to creating patent infringement under the doctrine of equivalents. This creates a similar question of how the law proceeds with potential infringement claims. In the case of AI-generated infringement, could the platform itself be culpable of infringement as well as the user? This seems particularly true in patents because the underlying analysis and data are likely not known to the user and the output is the only thing the user sees. For example, within pharmaceutical patents, the chemical compounds used for a new output could infringe on the patent of an existing medicine. It would require deep analysis of the user's actions and AI programs to fully uncover such a scenario. Conversely, the speed and accuracy of AI at processing large amounts of data could make the tool a cost saver for those trying to uncover infringement. There is also a question of what happens as AI becomes more sophisticated and can implement a patented process on its own. Where will the liability be in that scenario, and how should platforms address this potential issue?

Trade secrets are another area of IP that has limited impact on communicators, yet it raises serious legal questions. A trade secret must derive its value from not being known, and the owners must make legally reasonable efforts to keep it secret. Unlike most forms of IP, trade secrets are protected under both state and federal law.[62] There is no registration process as the property right emerges from actions of keeping content secret. It does overlap in some ways with patents as some patentable material could have been be protected by a trade secret (but not always). However, trade secrets and AI raise unique concerns that implicate privacy (a topic covered more in depth in Chapter 5). For example, what happens to a trade secret's status if the content of the secret is absorbed in an AI platform?

Trade secret appropriation, the process by which an unauthorized person gains access to a trade secret can happen more easily through AI's unauthorized access, scraping, or reverse engineering capabilities.[63] Similar to patents, AI can assist in monitoring proprietary content by detecting anomalies that flag unusual access and enabling audit controls for the use of sensitive information. While lawsuits involving AI and trade secrets have been relatively limited so far, the potential for litigation is growing as users become more active on AI platforms. It is easy to envision scenarios where disputes arise when a user inadvertently inputs proprietary information into a system only to have that content captured and replicated elsewhere. For communicators, this may have particular relevance in proprietary client lists, which, under certain circumstances, can constitute a trade secret.

Communicators as Creators: What AI Means for the Industry

Communicators are creators of content, and content control stems directly from IP ownership. The ability to produce ownable and controllable property is essential for many communication functions from marketing, public relations, advertising, brand management, reputation management, crisis communication, and journalism. As AI has proliferated, it has created the ability to create large amounts of content with apparent ease enabling communicators in small offices and limited resources to leapfrog over personnel challenges and fully engage with content production at scale. It has also provided those with limited technological ability, such as a communicator with basic photoshop capabilities, to use AI to produce high-quality low-cost content. However, as IP law struggles to catch up with technological innovation obvious problems arise. Perhaps the most troubling for the communication industry is the requirement of humanness in the creation of legally protected copyright, and the seemingly unregulated nature of AI that can produce scores of infringing contents.

Part of this discussion is also the role of the individual in verifying their work. While this call for communicator accountability seems rational and reasonable, it does not consider the feasibility of verification. Almost everyone recognizes the logos of McDonald's, Apple, Coca-Cola, or Mercedes, but what about those millions of marks that are not part of everyday use in commerce? Avoiding copyright infringement seems like it is a matter of due diligence, but how does a communicator really know they aren't infringing on an obscure work that was included in a massive data set within an AI platform? The power of AI is rooted in the big data that it leverages for high-quality output, but sourcing that data and recognizing it within a transformative context is a challenge for both technology and human users. Current IP law also does not seem to recognize that the value of AI lies in the ability to create new, and valuable content with ease. Requiring a human component devoid of the technology places a burden on the user. A brightline rule of human involvement also seems like a shifting legal expectation that is highly subjective. It also undercuts the technological reality that prompt writing is becoming less important as AI becomes more sophisticated. The future of autonomous AI also challenges this contemporary reality of use and will likely frustrate lawmakers, regulators, and lawyers alike.

Ownership of the content also presents new issues as well. AI personhood seems to many like a far-fetched sci-fi reality. However, is it analogous to corporate personhood, which has been acknowledged in the U.S. for over two centuries. AI ownership of AI-produced content may reach an inflection point faster than anticipated. In the field of patent development, it is not hard to imagine a scenario where an AI platform used by a researcher creates in concert with a user a valuable medication that can be marketed to many consumers. In that scenario would the platform cede ownership to the user, especially since the platform's data and algorithm likely played the primary role in the development of the new property? This type of scenario could be the be the future of AI IP litigation for years to come. It will cause the law that will have to reconsider age-old norms of content, transformity, and human creation.

Discussion Questions

1 What area of IP is most exposed to the proliferation of AI?
2 What level of human involvement should be required for AI generated content to receive protection?
3 What is the biggest issue currently facing IP in the age of AI? What can communicators do to protect their work?
4 What are the benefits for content creators in the age of AI? What can the law do to help them with their work?
5 Hypothetical: Suppose you are creating a new logo for a company, and you write the following prompt: "create a logo for a hotel resort on the ocean. Use bright and colorful images that reenforce a beach scene. Incorporate dolphins, starfish, and a beach umbrella into the design." The AI provides a high-level logo that you want to use. What IP issues are present? How would you combat potential infringement? Under what circumstances would you feel that you could use this in commerce? What type of IP protection would it receive (assuming it's not infringing any existing IP)?

Notes

1 Feist Publications, Inc. v. Rural Telephone Service Co., 499 U.S. 340 (1991).
2 17 U.S.C. § 102(b).
3 Atari, Inc. v. North American Phillips Consumer Electronics Corp., 672 F.2d 607 (7th Cir. 1982) (aspects of a video game like a maze, eating dots, or moving players are not copyrightable).
4 17 U.S.C. § 102(a) (1–8).
5 See, e.g., Cartoon Network LP v. CSC Holdings, Inc., 536 F.3d 121, 127–30 (2d Cir. 2008) (holding that data temporarily stored in RAM is not fixed because it is not sufficiently permanent); Williams Electronics, Inc. v. Arctic International,

Inc., 685 F.2d 870, 876–77 (3d Cir. 1982) (finding fixation in video games as the audiovisual elements are embodied in ROM chips); Midway Mfg. Co. v. Arctic Int'l, Inc., 704 F.2d 1009, 1012–13 (7th Cir. 1983) (determining that audiovisual components of arcade games are fixed because of their repeated display); Baltimore Orioles, Inc. v. Major League Baseball Players Ass'n, 805 F.2d 663, 674–75 (7th Cir. 1986) (holding that live broadcasts are fixed when recorded simultaneously); Stern Electronics, Inc. v. Kaufman, 669 F.2d 852, 855–56 (2d Cir. 1982) (ruling that audiovisual displays generated by computer programs are fixed when stored in ROM chips).

6 Gaffar Hafiz and Saleh Albarashdi. "Copyright Protection for AI-Generated Works: Exploring Originality and Ownership in a Digital Landscape." *Asian Journal of International Law*, 15(1):23–46.

7 Gaffar and Albarashdi, "Copyright Protection for AI-Generated Works."

8 Urantia Found. v. Kristen Maaherra, 114 F.3d 955, 957–59 (9th Cir. 1997).

9 Naruto v. Slater, 888 F.3d 418, 426 (9th Cir. 2018).

10 U.S. Copyright Office, *Compendium of U.S. Copyright Office Practices*, 3rd ed. (Washington, DC: U.S. Copyright Office, 2021), accessed November 25, 2024, https://www.copyright.gov/comp3/docs/compendium.pdf.

11 Ibid, 21.

12 U.S. Copyright Office, *Compendium of U.S. Copyright Office Practices*, Chapter 300, 21–22. This quotation cites an older USCO document from 1965, U.S. Copyright Office, *Annual Report of the Register of Copyrights 1965* (Washington, DC: U.S. Copyright Office, 1965), accessed November 25, 2024, https://www.copyright.gov/reports/annual/archive/ar-1965.pdf.

13 U.S. Copyright Office, *Compendium of U.S. Copyright Office Practices.*

14 U.S. Copyright Office. (2023). *Copyright Registration Guidance: Works Containing Material Generated by Artificial Intelligence.* Federal Register, 88(51), 16190–193. Retrieved from https://www.federalregister.gov/documents/2023/03/16/2023-05321/copyright-registration-guidance-works-containing-material-generated-by-artificial-intelligence

15 U.S. Copyright Office, *Copyright Registration Guidance: Works Containing Material Generated by Artificial Intelligence*, March 16, 2023, https://www.copyright.gov/ai/ai_policy_guidance.pdf.

16 Wes Davis, "AI generated art cannot be copyrighted, rules a U.S. Federal Judge, The Verge, August 18, 2023, https://www.theverge.com/2023/8/19/23838458/ai-generated-art-no-copyright-district-court; *Thaler v. Perlmutter*, No. 1:22-cv-01564 (D.D.C. Aug. 18, 2023).

17 U.S. Copyright Office, *Registration Decision Regarding Zarya of the Dawn*, February 21, 2023, https://www.copyright.gov/docs/zarya-of-the-dawn.pdf.

18 U.S. Copyright Office, *Registration Decision Regarding Zarya of the Dawn*, 9–10.

19 U.S. Copyright Office, Copyright and Artificial Intelligence Part 2: Copyrightability, January 2025, https://www.copyright.gov/ai/Copyright-and-Artificial-Intelligence-Part-2-Copyrightability-Report.pdf

20 17 U.S. Code § 106 (1–6)

21 17 U.S.C. § 302.

22 Feist, 499 U.S. at 340; Fourth Estate Public Benefit Corp. v. Wall-Street.com, 586 U.S. 296 (2019).

23 Arnstein v. Porter, 154 F.2d 464 (2d Cir. 1946); Sid & Marty Krofft Television Prods., Inc. v. McDonald's Corp., 562 F.2d 1157 (9th Cir. 1977); Three Boys Music Corp. v. Bolton, 212 F.3d 477 (9th Cir. 2000); Newton v. Diamond, 388 F.3d 1189 (9th Cir. 2004).

24 Three Boys Music Corp., 212 F.3d 477\.

25 Sid & Marty Krofft Television Prods., Inc., 562 F.2d 1157
26 Williams v. Gaye, 895 F.3d 1106 (9th Cir. 2018).
27 Sheldon v. Metro-Goldwyn Pictures Corp., 81 F.2d 49 (2d Cir. 1936).
28 Newton v. Diamond, 388 F.3d 1189 (9th Cir. 2004).
29 17 U.S.C. § 507(b)); Petrella v. Metro-Goldwyn-Mayer, Inc., 572 U.S. 663 (2014).
30 17 U.S. Code § 107.
31 Campbell v. Acuff-Rose Music, Inc., 510 U.S. 569 (1994).
32 Sony Corp. of America v. Universal City Studios, Inc., 464 U.S. 417 (1984).
33 Harper & Row Publishers, Inc. v. Nation Enterprises, 471 U.S. 539 (1985).
34 Sony Corp. of America v. Universal City Studios, Inc., 464 U.S. 417 (1984).
35 Andy Warhol Foundation for the Visual Arts, Inc. v. Goldsmith, 598 U.S. 508 (2023).
36 Ibid.
37 Charles Pulliam-Moore, "Blade Runner 2049 Studio Sues Elon Musk over Copyright Infringement," *The Verge*, October 21, 2024, https://www.theverge.com/2024/10/21/24276092/alcon-entertainment-blade-runner-2049-tesla-musk-warner-bros-discovery-copyright.
38 Authors Guild v. OpenAI Inc., 23-CV-8292 (SHS) (S.D.N.Y. Apr. 1, 2024); Getty Images (US), Inc. v. Stability AI, Inc., No. 1:23-cv-00135 (D. Del. filed Feb. 3, 2023), https://docs.justia.com/cases/federal/district-courts/delaware/dedce/1:2023cv00135/81407/1; Andersen v. Stability AI Ltd., 23-cv-00201-WHO (N.D. Cal. Aug. 12, 2024); Silverman v. OpenAI, Inc., No. 3:23-cv-03416 (N.D. Cal. filed July 7, 2023); The New York Times Company v. Microsoft Corporation and OpenAI, Inc., No. 1:23-cv-11195 (S.D.N.Y. filed Dec. 27, 2023), https://nytco-assets.nytimes.com/2023/12/NYT_Complaint_Dec2023.pdf.
39 Blake Brittain "U.S. Judge Trims AI Copyright Lawsuit Against Meta," *Reuters*, November 9, 2023, https://www.reuters.com/legal/litigation/us-judge-trims-ai-copyright-lawsuit-against-meta-2023-11-09/.
40 Authors Guild v. Google, Inc., 804 F.3d 202 (2d Cir. 2015).
41 Andy Warhol Foundation for the Visual Arts, 598 U.S. 508.
42 15 U.S.C. § 1127.
43 Abercrombie & Fitch Co. v. Hunting World, Inc., 537 F.2d 4 (2d Cir. 1976).
44 15 U.S.C. § 1051(a); § 1127.
45 15 U.S.C. § 1127.
46 Silverman v. CBS Inc., 870 F.2d 40 (2d Cir. 1989).
47 Crash Dummy Movie, LLC v. Mattel, Inc., 601 F.3d 1387 (Fed. Cir. 2010).
48 Park 'N Fly, Inc. v. Dollar Park & Fly, Inc., 469 U.S. 189 (1985).
49 Bayer Co. v. United Drug Co., 272 F. 505 (S.D.N.Y. 1921); King-Seeley Thermos Co. v. Aladdin Indus., Inc., 321 F.2d 577 (2d Cir. 1963); DuPont Cellophane Co. v. Waxed Products Co., 85 F.2d 75 (2d Cir. 1936).
50 15 U.S.C. § 1114, § 1125(a).
51 Polaroid Corp. v. Polarad Elecs. Corp., 287 F.2d 492 (2d Cir. 1961).
52 15 U.S.C. § 1127; Eat Right Foods Ltd. v. Whole Foods Mkt., Inc., 880 F.3d 1109 (9th Cir. 2018); Kellogg Co. v. Nat'l Biscuit Co., 305 U.S. 111 (1938); Louis Vuitton Malletier S.A. v. Haute Diggity Dog, LLC, 507 F.3d 252 (4th Cir. 2007); Rogers v. Grimaldi, 875 F.2d 994 (2d Cir. 1989); Sebastian Int'l, Inc. v. Longs Drug Stores Corp., 53 F.3d 1073 (9th Cir. 1995).
53 15 U.S.C. § 1115(b)(4); New Kids on the Block v. News Am. Publ'g, Inc., 971 F.2d 302 (9th Cir. 1992).
54 15 U.S.C. § 1125(c).

55 15 U.S.C. § 1127; U.S. Patent and Trademark Office, *USPTO Issues Guidance Concerning Use of AI Tools by Parties and Practitioners* (Apr. 10, 2024), available at https://www.uspto.gov/about-us/news-updates/uspto-issues-guidance-concerning-use-ai-tools-parties-and-practitioners.
56 35 U.S.C. §§ 1–390.
57 35 U.S.C. § 101; Diamond v. Chakrabarty, 447 U.S. 303 (1980) (bacteria are patentable if they are part of a manufactured system); Alice Corp. v. CLS Bank Int'l, 573 U.S. 208 (2014) (establishes a two-step system for when an abstract idea is unpatentable. Essentially the court looks to whether the content is patent ineligible then the court looks to whether the ineligible concept can be made eligible by an "inventive concept."
58 35 U.S.C. § 102; Egbert v. Lippmann, 104 U.S. 333 (1881) (public use of an invention prior to registration invalidates the patent); Graham v. John Deere Co., 383 U.S. 1 (1966) (sets a three-prong test for obviousness).
59 35 U.S.C. § 103; KSR Int'l Co. v. Teleflex Inc., 550 U.S. 398 (2007).
60 35 U.S.C. § 112; Ariad Pharm., Inc. v. Eli Lilly & Co., 598 F.3d 1336 (Fed. Cir. 2010).
61 Graver Tank & Mfg. Co. v. Linde Air Prods. Co., 339 U.S. 605, 608 (1950); Warner-Jenkinson Co. v. Hilton Davis Chem. Co., 520 U.S. 17 (1997). This is a very abbreviated overview of this area of law. There are subparts to infringement as well that discuss direct infringement and the induced or contributory infringement that falls under indirect infringement.
62 18 U.S.C. §§ 1836–1839; See Uniform Trade Secrets Act (1985), National Conference of Commissioners on Uniform State Laws, available at https://www.uniformlaws.org/committees/community-home?CommunityKey=3a2538fb-e030-4e2d-a9e2-90373dc05792; Cal. Civ. Code §§ 3426–3426.11 (California's enactment of the UTSA); Fla. Stat. §§ 688.001–688.009 (Florida's enactment); Tex. Civ. Prac. & Rem. Code §§ 134A.001–134A.008 (Texas's enactment).
63 hiQ Labs v. LinkedIn Corp., 31 F.4th 1180 (9th Cir. 2022). This case is more about data scraping than trade secrets, but it provides an overview of the type of technological issues trade secrets and AI can present.

5

AI AND DISCRIMINATION

A "New Civil Rights Frontier"

Chapter Overview

This chapter examines AI use and discrimination. Specific attention is paid to the patchwork of U.S. laws at the federal, state, and local levels that attempt to combat AI discrimination in a variety of sectors, particularly employment. This system is contrasted with the European Union's (E.U.'s) AI Act, which categorizes AI according to risk and mandates certain actions to ensure fairness. The legal and philosophical approach of combatting discrimination in AI is discussed with an analysis of the geopolitical and technological consequences of the divergent U.S. and E.U. systems. The chapter concludes with an analysis of whether there can be a harmonized global approach to combatting AI discrimination and the legal and ethical challenges such as system presents.

Keywords: Discrimination, Employment, AI Audit, Algorithmic Bias, High-Risk AI

Artificial intelligence has been called the "new Civil Rights frontier" by federal regulators in the U.S. government.[1] Part of the reason is that AI is now used in a way to process vast amounts of information make quick decisions on important issues such as hiring, annual evaluations, and admissions. That speed allows for quicker decisions, and as Chapter 2 discussed, there is a natural human tendency to think that technology-driven solutions are more accurate and less biased than those made by human beings. This rise of decision-making in AI presents many opportunities to combat discrimination because AI platforms can be programmed to be objective and limited in their biased assumptions. However, the problem with these underlying assumptions is that AI is not devoid of bias.

DOI: 10.4324/9781003426561-5

Like human decision-making, AI discrimination can come from biases and prejudices embedded in its thought processes. However, unlike humans, AI bias is sometimes even less transparent. This raises unique issues for users who over-rely on AI outputs without giving much thought to how the platform makes decisions. For example, suppose an industry uses AI to screen job applications for an entry-level position in customer service. Part of the platform uses data from prior successful hires, which shows that the best candidates in the past are college-educated, young, and urban candidates. The screening of the new applicants may use that data to screen for candidates, which replicates the applicant pool of past successful hires. That leaves out applicants who would be qualified for the job, but do not meet the demographic characteristics of the prior hires. These screened-out applicants may be from lower-income families or from rural areas, but are otherwise qualified for the job, perhaps even more qualified than the prior hires. The screening may also look for more nuanced data points that provide a replicative biased candidate pool. Because of the preference for college educated, urban, young professionals, there may be a selectivity bias for people who worked internships at well-known companies. It may also privilege applicants who live in urban areas, which may correlate to people who have short driving distance commutes. The system may even look for phrases and words that privilege applicants that use certain phraseology. This may even be nuanced language such as picking applicants for the pool that say things like "strategic planning" or "strategic communication" over applicants that use phrases like "community outreach" or "community development." The subtlety of that linguistic difference can mean that candidates who worked in corporate fields are more likely to be hired than those who come from the non-profit sector. This complex issue shows the issue with overreliance of AI. Suppose a hiring manager is not involved in the selection of the AI platform used for job screening or does not know how that system was even developed. They may be under the wrong assumption that the system is less biased than a human and rely on the system to provide a quick and refined list of potential candidates for interviews.

Interviewing is another area where AI discrimination is a major concern. AI job interviews are becoming commonplace within large companies with sizable applicant pools. This has become more commonplace with the staffing issues in human resources departments (HR). HR professionals are frequently overburdened and understaffed, which has translated into the embrace of automation in HR departments in the U.S. AI platforms, such as Alex, an AI job interview platform owned by the company Aprioia, provide much-needed automation of a highly time-intensive process. The scale of these types of technologies allows for AI avatar interviews, which process not only the interview content but also facial expressions, enthusiasm, and tone. Some people like this experience because it allows for a less intense interview experience which can focus more on candidate qualifications and less on perceptual issues that frequently cause nervousness and interviewee anxiety. However, AI can also facilitate discrimination in this scenario.

For example, suppose after the AI job screening that a job candidate interviews with an AI avatar. Their responses will be evaluated most likely using key phrases that the AI system is trained to look for. A candidate can be highly qualified, but not use the "right" words which results in a poor interview. Moreover, if the AI platform is looking at language patterns, it can provide derogatory results for pause frequencies for some candidates. The AI may view this as signs of poor confidence or poor communication skills. However, it may be a sign of different cognitive processing for thoughtful responses, which disadvantages certain types of thinkers or communicators who would be excellent candidates. Facial expression can also be part of the AI evaluation. This can be used to determine the likability of a candidate. However, cultural differences on facial expressions can provide situations where candidates are discriminated against because of cultural norms. For example, smiling is a Western cultural norm that is interpreted by many as showing enthusiasm and approachability. In east Asian cultures, it may be interpreted as showing a lack of seriousness. If the AI is using a dataset that does not consider cultural nuance of smiling, then the output would be a discriminatory result for non-smiling candidates. Body language as an area of analysis has grown in the last few decades and it is possible that an AI system may be populated with that data to code interviews. However, that "science" is questionable, especially if it does not contain the cultural descriptions and idiosyncrasies of micro-expressions.

The mitigation strategy for this and other types of AI discrimination or bias is a careful auditing of the system and questioning of how AI systems work. Within HR, there is a movement that encourages the purchasing and use of proprietary AI platforms that are built exclusively for a company. Using this type of system requires knowledge of the data that underpins the system, how often the data updated, what populations are included in the dataset, and whether the system is being fairness tested.

It is important to remember that artificial intelligence is predicated on human intelligence, and human history is filled with prejudices, preferences, biases, poor judgment, and discrimination. AI systems trained on that knowledge is no different, and as Chapter 2 illustrates, there is no replacement for human oversight and human understanding. Lawmakers and regulators have focused on discrimination of AI and recognize it as a major issue within the larger development of the technology. This chapter analyzes those issues by looking at recent attempts at this regulation, and how it attempts to integrate existing anti-discrimination laws into the larger context of AI. It also looks at E.U. approaches to discrimination, particularly the concern around using AI for active discrimination through the process of what is popularly known as social scoring, a process by which individuals are categorized or ranked by immutable characteristics such as finances, behavior, or just activities. This is then used to privilege or suppress certain people for opportunities such as employment, housing, loans, and even social interactions. China's social credit system is an example of this concept in place, but the concern is that AI helps facilitate that type of system which is inherently biased and limits personal freedom.[2]

Within the U.S. and E.U., the concern over discrimination with AI has multiple facets. These include employment, housing, credit lending, policing, and healthcare. Within the U.S. Title VII of the Civil Rights Act, the Fair Housing Act, and the Equal Credit Opportunity Act address discriminatory practices.[3] AI exacerbates the discrimination that these laws are meant to prohibit, and federal agencies, along with some state laws, have attempted to prohibit AI from intentionally and unintentionally perpetuated discriminatory outcomes. Within the E.U., the General Data Protection Regulation (GDPR) and the AI Act work together to prevent discrimination.[4] The AI Act in particular has focused on high-risk AI use and attempts to regulate discrimination that stems from those platforms. These laws focus on transparency, bias testing, and mandatory human oversight to combat the excesses of AI and minimize social inequalities. Communicators are especially impacted by these regulations given AI use in audience segmentation, message strategy, and data storage. Communication content also needs to be transparent and compliant with these laws, especially in heavily regulated sectors. However, these laws are a work in progress as they focus on structured, identifiable data-driven systems. Implicit bias, unstructured data, and the scalability of systemic oversight present challenges. Marginalized groups that do not fit into legally recognized protected classes also may fall into gray areas where discrimination exists but is not explicitly prohibited by law. As this chapter will show, establishing standards that combat discrimination presents more questions than answers as AI and technology outpaces law and regulation.

U.S. Federal Regulations and Employment Discrimination

U.S. federal law has a longstanding prohibition of employment discrimination dating back over 60 years. With AI, there is a particular concern that AI in job screening could facilitate a hiring process that is a violation of Title VII of the Civil Rights Act of 1964, which prohibits employment discrimination based on race, color, religion, sex, or national origin. The concern is not theoretical. The Equal Employment Opportunity Commission (EEOC) has investigated claims where AI has been used to perpetuate these biases intentionally or unintentionally. In addition to investigations, it has become actively involved in AI within employment decisions since 2021 when it launched its Initiative on Artificial Intelligence and Algorithmic Fairness, which, among other things, established an AI working group to assess how AI was being used within employment.[5] The concern over AI in employment is merited. Since the 2020s, AI use in employment decisions has proliferated from workplace monitors to AI interviewers. Human resource employees have indicated that as many as 98 percent of companies intend to use AI within their employment process from hiring to firing.[6] There have also been high-profile examples of AI going quite wrong in employment decisions. For example, in 2017, Amazon's resume screening system was dropped because it regularly screened out women. The problem was the system looked at aggregate applicant data for the prior decade, which skewed heavily male. The maleness of the application data then was replicated again in the real-time application screening processes.[7] Racial discrimination is also a concern. There is evidence that facial recognition software does much better at matching faces of light-skinned people than those with darker skin. In one study that looked at matching faces, the program had a 10 to 100 times more chance of mismatching faces of those with east Asian and black faces than that of whites.[8] In high-stakes decision-making, such as healthcare, a study found that AI does a much poorer job in identifying the needs of black patients than white patients based on algorithmic bias.[9]

This creates a question around what is the best practice in using AI for decision-making purposes, especially when there is so much that can go wrong with AI and its replication of bias and facilitation of discrimination. In a practical sense, there is another question of how safe is it to use AI in these types of high-stakes decision-making anyway. Those using AI to make employment decisions are unlikely to choose a platform to intentionally create discriminatory outputs. It is more likely that they are using the AI system thinking it will do the screening much faster and more efficiently than a human, and probably with a lot less bias. There's also the issue that the person or organization using AI typically hires a designer or engineer to create a platform for use. This third-party vendor use is something that presents a unique situation for many in the workforce as they are relying on the product they are purchasing, in this case AI, to work as intended and not create unintended consequences. However, the net result of discriminatory AI hiring can be legally catastrophic. What's the benefit of an AI system designed to save time and money if the company using it ends up in a class action discrimination lawsuit that costs millions? Moreover, who is at fault, the AI, the employer, the designer, or all of the above?

As mentioned above, subtle discrimination can occur when AI uses past employment data to screen applicants, which can result in a screening out of qualified candidates based on race, religion, sex, or national origin. Employers are responsible for these violations and the EEOC has issued guidance on how to avoid these types of claims. It is important to note that Title VII encompasses both what is called "disparate treatment," which is a type of explicit discrimination in employment, and tests and procedures which create a "disparate impact" or "adverse impact" on employment.[10] The liability of the employer is established under federal law, and an employer that uses these types of algorithms with adverse impacts are legally responsible even if they purchased the AI platform from a vendor. This places a legal due diligence on the employer to ask AI vendors questions around algorithmic fairness and data discrimination, as well as how these platforms can be tested for perpetuating biases in employment decisions. However, how far does this liability extend? Can it extend to the platform developers as well? The answer is one that is currently being sorted out in the courts.

AI discrimination in employment goes beyond just hiring. Consider this example. Suppose a company uses AI to evaluate productivity of workers to provide annual performance reviews. This analysis, which used to take weeks to facilitate, now can be done within a few minutes. Large amounts of data can be processed with a productivity score that identifies at-risk workers and identifies low-production workers who could be potentially terminated. This system is a classic example of how AI can be used in the workplace to evaluate performance, and it is also an example of how AI without proper controls and context can create discriminatory results. Suppose the results show a group of workers who have lower productivity. Are those workers all over 55 years old? Do those workers have physical disabilities? Those types of discriminatory outputs are exactly the type of concerns that U.S. agencies are concerned about with the introduction of AI within the workplace. For example, in 2022, the EEOC entered into a settlement with iTutorGroup, which provides English language services to users in China, based on a job screening AI platform that screened out tutors based on age (females over 55 and males over 60).[11] These types of cases are increasingly complex. AI vendors can likewise be civilly liable for discrimination under the theory that they operate as hiring agents on behalf of companies. In a recent lawsuit filed in the U.S. District Court for the Northern District of California, the court extended liability to an AI platform that allegedly screened applicants in a discriminatory manner. In that particular case, the plaintiff alleged that the AI system that used machine learning used AI to create behavioral screening through personality tests and assessments that revealed mental health disorders or impairments. This resulted in the denial of job offers for otherwise credentialed and qualified candidates. The judge in the case held that under agent theory of hiring the AI was a delegated screener of job applicants. The court held:

> [The third-party platform's] role in the hiring process is no less significant because it allegedly happens through artificial intelligence rather than a live human being who is sitting in an office going through resumes manually to decide which to reject. Nothing in the language of the federal anti-discrimination statutes or the case law interpreting those statutes distinguishes between delegating functions to an automated agent versus a live human one. To the contrary, courts applying the agency exception have uniformly focused on the "function" that the principal has delegated to the agent, not the manner in which the agent carries out the delegated function.[12]

This has major implications for those in the AI field actively involved with job screenings because it extends liability beyond the client engaging the AI system to the AI system itself. While the case is ongoing and this ruling may be subject to an appeal, it signals something significant about the legal accountability of AI within discrimination and employment law. Systems cannot hide behind clients for their accountability within AI issues.[13]

The EEOC has provided guidance around this specific issue of employment discrimination with AI. However, disparate impact is a legal concept that can be difficult to prove, and some have speculated that this may provide some cover to employers who are faced with discrimination allegations because they use AI in the hiring process. In fact, the legal concept of disparate impact is the byproduct of what the Brookings Institute calls a "patchwork of federal statutes, many of which the courts have weakened over the years."[14]

One major legal concept within this is the concept of selection rate, which AI is particularly well equipped to provide as an output. The selection rate is "the proportion of applicants or candidates who are hired, promoted, or otherwise selected."[15] The EEOC also uses the 4/5 rule or 80% rule in hiring analysis. This guideline identifies potential adverse impacts in employment practices by examining the outcome of certain hiring practices based on percentages. The EEOC provides this example in terms of AI:

> A personality test scored by an algorithm, the selection rate for Black applicants was 30% and the selection rate for White applicants was 60%. The ratio of the two rates is thus 30/60 (or 50%). Because 30/60 (or 50%) is lower than 4/5 (or 80%), the four-fifths rule says that the selection rate for Black applicants is substantially different than the selection rate for White applicants in this example, which could be evidence of discrimination against Black applicants.[16]

However, it is important to note that the 4/5 rule is not the law but is a guidepost for making decisions.[17] There are situations where it is not appropriate, such as when the applicant pool is a small size or when the applicant pool has large disparities in qualifications, e.g., degree status. Employers need to take note that the EEOC holds them responsible for these results even if they are relying on third-party AI vendors. The use of a pre-programming AI platform to make this predictive analysis is not an immunization from legal responsibility. Again, it reiterates the theme in AI development and utilization that human oversight is required, and, in this case, legally demanded. However, this does not mean that AI is banned from employment use. In fact, many organizations use AI to do resume scanning, job interviews, employment assessments, so-called "job fit" scoring for potential hires and promotions, and employee monitoring with great success.

Discrimination is not just part of hiring, and the U.S. federal agencies have been part of an ongoing effort to combat discrimination in other areas, such as housing. In 2023, the U.S. Department of Justice entered into an agreement with Meta, formerly Facebook Inc., over the platforms use of large language models that identified prospective users for housing advertisements. These ads were shown to users who fit certain protected characteristics under the Fair Housing Act. The platform was using a system known as "Lookalike Audience" or "Special Ad Audience" that matched users to certain pre-determined groups that were identified as prospective customers by the advertiser.[18] In 2024, a group of potential renters filed a class action lawsuit alleging that an AI system discriminated against them under a rental scoring system that marked them as at-risk tenants. While the company did not admit fault, the lawsuit resulted in a $2.2 million judgment in an out-of-court settlement.[19]

What these lawsuits demonstrate is that discrimination by AI presents novel issues to age-old issues of workplace, housing, and other forms of discrimination. Federal law has protections in place for these scenarios, but what AI is doing is presenting unique and sometimes hard-to-prove cases of discriminatory conduct. What will become more difficult to combat are nuanced examples of discrimination such as proxy discrimination when neutral data points within AI, such as zip codes, correlate to characteristics like race. Combatting algorithmic bias also presents logistical challenges under the law as many algorithms are legally protected trade secrets. This presents a barrier to plaintiffs trying to establish a discrimination case because the employer may be legally unable to provide the algorithm as part of discovery. Of course, there is a likelihood that there will also be allegations that the corrective bias measures in AI will produce a reverse bias. This discussion of algorithmic overcorrection is likely to be a politically and legally hot topic in the latter half of the 2020s.

State Antidiscrimination Laws and AI

While the U.S. federal government has acknowledged the role AI plays in discrimination, there are many areas of discrimination that are not addressed. What has emerged in the past few years is greater state involvement in discrimination and AI, particularly in discrimination in hiring. One of the first, and perhaps best known, local laws about AI and discrimination came in 2021 when New York City enacted a municipal code that required employers to conduct audits for bias in AI employment tools, commonly known as automated employment decision tools (AEDTs).[20] This law, known as Local Law 144, mandated AEDTs to have independent auditors, provide a summary of results, require applicants that have notices that their applications were being reviewed by AEDTs, and mandated that job candidates have alternative processes for evaluation. The law went into effect on July 5, 2023, and is enforced by the New York City Department of Consumer and Worker Protection (DCWP). Compliance has been mixed and one study suggested a large gap between those that are required to comply with Local Law 144 and those who actually do.[21] Part of the reason for this lack of compliance is the law's language provides a wide interpretation of who is actually subject to the regulation. Despite these issues, the law represents a watershed moment for local AI regulation as it was an early attempt to address algorithmic bias and data discrimination in hiring.

Colorado has also emerged as a leader in AI discrimination law enacting the Colorado Artificial Intelligence Act (CAIA) that will go into effect on February 1, 2026. The implication of the law is that developers and users of high-risk AI systems that make a "consequential decision" are subject to certain oversights and transparency requirements. These consequential decisions include education, employment, financial services, housing, healthcare, insurance, or legal services. Developers have a series of obligations when developing these high-risk systems including foreseeable uses, type of data used to train the system, documentation about evaluations, measures to mitigate discrimination, intended outputs, and intended use. Developers also have to display on their websites a disclosure of any high-risk AI they use or develop and any potential risks and discrimination.[22] The law is particularly concerned with consumer rights, and the CAIA mandates that consumers be informed with AI is making consequential decisions about them, especially when inaccurate personal data is used. The law is precedent setting in that it is one of the few U.S. laws that specifically operationalizes what high-risk AI is, and it places accountability on developers and deployers of AI systems as opposed to users. However, this law does not allow for individual lawsuits based on

AI discrimination. Rather the enforcement of the law is vested in the Colorado Attorney General who uses their centralized oversight treating these violations as a violation of deceptive trade practices under the Colorado Consumer Protection Act.[23]

Other states are following the example of Colorado. At the time of this writing, California, Georgia, Hawaii, Illinois, and Washington all have pending legislation that addresses potential AI discrimination in employment.[24] The significance of these laws is that they shift the perspective of how accountability and fairness are understood. In some sense, they have now become managers of algorithmic standards. Inherent in this responsibility is employers have to have a higher AI and algorithmic literacy, something that may be difficult (and expensive) to learn. Developers are also being held to a higher standard of accountability, particularly in their AI design. As the recent federal lawsuits involving the EEOC show, this liability of accountability for discrimination may extend to third-party vendors. This also creates a new dynamic to hiring. Potential employees may now look to transparency of AI systems and corporate accountability as prerequisites prior to submitting an application. However, the theme of human accountability remains. What these laws show is that humans are still held to the standard of accountability when dealing with fairness, transparency, and ethics, even when those decisions are mediated by machines, emphasizing that technology cannot serve as a scapegoat for systemic inequities or poor judgment. What employers and companies have to do is be proactive in their accountability. They have to understand algorithms like they would an employee. Their data vendors and developers should provide them with a data resume that includes information about the sources of data, algorithm evolution, and auditing tools. These organizations should also leverage their network of professionals, which may include human resources, ethicists, communicators, and IT, to create an audit committee that actively evaluates bias. Companies should also provide transparent AI disclosures both for compliance, but also for the positioning of their organization within the marketplace. This recognition of how AI impacts workers and the identity of an organization is the first step in embracing the new human-AI hybrid workforce.

The European Union's Approach to AI Discrimination

The E.U.'s AI Act addresses discrimination in a distinct way that focuses on larger system societal discrimination. The Act is legally consequential in that it articulates AI by degrees of risk, with risk being associated with human rights-based protections. The comprehensive scope of the act coupled with its proactive protections makes it unique in the regulation of AI. High-risk AI must meet strict nondiscrimination standards while also ensuring that AI does not engage in manipulative practices that cause harm or exploit vulnerabilities of people. The law defines AI as "high risk" when it is used for education, employment, policing, and social service access. Requiring mechanisms to combat discrimination and mitigate bias.

Part of the difference of the E.U.'s approach to discrimination lies in its focus on fundamental rights, such as equality, dignity, and privacy, that are articulated in the E.U. Charter of Fundamental Rights.[25] These rights differ from what the U.S. Constitution provides in that the E.U. Charter encompasses both liberal rights, e.g., freedom of speech, with modern social rights, such as healthcare, housing, and education. These rights are explicit and they include rights protecting people from data manipulation, discrimination, and even environmental protection. In the U.S., the closest thing to this level of rights protection is a patchwork of federal and state laws, such as the California's Consumer Privacy Act (CCPA) which represents the high-water mark for privacy rights in the U.S.[26] Given these differences, a comprehensive legal framework provided by the AI Act would likely face significant constitutional challenges in the U.S. both in structure and operation. Legislation such as the E.U.'s AI Act would likely face significant challenges under the concept of federalism and state's right to govern areas of law. But most significantly, the AI Act's prohibition of manipulation would face the biggest hurdles under the First Amendment. Blanket prohibitions on speech would face challenges under the content-specific speech analysis which places a high bar of protection of fully protected speech. There would also be challenges to bias mitigation and audits under the Fourth Amendment, and potentially under intellectual property protection for algorithms. Transparency obligations could also face First Amendment challenges under the prohibition of compelled speech, and corporate penalties and accountability could be challenged under the Fourteenth Amendment due process analysis.

Despite these one-to-one comparisons, the AI Act does present an interesting discussion about discrimination as it relates to social scoring. As mentioned above, social scoring has become a fear for many in Western democracies, and many point to China's social credit scoring system as an example of how data can be used to erode rights. Social scoring in its broadest sense is the practice of giving people scores based on their behavior or characteristics, which then is used to determine access to services, social privileges, and other opportunities. At its core, it is a way to categorize people based on their worthiness of certain freedoms and opportunities. It erodes human freedom and is a system that fundamentally controls society through surveillance penalizing people for their personal choices.

The E.U. AI Act specifically prohibits AI use for social scoring in Article V. In that article, there are express bans on certain types of AI use. Specifically, under Article V section 1b, it states that the E.U. prohibits:

> the placing on the market, the putting into service or the use of an AI system that deploys subliminal techniques beyond a person's consciousness or purposefully manipulative or deceptive techniques, with the objective, or the effect of materially distorting the behaviour of a person or a group of persons by appreciably impairing their ability to make an informed decision, thereby causing them to take a decision that they would not have otherwise taken in a manner that causes or is reasonably likely to cause that person, another person or group of persons significant harm.[27]

This section focuses on the manipulation or deception of others to facilitate a type of scoring. The act goes on to prohibit AI from evaluation of individuals as well stating that the E.U. prohibits:

> the placing on the market, the putting into service or the use of AI systems for the evaluation or classification of natural persons or groups of persons over a certain period of time based on their social behaviour or known, inferred or predicted personal or personality characteristics, with the social score leading to either or both of the following:
>
> i detrimental or unfavourable treatment of certain natural persons or groups of persons in social contexts that are unrelated to the contexts in which the data was originally generated or collected;
> ii detrimental or unfavourable treatment of certain natural persons or groups of persons that is unjustified or disproportionate to their social behaviour or its gravity.[28]

These bans implicate all sorts of behavior including aggregate cross-domain analysis such as using social media posts, employment records, and financial records to create a personal score that then determines the denial of loans, housing, or jobs. Ultimately what the E.U.'s AI Act does is acknowledge the risks within the quantification of culture. Social scores place a premium on numerically evaluating behavior and trust in place of human relationships. It goes beyond mere privacy concerns because it potentially quantifies morality and incentivizes behavioral conformity. This erodes the humanness of people and replaces nuanced evaluations with bureaucratized, calculable metrics. What the AI Act does is stand in place of that system recognizing that technical "fairness" is not necessarily the same as ethical and social justice.

While well intentioned, the E.U. AI Act's prohibition of social scoring is not without risk. Its blanket prohibition creates inadvertent risks of creating a moral blind spot within new technology. A categorical ban of AI evaluation could create a scenario where these technologies go underground where they are unregulated. This may result in what is known as "shadow innovation," where AI can be developed outside of E.U. controls because of overly restrictive regulations. This jurisdictional evasion actually allows the type of technology the E.U. seeks to ban to actually proliferate in an environment where the excesses and misapplication are much worse than ever anticipated. Of course, without universal standards of development and regulation, this is always a risk, but it is more of a risk when a large economic sector outright bans particular use. Additionally, blanket prohibitions of AI for analysis also overlook potential benefits of aggregate scoring. For example, there could be a public health use of aggregate human data for things like evaluating access to resources in areas like public health. By stigmatizing the use of aggregate data scoring there is the potential to overlook major innovations within the use of AI for public good. While well intentioned the E.U. could stagnate AI use and development creating a society that does not fully benefit from AI's technological innovation.

Implications for the Communications Industry

AI use to facilitate discrimination raises interesting and new questions about how we ensure a fair society. What AI allows is a type of proxy discrimination based on variables, such as zip codes or online purchasing, that may seem neutral, but in fact create judgments based on socioeconomic status. There is also a dynamism to AI decision-making, which allows for an AI platform to become more discriminatory over time by replicating and amplifying embedded biases. Unlike human bias, which likely remains static, AI bias can grow even more pronounced over time and do so in a covert way that may not be uncovered without stress tests and audits. The concept of intersectionality, the interconnected social categorizations such as race, class, disability, sexuality, and gender, is also an important change within discriminatory conduct. Intersectional identity challenges the one-dimensional view of identity and inequality within society showing that the impact of discrimination can be compounded by marginality within multiple groups. Because of AI's complex ability to examine aggregate data, it can create a process that facilitates intersectional bias and discrimination in a faster and more complete way than a human being. Traditional anti-discrimination laws, such as Title VII of the Civil Rights Act of 1964, do not anticipate that type of discrimination. It calls into question the workability of current regulations that did not anticipate this type of bias in decision-making.

The issue with discrimination within AI is rooted in what organizations are willing to do to ensure fairness and how fairness is operationalized. Minimal compliance with existing laws can result in ethical AI washing, a concept where minimal ethical compliance is done to be legally compliant, while permitting deeper more nuanced discrimination. Superficial audits create a false impression of compliance and progress without addressing system issues within the technology. There is also a risk within AI regulation that it actually benefits large AI players who are able to comply with regulations like bias audits, which squeeze out smaller competitors. What results in a monopolistic AI environment in which a few well-funded and connected companies dominate the business of AI. Small firms may not be equipped to handle compliance in the same way, thereby making them less competitive. This has been a reality for many types of business and is the root of the scholarly work regulatory capture and public choice theory. These regulations allow for a regulatory barrier to entry for less well-funded companies, potentially ones that may be better at anti-discrimination AI. This lack of diversity of platforms can lead to a system where echo chambers of acceptable bias exist because the companies can meet minimum governmental standards.[29] The net effects of this not only could be an accepted system of discrimination within the use of AI but also an undermining of public trust in the technology.

There are practical issues with discrimination within AI, notably a tradeoff between transparency and privacy. Laws like the E.U. AI Act mandate transparency measures to combat discrimination, particularly in high-risk systems. However, within those tradeoffs, there are concerns about trade secret integrity when it comes to algorithms, and also the disclosure of private information about individuals. The implementation of these transparency initiatives, particularly in the U.S. where there are strong trade secret laws, may be a challenge. Companies guard these secrets as part of maintaining them as property, and the requirement of transparency, in effect, can make this valuable property cease to exist.[30]

The biggest obstacle in combatting discrimination in AI is the lack of a uniform regulation. Fragmented regulations lead to inconsistent results, which perpetuate different forms of discrimination. However, the creation of a global AI standard is likely impossible given the different conceptualizations of privacy, property, and rights that exist globally. The closest thing to a uniform AI law would likely come from the European Union because their system has an outsized influence in the global marketplace. The so-called Brussels effect exists because of the regulatory influence of the E.U. and the market access that compliance provides for non-E.U. nations. The concept is rooted in the idea that there is a global soft power with the E.U. marketplace that creates a regulatory ecosystem that drives unform philosophical approaches to issues like privacy, and perhaps, artificial intelligence. This creates a global harmonization of laws and establishes clear definitions and approaches to legal issues. This impact of this may go beyond technological regulation, but a redefinition of AI innovation coupling it with ethical compliance. This could create unique results where AI could take on new dimensions and roles within society such as AI becoming part of public good and collective intelligence. Within the regulatory sphere AI could become part of a democratizing function within society where ethical AI becomes a norm and rogue unethical AI becomes part of cultural resistance similar to cryptocurrency. Conversely, the Brussels effect has a Eurocentric impact that could create an AI and algorithmic monoculture where AI becomes standardized.

Discrimination and its regulation could have long-term consequences for the global development of AI. The U.S. and E.U. represent two conflicting standards of AI development. The U.S. approach is rooted in market-driven solutions meant to protect against discrimination, while also promoting innovation. The approach can be best characterized as reactive. Laws, such as those in Colorado and New York City, focus on audits and opportunities for lawsuits to combat bad use of AI. The E.U.'s approach is more preemptive, where fairness and standards are mandated prior to the launch of platform. It mandates more deliberative development, which can stifle innovation and ultimately could make the E.U. less competitive in the creation of AI platforms. These two approaches could lead to a fractured AI landscape where the U.S. is more tolerant of the excesses and pitfalls of AI whereas the E.U. is more protective, but ultimately less innovative in development. The approaches could create a two-tiered system of development and the potential for different operations of common AI platforms depending on jurisdiction. This creates larger developmental concerns in the AI race where models consider larger questions of morality and justice along with cultural concepts of fairness. A reconciliation of these approaches could lead to a hybridized approach to AI that attempts to couple innovation with fairness with cutting-edge technology that is ethically grounded.

All of this has major implications for communicators who are ethical stewards and educators of AI use. Their position within organizations places them in the nexus of innovation and decision-making. Ultimately, the legal and ethical values that shape AI development are a derivative of cultural decisions. Communicators have the ability to shape these conversations and also employ these tools in a responsible way. Within the context of AI discrimination, communicators will not only manage public perception but can also steer the conversation as advocates of inclusivity and fairness within the AI field. They also can best articulate the transformative nature of AI and the benefits of the technology leveraged to enhance quality of life and society.

Discussion Questions

1 What is the most concerning aspect of AI discrimination and how should systems combat it?
2 What are the core philosophical differences in U.S. and E.U. approaches to discrimination? Which system is "better"?
3 Are AI audits the right way to combat discrimination? If you were working for a company that used AI audits, what would you need to do to ensure that the audit provided in the information you needed?
4 Is human oversight better to combat discrimination, or should AI systems monitor themselves? What is the inherent advantage to using AI to combat discrimination?
5 Suppose you are using AI to screen job applicants. You have excellent applicant pools, but the pools appear to have the same type of people: urban, college educated, East coast, mid-20s, females. What would you do to find out if the AI system was creating a biased result? Suppose the applicant pool is small, does that make a difference? What steps would you take to combat this homogenous pool? Is the solution AI based or human based?

Notes

1 Cat Zakrzewski, "Federal regulators call AI discrimination a 'new civil rights frontier,'" *Washington Post*, April 25, 2023, https://www.washingtonpost.com/technology/2023/04/25/artificial-intelligence-bias-eeoc/.
2 Katie Canalas and Aaron Mok, "China's 'social credit' system ranks citizens and punishes them with throttled internet speeds and flight bans if the Communist Party deems them untrustworthy," *Business Insider*, November 28, 2022, https://www.businessinsider.com/china-social-credit-system-punishments-and-rewards-explained-2018-4.
3 Title VII of the Civil Rights Act of 1964, 42 U.S.C. §§ 2000e et seq.; Fair Housing Act, 42 U.S.C. §§ 3601 et seq.; Equal Credit Opportunity Act, 15 U.S.C. §§ 1691 et seq.
4 European Union, *General Data Protection Regulation (GDPR), Regulation (EU) 2016/679 of the European Parliament and of the Council of 27 April 2016 on the Protection of Natural Persons with Regard to the Processing of Personal Data andon the Free Movement of Such Data and Repealing Directive 95/46/EC (General Data Protection Regulation,* Official Journal of the

European Union, L 119 (4 May 2016): 1-88, https://eur-lex.europa.eu/legal-content/EN/TXT/PDF/?uri=CELEX:32016R0679; European Union, Regulation (EU) 2024/1689 of the European Parliament and of the Council of 13 June 2024 Laying Down Harmonised Rules on Artificial Intelligence and Amending Certain Union Legislative Acts (Artificial Intelligence Act), Official Journal of the European Union, L'2024/1689 (12 July 2024), https://eur-lex.europa.eu/legal-content/EN/TXT/PDF/?uri=OJ:L_202401689

5 U.S. Equal Employment Opportunity Commission, "EEOC Launches Initiative on Artificial Intelligence and Algorithmic Fairness," October 28, 2021 accessed December 4, 2024, https://www.eeoc.gov/newsroom/eeoc-launches-initiative-artificial-intelligence-and-algorithmic-fairness.

6 Jack Kelly, "How Companies Are Hiring and Firing with AI," *Forbes*, November 4, 2023, https://www.forbes.com/sites/jackkelly/2023/11/04/how-companies-are-hiring-and-firing-with-ai/.

7 Jeffrey Dastin, "Insight: Amazon Scraps Secret AI Recruiting Tool that Showed Bias Against Women," *Reuters*, October 10, 2018, https://www.reuters.com/article/world/insight-amazon-scraps-secret-ai-recruiting-tool-that-showed-bias-against-women-idUSKCN1MK0AG/.

8 Patrick Grother, Mei Ngan, and Kayee Hanaoka, *Face Recognition Vendor Test (FRVT) Part 3: Demographic Effects*, NIST IR 8280 (Gaithersburg, MD: National Institute of Standards and Technology, 2019), https://nvlpubs.nist.gov/nistpubs/ir/2019/NIST.IR.8280.pdf.

9 Zaid Obermeyer, Brian Powers, Christine Vogeili, and Sendhil Mullainathan, "Dissecting racial bias in an algorithm used to manage the health of populations, *Science* 366, no. 6464 (2019): 10.1126/science.aax2342, https://www.science.org/doi/10.1126/science.aax2342.

10 U.S. Equal Employment Opportunity Commission, *Select Issues in Assessing Adverse Impact: Software, Algorithms, and Artificial Intelligence*, accessed December 4, 2024, https://www.eeoc.gov/laws/guidance/select-issues-assessing-adverse-impact-software-algorithms-and-artificial.

11 EEOC v. iTutorGroup, Inc., et al., Civil Action No. 1:22-cv-02565 (E.D.N.Y. 2022); U.S. Equal Employment Opportunity Commission, "iTutorGroup to Pay $365,000 to Settle EEOC Discriminatory Hiring Suit," accessed December 4, 2024, https://www.eeoc.gov/newsroom/itutorgroup-pay-365000-settle-eeoc-discriminatory-hiring-suit.

12 Mobley v. Workday, 2024 WL 3409146 (N.D. Cal, July 12, 2024), *6.

13 Ibid.

14 Chiraag Bains, "The Legal Doctrine that Will Be Key to Preventing AI Discrimination," *Brookings Institution*, September 13, 2024 accessed December 4, 2024, https://www.brookings.edu/articles/the-legal-doctrine-that-will-be-key-to-preventing-ai-discrimination/.

15 29 C.F.R. § 1607.16(R).

16 U.S. Equal Employment Opportunity Commission, *Select Issues in Assessing Adverse Impact: Software, Algorithms, and Artificial Intelligence.*

17 *See* 29 C.F.R. § 1607.4(D); Watson v. Fort Worth Bank & Trust, 487 U.S. 977 (1988).

18 U.S. Department of Justice, "Justice Department Secures Groundbreaking Settlement Agreement with Meta Platforms (Formerly Known as Facebook) to Resolve Allegations of Discriminatory Advertising," June 21, 2022, accessed December 4, 2024, https://www.justice.gov/opa/pr/justice-department-secures-groundbreaking-settlement-agreement-meta-platforms-formerly-known.

19 Jesse Bedayn, "Class Action Lawsuit on AI-Related Discrimination Reaches Final Settlement," *Associated Press*, November 20, 2024, https://apnews.com/article/artificial-intelligence-ai-lawsuit-discrimination-bias-1bc785c24a1b88bd425a-8fa367ab2b23.

20 New York City Council. *Int. No. 1894-A, Local Law 144 of 2021: Automated Employment Decision Tools Bias Audits.* Enacted July 5, 2023. https://www.nyc.gov/assets/dca/downloads/pdf/workers/Local-Law-144.pdf.
21 Lucas Wright et al., "Null COmpliance: NYC Local Law 144 and the challenges of algorithm accountability," *Proceedings of the 2023 ACM Conference on Fairness, Accountability, and Transparency (FAccT)*, June 5, 2024. https://doi.org/10.1145/3630106.3658998.
22 Colorado General Assembly, "Senate Bill 24-205: Concerning Consumer Protections for Interactions with Artificial Intelligence," Enacted May 17, 2024. https://leg.colorado.gov/bills/sb24-205
23 Colorado Revised Statutes, Title 6, Article 1: Colorado Consumer Protection Act. Available at: https://colorado.public.law/statutes/crs_title_6_article_1
24 Colorado General Assembly, *Senate Bill 24-205: Colorado Artificial Intelligence Act (CAIA)*, enacted May 17, 2024, https://leg.colorado.gov/bills/sb24-205; Illinois General Assembly, *House Bill 5322: Illinois Commercial Algorithmic Impact Assessments Act*, https://legiscan.com/IL/text/HB5322/id/2921992; New York City Council, *Int. No. 1894-A, Local Law 144 of 2021: Automated Employment Decision Tools Bias Audits*, enacted July 5, 2023, https://www.nyc.gov/assets/dca/downloads/pdf/workers/Local-Law-144.pdf; California Civil Rights Council, *Proposed Regulations for Preventing AI Discrimination*, released May 2024, https://calcivilrights.ca.gov/2024/05/17/civil-rights-council-releases-proposed-regulations-to-protect-against-employment-discrimination-in-automated-decision-making-systems; Georgia General Assembly, *House Bill 890: AI Discrimination Protections*; Hawaii State Legislature, *House Bill 1607: AI and Anti-Discrimination Protections*, https://labor.hawaii.gov/hcrc; Washington Legislature, *Washington Law Against Discrimination (WLAD)*, RCW Title 49, Chapter 49.60, https://apps.leg.wa.gov/RCW/default.aspx?cite=49.60.
25 European Union, *Charter of Fundamental Rights of the European Union*, 2012/C 326/02, October 26, 2012, https://eur-lex.europa.eu/legal-content/EN/TXT/?uri=CELEX:12012P/TXT.
26 California Legislature, *California Consumer Privacy Act (CCPA) of 2018*, Cal. Civ. Code § 1798.100–1798.199.100 (2018), https://oag.ca.gov/privacy/ccpa.
27 European Union, *EU Artificial Intelligence Act: Article 5 – Prohibited AI Practices*, accessed December 6, 2024, https://artificialintelligenceact.eu/article/5/.
28 European Union, *EU Artificial Intelligence Act: Article 5*.
29 George J. Stigler, "The Theory of Economic Regulation," *The Bell Journal of Economics and Management Science*, 2, no. 1 (1971): 3–21; Ernesto Dal Bó, "Regulatory Capture: A Review," *Oxford Review of Economic Policy*, 22, no. 2 (2006): 203–25; Amitai Etzioni, "The Capture Theory of Regulations—Revisited," *Society*, 46 (2009): 319–23; Elizabeth Warren, "Corporate Capture of the Rulemaking Process," *The Regulatory Review*, 14 June 2016, https://www.theregreview.org/2016/06/14/warren-corporate-capture-of-the-rulemaking-process/.
30 It is important to note that within the U.S. trade secrets are largely protected under state law which typically follow some version of the Uniform Trade Secrets Act (USTA). There is also federal protection of trade secrets under the Defend Trade Secrets Act of 2016 (DTSA), U.S. Code, Title 18, §§ 1836–1839. In the E.U. trade secrets are protected under the Trade Secrets Directive (Directive (EU) 2016/943), European Union. *Directive (EU) 2016/943 of the European Parliament and of the Council of 8 June 2016 on the Protection of Undisclosed Know-How and Business Information (Trade Secrets) Against Their Unlawful Acquisition, Use, and Disclosure.* Official Journal of the European Union, L 157, June 15, 2016, pp. 1–18.

6

AI AND LIABILITY

Determining Legal Responsibility

Chapter Overview

This chapter examines the core concepts of liability for artificial intelligence (AI) in the U.S. and E.U. The philosophical underpinnings of liability are discussed through the historical development of negligence and strict liability within the common law system of Great Britain and the U.S. The chapter then examines contemporary attempts to define AI liability in the European Union and the U.S. with a focus on how the two systems approach AI from a rights-based protection (E.U.) and a market-driven innovation approach (U.S.). The chapter concludes with a discussion of the future of liability and the technological difficulty in assigning fault in AI systems that utilize opaque, black box designs.

Keywords: Liability, Negligence, Strict Liability, Product Liability, Black Box, E.U. A.I. Act

Who is legally responsible for the output of artificial intelligence (AI)? Consider this scenario. Suppose AI is used to create custom news articles and video reports for users with simple prompts. This creates news information in a highly realistic format using what is commonly referred to as deepfakes as anchors to deliver the news. One report provides news about a well-known CEO and states he is under federal investigation for fraud. This clip includes the CEO's likeness and appears highly believable and realistic. This clip is then posted by the user and it goes viral on social media. The user truly believes this report is true, but knows it was AI generated with AI deepfake anchors. The reality is none of the story is true, and it was generated by a hallucination in the AI platform based on

DOI: 10.4324/9781003426561-6

a feature of the data and algorithm in the AI. The system itself is a black box, meaning that its processes are not transparent to the user. The user's post is shared throughout social media and actually leads to a decline in the CEO's company's stock prices. The CEO files a defamation suit for his damaged reputation and the stock prices. Who is legally at fault? The user for the initial prompt? The user because of the subsequent post? The AI platform for creating the untrue content? The AI designer for creating an algorithm and data set that gives false information? The other users who reposted the content making it go viral? These questions get to the larger issue of AI liability. How can liability extend to users who rely on a technology without fully understanding its processes, and how can a company that produces technology that is an autonomous agent be held responsible for its actions?

The nuanced challenge of liability within AI exists when a multilayered system in which users, developers, platforms, and the AI system work in an interconnected method to produce content. This is made even more complicated by the fact that AI is oftentimes working in a black box, meaning the internal decision-making mechanism is opaque and not easily understandable by humans. This opaqueness of AI presents understandability issues not only for users, who may just have a shallow understanding, but also for developers. Deep learning neural networks can learn very complex data using millions of small incremental changes to the data to increase accuracy. These iterative adjustments are guided by the algorithm, which creates a refinement within the system that can recognize patterns "better" and create "better" outputs. This creates complex liability issues for AI platforms because the results can be unpredictable. This also presents a question about legal accountability. If the AI system is creating bad decisions, then shouldn't it have legal responsibility as well? Conversely, if a human being is using AI to make decisions without verification and proper oversight, shouldn't they be held legally responsible as well? This is compounded when thinking about the AI system's own outputs because developers play the role of initial creation of the system, but the adjustments made by the AI later on are not the result of developer decisions but the AI's decisions.

All of this presents a larger question of duty of care, the core foundation of tort law, particularly the legal principle of negligence. Over the past two centuries, negligence standards have developed that require individuals to act with reasonable care to prevent harm. Duty is present when there is a legally recognized obligation of a person or entity toward another. This concept of duty of care is well established in U.S. tort law and was developed in an era where personal injury was a primary concern for companies, especially railroads.[1] Elsewhere duty is also an established legal concept, especially within E.U. member states that follow E.U.'s Principles of European Tort Law (PETL) established by the collection of academics in the European Group on Tort Law. The PETL Article 4:103 defines duty this way:

> A duty to act positively to protect others from damage may exist if law so provides, or if the actor creates or controls a dangerous situation, or when there is a special relationship between parties or when the seriousness of the harm on the one side and the ease of avoiding the damage on the other side point towards such a duty.[2]

The PETL is a set of proposed guidelines that are meant to create uniformity within different E.U. countries' tort laws. While there are idiosyncrasies within these member nations' laws, the foundation of duty is similar to that in the U.S. These duties are rooted in the concept that damage from actions (or lack of care) is foreseeable, there is a relationship between parties that results in duty, and there is an expectation of reasonableness of this expectation of duty. AI poses significant philosophical challenges to these legal principles. Part of the challenge is that autonomous AI systems and black box models do not allow for a full understanding of the mechanics of their outputs. As AI becomes more autonomous, the unintended consequences of the system create a higher rate of emergent behaviors, which are non-obvious side effects of a combination of capabilities.[3] How courts will handle these new issues is a topic of discussion that will play out as more AI litigation continues in the next decade. Understanding the stakes, and the role of humans in mitigating risks, is an important aspect of AI law and practice.

General Overview of Legal Liability in AI

Legal liability is rooted in the concept of accountability, which has a foundation that go back to ancient law. Understanding AI's legal responsibilities and accountabilities requires an understanding of the core concepts of duties and accountabilities. While most lawmakers are probably not trained in the historic underpinnings of legal responsibility, it is important for those trying to configure new AI liability laws to understand how the concepts of duty, negligence, and liability were created and why they were established in tort law. A theme emerges from this history that shows technological innovation has frequently caused lawmakers to rethink how legal responsibility works, and how much responsibility a person, corporation, and technology have when someone is harmed.

The core of legal responsibility is the concept of proportionality between harm and consequence. That is, a person or company should be held accountable proportionately to the transgression or harm. As a legal philosophy liability's roots go back to ancient times with Hammurabi's Code from 1754 B.C. which introduced the idea of "an eye for an eye" known as *lex talionis*.[4] This level of liability of personal retribution has been replaced over the past millennia with more sophisticated concepts of civil liability that includes strict liability, actual malice, and negligence. Many cite Hammurabi's Code as a harsh reality of retribution and vengeful justice, but it is also about proportionality under the law. For example, modern concepts of harm allow for certain types of damages. But those damages cannot be disproportionate to the harm caused. The legal concept of negligence is important in understanding this legal accountability and expectations. Negligence, which is the failure to exercise ordinary care, had origins going back to Roman law where there was a culpa (fault) standard, which has intentional (dolus) and carelessness (culpa) standards for certain damages. The concept that a person would exercise ordinary care was also rooted in Roman law where a person was expected to act with prudence. By the 1500s, there began a standard of care associated with duty, reflected in the English common law writ of duty of care and contractual duties. By the Industrial Revolution technological development refined the concept of care and negligence through a series of cases beginning with *Vaughan v. Menlove*, an 1837 case that established the reasonable person standard. This standard has survived into the 21st century essentially intact.[5] There is the concept in tort law that a person is expected to act with an objective standard of ordinary care, which is not particularized to the individual's abilities. By 1856, another landmark case *Blyth v. Birmingham Waterworks Co.*, established that negligence was a failure to do something a reasonable person would do.[6] This definition would go on to inform the negligence standards in courts globally. By the 1880s, the concept of foreseeability became part of negligence when a case held that a duty of care exists when a party can foresee a potential harm. Later that foreseeability concept would be extended to when an individual was held to have a duty of care when it is foreseeable that others would be affected by their actions.[7]

These core concepts of negligence and duty would be imported into U.S. law and shape it as it developed in the late 19th century.[8] Today classic negligence requires four elements: duty, breach of that duty, causation, and harm.[9] In the U.S., plaintiffs must show actual cause (cause in fact) and proximate cause (legal cause). Sometimes cause in fact is called but-for causation, which means but for the action the harm would not have resulted. Proximate cause examines the foreseeability of the event. These concepts are essential in ascertaining fault in a lawsuit. For example, suppose that an AI system is used for employment screening, and its results are a discriminatory hiring pool in which demographic features of candidates are the determinative reason why people are rejected. A job applicant is rejected based on this discriminatory system. In their lawsuit, the job applicant plaintiff would argue but for the discriminatory screening process, they would have been selected for an interview. Proximate cause looks at whether these actions were foreseeable. In the same scenario, the applicant/plaintiff would need to show that the AI system was foreseeably discriminatory. This looks at the type of harm in the case. Was the harm of being screened out indirect, or what it highly related? In this case, the foreseeability would be likely very proximate because biased AI data training resulting in discrimination is foreseeable. Now, the reality of this scenario is that there are many more facts in play that are not presented, and there is a high likelihood that in a real case like this, there would be significant disagreement over the causation. However, this illustrates the way negligence cases, including discrimination cases, involving AI would be litigated.

However, there is a complicating variable in cases involving technology. In some instances, the law states a party is held liable for damages regardless of fault, intent, or negligence. It is a standard where the defendant is held legally responsible because they engaged in a certain type of activity. This applies in product liability, certain ultra-hazardous activities, and, in some cases, with animal ownership. Within AI the idea of strict liability is important because some of the AI in question could fall under a product liability case where a system is defective. There is also the potential that AI could be held strictly liable if the activities it is engaged in are considered abnormally dangerous. That raises the specter of potential lawsuits that would be very difficult for AI companies to defend and ones in which AI could potentially be legally responsible for significant sums of money. The answers to these questions are rooted in whether AI is considered a product or a service, and how autonomous decision-making will evolve over time as AI technology improves.

The concept of strict liability has evolved alongside technological advancements, and the current state of AI mirrors many of the technological revolutions of the past. With the advent of the industrial revolution, courts, especially in the U.S., moved from a concept of English common law writs where liability was based on injury alone to providing certain levels of liability based on the status of the wrongdoer. In the 19th century, there was a proliferation of injuries from large factories and railroads prompting the creation of modern tort principles. British law created the concept of strict liability in 1868 with the case *Rylands v. Fletcher*, which established the precedent that a person is automatically liable when they do something that is highly dangerous and likely to cause injury.[10] This case involved the creation of a reservoir on land with many open shafts. The reservoir builders did not close the shafts and when the reservoir was filled with water the mines flooded. The House of Lords ruled that even though the reservoir builders were not negligent, they were still liable under the concept of strict liability because they were engaged in highly dangerous work with water that had a high likelihood of injury.[11]

Rylands v. Fletcher was a significant case for tort liability in other common law systems, notably in the U.S.[12] The case's precedent established the legal standard that when ultra-hazardous materials are used there is an increased accountability because of the likelihood and risk of significant injury. Early 20th-century U.S. jurisprudence bears this out. Courts began recognizing that companies owed a duty to customers and established the concept of product liability law.[13] Then courts introduced the concept of strict liability in the mid-20th century. Courts established the concept that manufacturers owed a duty under strict liability for defective products even if the company was not negligent in their manufacturing.[14] This was reflected in the 1965 Second Restatement of Torts, which is a model rule created by the American Law Institute, that argued that product liability existed even without the proof of negligent behavior.[15] By the 1970s, product liability became closely intertwined with the standard of strict liability, and this theory became attached to other areas of wrongdoing such as environmental regulations, such as the Comprehensive Environmental Response, Compensation, and Liability Act of 1980 (CERCLA).[16]

In contemporary society, strict liability continues to be applied to activities that have certain high-level risks. As a concept, it has evolved alongside technological growth. Today with AI's use in areas like autonomous vehicles, medical AI, and AI predictive analysis, courts and lawmakers may revisit strict liability's application. Today, there are no cases in the U.S. where strict liability is imposed on AI, but there are certainly examples of high-risk AI cases that call the technology's impact on society into question. For example, Character.AI has been sued because of the suicide of a 14-year-old boy after he had extensive AI interaction with a chatbot. The plaintiff argued that the platform created a dangerous situation where safety measures were not taken. In that case, the chatbot, named after a *Game of Thrones* character Daenerys Targaryen, was used by the teen in a highly personal way. It is alleged that the interactions with the chatbot became so personal that he developed other problems with schoolwork. Ultimately after cryptically engaging with the chatbot the teen committed suicide. His mother filed a lawsuit in the U.S. District Court for the Middle District of Florida for wrongful death under the theory that Character.AI had a defective design that was not tested for potential harm, especially to minors.[17] This case is rooted in both negligence and strict liability for product liability for failure to warn about the platform's addictive quality and adverse impact. While at the time of this writing this case is ongoing, the issue of AI, especially its impact on minors, has received high levels of attention. In 2023 the National Association of Attorneys General issued a letter demanding Congress to study AI and its harmful impact on children.[18] This concern shows that the liability and risks of AI, especially on vulnerable populations like children, may be a starting point for broader discussions of regulation and accountability. In some circumstances, given that impact of children, particularly those who may suffer from mental health issues or other disabilities, may be outsized there could be the potential for AI regulation to impose strict liability or higher-level standards of legal accountability.

What these types of cases demonstrate is that the legal accountability of AI is still being sorted out. These standards of fault also highlight the issue of human oversight and platform accountability. If AI is held to the standard of negligence, fault may hinge on the human oversight of the platform. For example, did the programmers, developers, or users use reasonable care in preventing a foreseeable harm? This fits the scenario where a user utilizes AI for generative content that is flawed and then acts upon it. It is traditional tort law, and it fits within the known concept of liability in countries like the U.S. and E.U. However, as AI develops into a more sophisticated system that has higher levels of autonomy, a negligence standard may not work. What is foreseeable with an AI system that has its own power to think and act? How can there be human oversight in that situation? Does that make having an AI system similar to keeping a wild animal or engaging in explosive detonation, which are the type of ultrahazardous activities that warrant strict liability? This may create a situation where the law treats AI not as a service but as a product. If that is the case, then what are the net effects? That standard, while beneficial to those who are injured by AI, may serve as an obstacle to development. There is also the issue of asymmetrical burden on tech industries. AI developers are in the best position to correct algorithmic or data harms. By allowing for a negligence standard to apply to AI, lawmakers would permit a legal accountability that is not so restrictive. This acknowledges the reality of AI where complete control of systems is an impossible standard to meet or maintain.

Strict liability is also a controversial legal standard, and the impact of the standard can be crippling to certain industries. For example, prior to 1964, some states had a strict liability standard for defamation cases. That was overturned by the U.S. Supreme Court in the famed case *New York Times v. Sullivan*.[19] That case actually raised the fault level for public officials from negligence to actual malice, which is an even higher standard of fault. The reasoning was that strict liability for defamation had unintended consequences for free speech and the press. That fear of a chilling effect was enough for the court to constitutionally ban it as a legal standard for those types of cases. This philosophical rationale could be extended to technological innovation where glitches and errors of AI could result in a stagnation of development because of an overly punitive tort system.

However, there are even more unanswered questions in this analysis of fault. Suppose the damages of a negligent act include AI along with a network of other actors. In that scenario, fault becomes highly decentralized with multiple defendants, including AI, holding legal responsibility. In that scenario who is going to be held legally responsible and is there a situation where the liability has different standards of fault including strict liability and negligence depending on the status of the defendants? Situations with multiple actors are encompassed in the legal concept of joint and several liability where multiple parties have various degrees of fault. Under this legal doctrine, a plaintiff can recover 100 percent of the judgment from any of the parties involved. In the U.S. this liability standard varies by state with some states having pure joint and several liability, modified joint and several liability, or several liability.[20] Outside the U.S., this standard varies by country. The net result is that contributors to AI platforms, especially if they are small entities, may be reluctant to participate in programs because of the fear of liability. Another principle of negligence that may impact AI liability is contributory negligence, that is a doctrine that holds that when a party is contributing to their harm then they cannot recover any damages.[21] It is a harsh rule, but it is followed in some jurisdictions. For example, suppose an AI system for a driverless car produces a crash. However, the injured driver who sued was going 5 miles over the speed limit. In that scenario, the injured driver may be barred from recovery because of his contributory negligence. Such situations underscore how AI liability is not limited to systems themselves, but users for their contributions and decisions to AI outcomes.

The role of liability in AI also presents novel questions previously unanswered by law or technology. Could AI liability create new industries, such as AI liability insurance, that would protect AI from fault-anticipating lawsuits. Could AI indemnify itself with user agreements that remove all levels of fault? That works so long as there is a user relationship with the platform. As AI becomes more technically sophisticated this type of agreement becomes obsolete as autonomous AI does not have a user or any agreement that restricts its behavior. So, as AI evolves from a tool to autonomous actor, liability shifts from human to machine through a method of distributed fault. In that situation, indemnity user agreements and AI personhood could blend to create a situation where AI becomes the manager and enforcer of its own self-executing system where liability has nothing to do with human or corporate oversight.

Standards and Differences in AI Liability U.S. versus E.U.

Globally the U.S. and E.U. present the major regulatory frameworks for analyzing and shaping AI liability. However, these frameworks differ in their approach. The E.U.'s approach can best be described as tiered. The AI Act, the Product Liability Directive (PLD), and the proposed AI Liability Directive (AILD) directly address liability of the technology.[22] These laws emphasize auditing and transparency as the primary means of regulating AI liability and use. In contrast, the U.S.'s approach on liability is rooted in its historical view of negligence, strict liability, and product liability. The federal system in the U.S. makes this approach decentralized, largely governed through state law. In the U.S., the plaintiff has the burden of proving the legal standard of fault and showing damages. In that regard, the U.S.'s liability has a reactive quality forcing those harmed by the technology to bring lawsuits. There is some contextualized AI liability as well where federal agencies, such as the Food and Drug Administration (FDA) or FTC, regulate sectors of AI. That is somewhat akin to preventive risk management systems like that of the E.U., but not completely. The U.S. looks to self-regulation as the primary means of quality control for AI, which serves the larger U.S. priority of fostering an economic and regulatory environment that promotes AI innovation and development.

Within the E.U. the regulation of AI's liability is largely governed by the AI Act and other existing laws that mandate certain levels of legal responsibility. The AILD is a proposed law that is not yet enacted, but it shows the underpinning of E.U. liability philosophy. In June 2024, there was some concern raised by the European Parliament and Council, which, among other things, questioned the AILD's overlap with existing E.U. laws such as the PLD. The biggest impact of the AILD is that it creates a rebuttal presumption of causality for those harmed by AI systems. The underpinning of this approach is it lowers the burden of proof for those plaintiffs bringing suits. The AILD would exist within a larger E.U. system where national liability laws provide some avenues for compensation. These systems range in their application of fault from negligence to strict liability. Most notably in the E.U. is that the PLD provides for strict liability for harm based on product liability with a statute of limitations of 10 years. The PLD, national liability laws, and the proposed AILD would create three legal avenues for those harmed by AI. Notably, the PLD could provide for a highly pro-plaintiff strict liability standard for AI casting the technology as a product rather than a service. While the E.U. does not have a solidified system of liability for AI one thing they are concerned about is legal fragmentation between nations. It is entirely possible for a combination of strict liability, negligence, and presumptive fault to develop within the E.U. depending on the risk factor of the AI platforms.[23]

One of the things the AILD recognizes is that legal fault within AI is different than traditional fault claims based on negligence. Those lawsuits are rooted in the concept of proving a party did or did not perform a duty in the physical sense. However, within AI, the ability to demonstrate legally that there is fault can be prohibitively expensive because of the black box structure of AI. Because of that, the AILD supports the creation of a uniform standard of fault, which lowers the barrier to lawsuits by creating presumptive fault. Additionally, the AILD advocates for standardized E.U. AI fault because it ultimately helps businesses position themselves in developing AI systems. Having brightline fault guidelines that are standardized throughout the E.U. allows for more predictability within AI development.[24] A harmonized legal framework that creates lower barriers to lawsuits ultimately supports the E.U.'s mission of creating accountability for AI and protection of public safety.

Of course, there are criticisms of this approach to AI, which is one of the reasons the AILD has not been enacted into law. One is the increased compliance burden ultimately can create a deterrence of innovation. Lowered barriers for lawsuits also can encourage litigation, which can create frequent, expensive, and unfounded legal issues for AI developers. Moreover, the operationalization of non-compliance creates risks for enforcement and development of AI. But other issues with these types of liability laws also affect the larger AI development. These laws can chill risk-taking within AI, and perhaps stunt open-source AI development. The presumption of fault also challenges what many see as a fundamental aspect of Western law, which requires plaintiffs to prove their cases. This burden shifting can create complex legal scenarios as the line between human and AI error blurs. It seems that the AILD could be viewed as having the philosophy that AI is more than a tool for humans to use but is an autonomous legal entity. If AI takes on the burden of liability, does that open the door for AI to enjoy the benefits of individual rights and ownership?

There are also issues with cross-border issues, particularly with the U.S. The AILD and AI Act have cross-border implications when E.U. courts have standards that apply to U.S.-based companies. One of the obvious issues is the potential requirement of disclosure of algorithms for high-risk systems. While the AI Act emphasizes audits and transparency for AI systems, the AILD, if enacted, would give national courts the ability to order disclosure of evidence for high-risk AI. The reason for this compelled disclosure is plaintiff access to important evidence for their lawsuit. The AILD recognizes that this evidence request needs to be "necessary and proportionate" to support a lawsuit. However, it presents potential conflicts within the U.S. for companies that may protect algorithms under trade secret law. This can lead to bigger legal issues involving data sovereignty, intellectual property protection, and trade. Similar to the concept of forum shopping, where a plaintiff brings a lawsuit in the most favorable system, this type of system could create AI liability tourism where plaintiffs bring lawsuits in E.U. jurisdictions that are plaintiff-friendly. This also can create a highly balkanized AI market where there is less international cooperation. The net effect of this can impact consumers who may not have access to certain AI platforms with their fullest power because of concerns over cross-border liability.

In the U.S., AI liability falls into the historical structure of legal responsibility through tort law, product liability, and contracts. Plaintiffs must prove liability through the causation framework, which ranges in standard from negligence to product defectiveness. Proving these claims requires evidence, which is governed through the state or federal rules for civil procedure and discovery. It is an expensive process, and the U.S. legal system does not provide a lowered barrier to lawsuits in order to facilitate the ease of access to materials. Given the technological and legal realities of algorithmic trade secrets and black box AI systems, the U.S. discovery system for AI lawsuits would be expensive and perhaps overwhelming to the average litigant.

The U.S. also uses a fragmented approach to certain types of claims. For example, discrimination claims by AI are governed by the Equal Employment Opportunity Commission (EEOC) whereas claims around consumer rights and AI would be handled by the FTC. Should antitrust issues with AI arise, then the Department of Justice, Antitrust Division would use existing antitrust laws to address those potential violations. Having a unified AI Act similar to that of the E.U. would likely not occur in the U.S., at least not in a comprehensive way. Part of this is the fragmentation of the federalist legal system and the further specialization of federal agencies. There is also a preference for industry self-regulation. Large AI companies, such as Microsoft, Google, and Open AI, have led the way on self-regulation, offering self-regulatory principles of AI development and implementation.[25] These self-regulations operate as a type of soft law, that indirectly shapes the legal interpretations in cases. It also allows for the U.S. to encourage rapid adaption to technological changes, which is a U.S. geopolitical priority. The negative impact of this type of approach is that it allows for a myriad of rules that provide inconsistent experiences and safety. These self-imposed guidelines become the de facto "standard of care" in terms of negligence, which has the effect of insulating large corporations from legal responsibility.

The outcome of this type of system may produce unexpected results. As E.U. law has shown, there is something evidentiarily different about the black box technology of AI. Its structure provides a barrier for plaintiffs who need to find information to bring successful suits. Flipping the burden to the defendant seems unlikely in the U.S. (and for that matter probably the E.U. as well). However, that discussion shows a larger awareness of the litigation issues around a technology that is rooted in secrecy. There is also the question of derivative liability when proprietary platforms are created for companies and then managed by third-party operators. That has already been a question explored in U.S. discrimination law and is one that is likely to continue in other areas as well. This might result in a higher level of contractual agreements around AI use not only between users and platforms but also companies and third-party vendors. Those contracts might directly address liability issues and provide for certain required audits or analysis, not to mention indemnity. AI litigation also may provide for more psychological harm-based lawsuits under the theory of emotional distress. This may be more of an issue as chatbots become more commonplace and potentially take the place of human contact for many users. Their emotional and personal attachment to them may lead to future discussions of duty of care for designers and even the rise of questions about negligent infliction of emotional distress.

Avoiding Legal Liability with AI: Issues for Communicators

Those working in the field of communication are uniquely exposed to some of the liability issues of AI. How can a communicator avoid some of the legal pitfalls of AI? What responsibility do they have as individual users of AI to avoid leveraging the technology in a way that leads to legal liability? How should they communicate to others about AI and its limits? These are all questions that have no clear-cut answer, but they serve as starting points for a larger discussion that must be had within the communication industry. Acknowledging the limits and risks of AI while also understanding the contours of liability puts communicators in a unique position to influence the field and also impact the way AI is used.

One of the first things communicators should acknowledge within AI liability is that they can be the reason their company gets sued. Human verification is the theme of responsible AI use. Verifying information and complying with current laws ultimately falls to the communicator, not their tools. For example, if a communicator was using AI to create advertising content, then they must follow the same laws around false advertising as they normally would. Claims that require substantiation still require that regardless of AI. Communicators also need to be aware that AI content has accuracy issues, and also has the potential to create hallucinated content that may create legal problems. The AI output from a generative platform can become evidence along with the prompt written by the communicator. This is the reason why understanding the limitations and the best practices for AI use is so important.

Chatbots provide invaluable opportunities for improved customer service. However, within communication leveraging this technology also presents certain risks. Accuracy of information along with the evolving issue of emotional distress claims can mean that chatbots can be a growing source of liability. Anthropomorphic AI systems, i.e., platforms that have a very human like quality, will only make these types of platforms more prolific. Understanding their limits and perhaps providing warning labels and disclaimers of their abilities can be important communications that limit liability. For example, suppose a user asks a chatbot for health information, then relies upon it to their detriment. Suppose the user dies from this disinformation. There is no immunity for AI under U.S. federal law or E.U. law. Understanding the limitations of the technology is not only essential for communicators creating content but also a fundamental responsibility for them to educate the public about these limitations. That education may prove crucial to civil liability. This also presents an issue about expectations. Human-like chatbots may create user expectations that are higher than those of other forms of AI. This can result in standards of care that are different for those platforms that have a higher level of anthropomorphic qualities.

The gathering of data to train AI also presents legal and ethical issues. While privacy is discussed in more detail in Chapter 7, the liability for gathering that data presents important considerations. Data, particularly that from customers, used to create an AI system may require clear disclosures and transparency. For those communicators working in a global practice with a E.U. presence, it is important to acknowledge that the standards for disclosure and privacy are different than those in the U.S. The General Data Protection Regulation (GDPR) codifies privacy standards for the E.U., which are much more robust than those in the U.S. Communicators need to be conscious that in global practice the standards of privacy, just like the standards of AI liability, differ. Understanding the "law" not only requires a working knowledge of U.S. regulations but also of E.U. standards.

Communicators have much to offer in terms of design for maximized user experience. Leveraging the power of AI also makes for more targeted and higher-quality communications. However, the issue of liability for communicators is that the presence of AI does not divest humans of responsibility. One of the most impactful ways communications resonate is by understanding the nuanced aspects of human understanding. Communicators bring that knowledge with them during the decision-making process. It would be prudent for communicators to leverage that knowledge in the larger decision-making process in AI from development to implementation.

Liability within AI has significant consequences for users and developers. As the ethical and societal concerns about AI grow the underlying issue is one of accountability and human oversight. As the issue of liability shows, these two principles of governance and accountability are crucial in setting ethical and legal boundaries. It is important that AI remain under human control and have human oversight for it to be leveraged for societal betterment. The answer to how to hold AI accountable presents conflicts of priorities. On the one hand developers and AI platforms need to be responsible for their products. This is even more important because these products often have opaque systems that are difficult to understand. There should not be a responsibility gap between the programmers and the platforms where AI systems can create detrimental results with no accountability. On the other hand, AI is a tool that should be controlled by humans. Human users leverage the platforms for certain outputs, and those human interactions serve as a basis for the outcomes of AI use.

There are also issues that create an interplay between legal accountability and innovation. The more accountable AI is, there is a risk that the less innovative the technology becomes. Risk-adverse programmers and designers may be reluctant to leverage the technology to its fullest capacity because of fears of litigation. In the global AI race, markets that have less restrictive regulations have an advantage. Countries that strictly regulate AI may create a more hostile environment for AI developers, which, in turn, limits innovation. This tension between innovation encouragement and regulation is highlighted in the liability differences between the U.S. and E.U.'s approach to AI. It is also the basis of the AI approach of the Trump administration and the President's 2025 Executive Order Removing Barriers to American Leadership in Artificial Intelligence.

One of the challenges of AI liability is fitting the technology within a preexisting notion of agency and legal responsibility. The current legal frameworks of liability look at AI as either a tool of human action or a product that can become defective. Instead, there could be a shift in the legal understanding of causality and responsibility. Perhaps AI is a different type of action that operates in a space between human control and product performance. This could lead to lawsuits that emphasize the joint and several liability of AI design. This would represent a powerful shift in the understanding of products where a product would have defined obligations with moral and ethical agency (similar to a corporation). This could lead to new structural oversights such as AI insurance or accountability bonds through financial guarantees for potential liabilities. Obligations also could shift as AI becomes more autonomous, and the legal concept of liability and expectations could shift as AI evolves in its own design.

The esoteric legal concept of liability really is about the larger societal concern about AI's impact on the human. Questions like who is in control, what power does AI have, and how much responsibility do humans and machines have to make life better are the underpinnings of a discussion on AI agency. The E.U. and U.S. present two systems that are trying to balance human dignity and collective welfare against individual responsibility and market-driven innovation. There is no clear-cut answer, and the larger legal debate over AI liability will uncover far more questions than answers. The innovation of AI also presents the question of can legal responsibility exist without human intention? That question requires humans to reimagine their understanding of accountability and justice. AI's growth and development may present a new reality where it can make choices that are divorced from the intention of their creators. When that occurs is it possible to legally hold creators or users accountable? Machine accountability and algorithmic agency may be new concepts the law needs to examine alongside the larger philosophical dimensions of free will, morality, and agency. This presents a larger issue of reimagining responsibility itself, and legal accountability becomes de-humanized. Can justice exist in that environment? Can accountability exist without intention or consciousness? Those are questions lawmakers and courts will grapple with in the years to come.

Discussion Questions

1. What responsibilities do AI designers and programmers have in determining the type of outputs their systems have?
2. Does human oversight mean that humans should always be held responsible for the byproducts of their AI use? In what situations would humans not be held responsible?
3. Is it fair to hold AI platforms presumptively responsible for their outputs? Does that type of system stifle innovation?
4. The U.S. and E.U. offer radically different approaches to AI consumption. Which system is better? What is the global impact of these competing systems of liability?
5. Scenario: Suppose a large company uses an AI-powered customer service chatbot that uses machine learning that evolves over time

based on customer input. The system is tested and audited and seems to be doing well, especially in the first few months of its utilization. One day a customer asked the chatbot if a weight loss supplement the company sells is safe to use while taking a particular medicine. The chatbot states that taking the medicines together, which is untrue. The customer purchases the product and uses it. She is not injured, but the supplement does not meet her expectations. She files a lawsuit for false advertising. Who is at fault? Does the intent or autonomy of the system make a difference? Suppose she is injured, does that change the issue? Should this fault of the AI platform be considered human error or a product liability? How would this case's outcome differ in the U.S. versus the E.U.?

Notes

1 Palsgraf v. Long Island Railroad Co., 248 N.Y. 339 (1928)
2 European Group on Tort Law, *Principles of European Tort Law*, Art. 4:103, "Duty to Protect Others from Damage,"
3 Katherine Miller, "AI's Ostensible Emergent Abilities Are a Mirage," *Stanford Institute for Human-Centered Artificial Intelligence (HAI)*, May 8, 2023, https://hai.stanford.edu/news/ais-ostensible-emergent-abilities-are-mirage. There is some question as to the power and impact of emergent behavior. In this article Miller challenges the notion that emergent behaviors are greater than the sum of their parts of AI.
4 Morris J. Fish, "An Eye for an Eye: Proportionality as a Moral Principle of Punishment." *Oxford Journal of Legal Studies* 28, no. 1 (2008): 57–71.
5 *Heaven v. Pender*, (1883) 11 QBD 503 (CA).
6 *Blyth v. Birmingham Waterworks Co.* (1856) 11 Exch. 781, 156 ER 1047.
7 *Donoghue v. Stevenson*, [1932] AC 562 (HL).
8 Anthony Gray, "The Historical Development of the Fault Basis of Liability in the Law of Torts," in *The Impact of Law's History: What's Past is Prologue*, eds. Sarah McKibbin, Jeremy Patrick, and Marcus K. Harmes (Cham: Palgrave Macmillan, 2022), 105–30.
9 Dan B. Dobbs, Paul T. Hayden, and Ellen M. Bublick, *The Law of Torts*, 2nd ed. (St. Paul, MN: West Academic Publishing, 2011), 231–45.
10 *Rylands v. Fletcher* [1868] UKHL 1, (1868) LR 3 HL 330.
11 Ibid.
12 Ibid.
13 *MacPherson v. Buick Motor Co.*, 217 N.Y. 382, 111 N.E. 1050 (1916).
14 *Escola v. Coca-Cola Bottling Co. of Fresno*, 24 Cal. 2d 453, 150 P.2d 436 (1944).
15 American Law Institute, *Restatement (Second) of Torts* § 402A (1965).
16 Comprehensive Environmental Response, Compensation, and Liability Act of 1980, 42 U.S.C. §§ 9601–75.
17 Kevin Roose, Can a Chatbot be blamed for a Teen's Suicide?," *New York Times*, October 23, 2024, https://www.nytimes.com/2024/10/23/technology/characterai-lawsuit-teen-suicide.html.
18 National Association of Attorneys General, "54 Attorneys General Call on Congress to Study AI and Its Harmful Effects on Children," Press Release, September 5, 2023, https://www.naag.org/press-releases/54-attorneys-general-call-on-congress-to-study-ai-and-its-harmful-effects-on-children/.

19 *New York Times Co. v. Sullivan*, 376 U.S. 254 (1964).
20 "Contribution Actions in All 50 States," Matthiesen, Wickert & Lehrer, S.C., last modified March 2013, https://www.mwl-law.com/wp-content/uploads/2013/03/contribution-actions-in-all-50-states.pdf.
21 "Contributory Negligence." Law.com, September 1, 2015. https://dictionary.law.com/Default.aspx?typed=contributory%20negligence&type=1
22 Council of the European Communities, *Council Directive 85/374/EEC on the Approximation of the Laws, Regulations and Administrative Provisions of the Member States Concerning Liability for Defective Products*, July 25, 1985, Official Journal of the European Communities L 210, 29–33, https://eur-lex.europa.eu/legal-content/EN/TXT/?uri=CELEX%3A31985L0374; European Commission. *Proposal for a Directive of the European Parliament and of the Council on Adapting Non-Contractual Civil Liability Rules to Artificial Intelligence (AI Liability Directive)*, September 28, 2022, COM(2022) 496 final. https://ec.europa.eu/commission/presscorner/detail/en/ip_22_5737; European Union, Regulation (EU) 2024/1689 of the European Parliament and of the Council of 13 June 2024 Laying Down Harmonised Rules on Artificial Intelligence and Amending Certain Union Legislative Acts (Artificial Intelligence Act), Official Journal of the European Union, L'2024/1689 (12 July 2024), https://eur-lex.europa.eu/legal-content/EN/TXT/PDF/?uri=OJ:L_202401689
23 European Parliamentary Research Service, *Briefing: AI Liability Directive—Digital and Product Liability Rules for the AI Era*, EPRS_BRI(2023)739342, June 2023, accessed December 10, 2024, https://commission.europa.eu/business-economy-euro/doing-business-eu/contract-rules/digital-contracts/liability-rules-artificial-intelligence_en
24 European Commission, *Proposal for a Directive of the European Parliament and of the Council on Adapting Non-Contractual Civil Liability Rules to Artificial Intelligence (AI Liability Directive)*, COM(2022) 496 final, September 28, 2022, https://eur-lex.europa.eu/legal-content/EN/TXT/?uri=CELEX%3A52022PC0496.
25 Google, *AI Principles: Responsible AI Practices*, accessed December 10, 2024, https://ai.google/responsibility/principles/; Microsoft, *Responsible AI Principles*, accessed December 10, 2024, https://www.microsoft.com/en-us/ai/responsible-ai; OpenAI, *AI Safety and Responsibility*, accessed December 10, 2024, https://openai.com/safety/.

7

AI AND PRIVACY

Chapter Overview

This chapter examines AI privacy regulations in the U.S. and European Union. Specific attention is paid to the differences in the legal concept of privacy within the two systems, and how each system approaches privacy regulation from either a market-driven or human rights-based approach. The chapter concludes with the argument that privacy will present many transparency and crisis-related issues for communicators, and that communicators will be placed in a position to navigate AI user expectations in the future. The chapter predicts that AI ethics will likely be a driving force in industry norms as the law has struggled to address nuanced privacy issues.

Keywords: Privacy, AI Act, General Data Protection Regulation, Black Box AI, Information, Personal Data

No other AI topic has received as much attention and concern as privacy. The use, collection, and protection of personal information that is then used to train machine learning models is the lifeblood of AI. However, the information used for this type of work includes biometric data, browsing histories, geolocation, and other very personal content. The major issues this presents include user content protection, re-identification of anonymous information, and the accessibility of data within the black box structure of AI. The sheer amount of personal data that is collected, stored, and analyzed by AI is tremendous. This is only going to grow as AI becomes more embedded in daily life through personal assistants, such as Siri and Alexa, and recommendation engines, such as Netflix and Amazon. This

DOI: 10.4324/9781003426561-7

ubiquity of AI in society means that the small actions in our lives can leave behind traces of data that are then trained to create even more power and control through AI.

These technological issues of privacy have centered the discussion around a few key topics. One is data ownership and consent. Because AI relies on personal data there are questions about who owns this information and how was consent given to give this data to the platform. Sometimes consent is given unwittingly through terms of service, which data brokerages can then collect and sell to train AI models. As more companies store this personal information, it becomes difficult for people to withdraw their information. This creates real problems for those systems that use machine learning to develop AI. Sometimes anonymous information can be re-identified in the quest to find patterns. It also can infer private information without explicit input, such as that used in predictive analytics. This means that AI, even if carefully developed to keep private information private, can still create content that may identify or infer private details of someone's life.

This type of breach is particularly troubling in highly regulated fields like healthcare, finance, and education. These data breaches are costly, and if the servers for AI are hacked, sensitive information can be leaked, causing a myriad of harms to people and organizations. This information also can be unwittingly leaked during data training. Large language models use sensitive information, such as names, addresses, or personal stories, to encode part of the model's knowledge. This underlying knowledge can be reproduced later in a separate inquiry. For example, suppose a person uses a generative AI platform to draft a personnel review. The user provides sensitive, personal information about the employee undergoing review. Later, another user in a separate company asks for a draft form letter for a personnel review. The AI system could produce the first letter, inclusive of the private information, to the second user. That unintentional resurfacing of data presents a host of privacy issues, not to mention potential proprietary information of the company. This memorization of sensitive data happens because the LLM learns sequences. This becomes more problematic if the platform is trained on small, repetitive tasks in which the model becomes overfitted. Mitigation of these risks includes minimizing the amount of personal data used in AI systems, the utilization of noise to anonymize personal data, training models locally rather than centrally, and verifying how data is going to be used or stored when purchasing proprietary AI models.

Many of these data concerns are rooted in the structure of AI itself. AI is thought of as open or closed source. Open-source AI poses significant threats to privacy because of the accessibility of the publicly available data sets. Sometimes these open-source models can re-identify people in previously anonymized data. Open-source AI permits public access to its codes and algorithms and generally allows transparency. Despite its democratized effect to AI, it also provides for an opening or bad actors to exploit this transparent system. For example, deepfakes, those hyper-realistic AI-generated images and videos, can be developed through open-source AI. While not all deepfakes are the byproduct of open AI, they are the most commonly used deepfake tools. They provide access to generative adversarial network (GAN) frameworks, which are used for creating synthetic images, videos, and audio. Platforms allow users to create this content because of the level of access they provide to pre-trained models. The more diverse the dataset, the more realistic the deepfake content will be. Closed-source AI does not allow for access to source code and operates with stricter privacy protections and content controls. Because deepfake generation requires direct access to model architecture, training parameters, and weights, users in closed-source AI does not receive the same level of attention in the discussion of deepfakes as open sourced AI. Deepfake generation requires the ability to train or customize models which are only accessible if the platform allows access to the model architecture and weights. These closed-source platforms also restrict access to source code and may embed watermarks on AI generated platforms. This does not mean that no synthetic images or audio can be made on closed-source platforms. Part of the reason is the deepfake may be of higher quality and harder to detect.

All of these issues focus on the technology of AI, but laws and regulations are also providing users with recourse for privacy concerns. The leader of AI privacy regulation is the European Union, which already has a robust protection of privacy in the General Data Protection Regulation (GDPR), which pre-dates the explosion of personal AI use.[1] However, in the U.S., there are also privacy laws at the state and federal levels that can address some of the issues within AI. Perhaps the most protective of these laws is the California Consumer Privacy Act (CCPA), a law that mirrors on many of the privacy protections found in the E.U. Of course, new regulations on AI privacy are under consideration.[2] The 2024 the E.U. AI Act provided for greater privacy protections specifically addressing the protections of human data in high-risk AI.[3] Some states in the U.S. have also provided for specific transparency standards for AI tools, such as those in healthcare. At the federal level, the U.S. has no comprehensive AI law, but there is a recognition that privacy should be protected with the widespread use of AI. At the time of this writing, China also has upcoming AI legislation that mirrors many of the protections addressed in the E.U. AI Act.

All of these regulations demonstrate there is a shift in law and regulation to risk-based oversight of AI. However, they also demonstrate the challenges of regulating a highly complex technology. The excesses of AI are feared by society, and lawmakers' concerns for surveillance, discrimination, and control are legitimate. AI may be a position soon where it can not only make predictions but also control individuals' lives. That is a system that lawmakers want to proactively prevent while encouraging technological innovation for the betterment of society. As this chapter will show, that is a very delicate balance.

U.S. Regulations on AI Privacy

Privacy laws in the U.S. are generally a sectoral, market-driven regulations that focus on areas such as consumers, healthcare, lending, and individual control over some personal information. It contrasts sharply with the rest of the world, particularly the European Union, which has a rights-based philosophy that is governed through comprehensive laws, such as the GDPR.[4] Privacy law in the U.S. is heavily segmented with laws such as Health Insurance Portability and Accountability Act (HIPPA) in healthcare or Family Educational Rights and Privacy Act (FERPA) for students in education.[5] Because U.S. law is predicated on a federal system there is also cross-section of state laws that provide a patchwork of protections. The U.S. also tends to be more business friendly in its concept of privacy rights, which makes AI regulation have a distinctly pro-innovation market-driven approach. This means that the regulations on AI, as with other technologies, tend to not be up-front and precautionary. Instead, they can best be described as reactive in which consequences of privacy violations only occur after a triggering event. For those in AI development, this is a much friendlier system, but it also provides for greater barriers to those plaintiffs who have been harmed. The expense of bringing lawsuits means that plaintiffs in the U.S. system may be much more reluctant or unable to bring legitimate claims for privacy violations.

State Regulation of AI Privacy

The fragmented state regulation of AI privacy poses some challenges for companies working in multiple states where legal inconsistencies may exist. Because there is no comprehensive federal AI privacy law, states have been able to create their own regulations. Part of the reason for this is the political gridlock within Washington D.C., and also the ease of passing state laws in legislatures that may have more bipartisan cooperation or dominance of one political party. Within the U.S., the most comprehensive state privacy law is the CCPA, which was passed in 2018 and went into effect in 2020.[6] It has much of the same legal undertones as the E.U.'s

GDPR[7]. There is an emphasis on personal control of data, transparency requirements for businesses, and measures for accountability for those collecting data. There are limits to the law, however. It applies to California residences and requires data transparency. Among the rights it provides, some are as follows:

- The right to know about the personal information a business collects about them and how it is used and shared;
- The right to delete personal information collected from them (with some exceptions);
- The right to opt-out of the sale or sharing of their personal information; and
- The right to non-discrimination for exercising their CCPA right[8]

In 2020 California voters approved Proposition 24, The California Privacy Rights Act of 2020 (CPRA), which amended the CCPA to include two more rights:

- The right to correct inaccurate personal information that a business has about them; and
- The right to limit the use and disclosure of sensitive personal information collected about them.[9]

Within AI the CCPA has particularly close application, even though the law itself does not mention AI or machine learning. Under the CCPA designers of AI would need to disclose how data was being used to train AI models and any privacy issues. Because the CCPA allows for access, delete, and opt-out data rights, there would be direct implications on AI development. This would likely require an anonymized or deidentified data under the law. There would also be legal issues with black box models as the CCPA has provisions that impact privacy. Within California, there are also issues with third-party AI vendors who would have to comply with CCPA requirements particularly in terms of customer explainability and requirements. This also has implications for California AI systems because of the CPRA, which has strict rules concerning privacy rights for California consumers.

The CPRA took effect on January 1, 2023, and it is viewed as a compliment to the CCPA. It has significant implications for AI because it regulates what it calls "sensitive personal information" (SPI), which includes race, ethnicity, health data, sexual orientation, and physical location.[10] Under this law, companies are required to allow consumers to limit the use of their SPI. Similar to the purpose of the E.U. AI Act, the guiding philosophy of the CPRA is protection of human data that can be used for high-risk activity. AI is certainly impacted by this law, especially if the AI platforms are using the data for training datasets. This is governed through the CCPA, which has enforcement power to investigate and sanction those in noncompliance. This means that within the structure of AI platforms, the CPRA would require some mechanism for data deletion and potentially could mandate models be retrained if found in violation of the law.

It is important to note that while this law may create a standard for AI creation, they are California laws and not national. However, California is the 5th largest economy in the world with a GDP of $3.9 trillion in 2023.[11] This results in an outsized extraterritorial effect of its laws, sometimes called the California effect, in which other states comply with these standards in order to do business within the state.[12] So, if a company was truly national in scope, it may comply with California law, which is the most restrictive, in order to have a 50-state presence. Moreover, large tech companies, such as Google Meta, Amazon, and Microsoft, find it easier to comply with stringent standards in order to have the largest business presence. This is why some states, like California, have an outsized impact on their business model and legal compliance (it's also why E.U. standards are often imported into the U.S. by these companies).

California is not the only state with robust privacy laws. Both Virginia and Colorado have protections for privacy and data that include protections on data collection, consent, and deletion rights.[13] Neither of these laws are directly about AI, but like the California laws do have an indirect impact on the technology. Virginia's Consumer Data Protection Act (VCDPA) went into effect in January 2023 and provides consumers rights for their personal data including:

- Confirm if the controller is actually processing their personal data.
- Correct inaccuracies in the consumer's personal data that is collected by the controller.
- Delete personal data provided by or obtained about the consumer.
- Obtain copies of the personal data collected by the controller.
- Opt out of the processing of personal data for purposes of targeted advertising, the sale of personal data, or further profiling.[14]

This has implications for AI because it requires explicit consent before collecting data, and it also can limit how companies can train data. There is also a consumer right to correct data, which can also impact AI system, particularly chatbots used for customer interactions. While the VCDPA does not provide for private lawsuits based on violations, it does provide the Virginia Attorney General with the power to impose fines of up to $7,500 per violation. This may create a major impact on companies and push them to take certain mitigation approaches to development.

Colorado has a similar consumer rights privacy law known as the Colorado Privacy Act (CPA).[15] Similar to California and Virginia, it too provides consumers with specific rights on data control. It also provides enforcement through the Colorado Attorney General and individual District Attorneys. Illinois also has a medical data privacy law, the Biometric Information Privacy Act (BIPA), which protects biometric data and makes companies using this data provide disclosure and a high standard of care. The Illinois law stands out because of its high level of restrictions and its $1,000–$5,000 sanction per violation. AI has been directly impacted by BIPA with related litigation surging in 2023.[16] One notable case, which was settled in June 2024, involved Clearview AI. In that case, Clearview was sued for scraping images from public websites in what constitutes biometric facial geometry. These images came from websites to compare to other content. For example, a face on a security camera of a suspected shoplifter could be compared to an AI database of faces pulled from the internet.[17] The settlement in that case was also unusual in that in the class action plaintiffs received 23% of Clearview AI as a negotiated settlement, which valued at approximately $52 million.[18]

States continue to develop AI laws to protect consumer privacy. The National Council on State Legislatures, a non-partisan association that advances the integrity of state legislatures, has tracked state laws on AI.[19] In the 2024 legislative session, it found that at least 45 states, Puerto Rico, the Virgin Islands, and Washington D.C. introduced laws regulating AI. These laws cover a vast amount of AI issues, and many of them are establishing AI workgroups. However, privacy is a primary concern of many of these states. These laws range in focus. At the time of this writing California has a pending law entitled the Data Digester Registration Act, which would require data digester, i.e., a system that takes raw data and processes it into action, to register with the CPPA.[20] New York has a pending State Privacy Act that would require companies to disclose how they deidentify personal information and safeguard data sharing.[21] Rhode Island has a pending bill entitled Generative Artificial Intelligence Models Regulations that would authorize the state's Attorney General to adopt rules to investigate privacy issues within AI platforms such as ChatGPT.[22] Virginia has a pending/carryover bill for the Joint Commission on Technology and Science that would require it to study the impact of AI particularly focusing on data privacy and misinformation.[23] These state laws foreshadow much of the larger discussion at the federal level. One of the downsides to state regulation is the inconsistent rules for AI platforms. This could create states that are more or less favorable to AI development and could potentially open AI platforms up to litigation for actions that would be legal in some jurisdictions but not in others.

U.S. Federal Laws on AI Privacy

At the federal level AI regulation faces political hurdles. There is a general recognition that privacy rights are important, and that AI poses many risks for user data. Some of these concerns center on consumers while other concerns focus on vulnerable populations such as children. The 2022 Blueprint for an AI Bill of Rights (Blueprint) published by the White House Office of Science and Technology Policy (OSTP) highlighted privacy as a major concern. The Blueprint was aspirational and not law. It outlined core philosophical beliefs that the Biden administration thought should be part of AI regulation. Privacy rights were described this way:

> You should be protected from violations of privacy through design choices that ensure such protections are included by default, including ensuring that data collection conforms to reasonable expectations and that only data strictly necessary for the specific context is collected. Designers, developers, and deployers of automated systems should seek your permission and respect your decisions regarding collection, use, access, transfer, and deletion of your data in appropriate ways and to the greatest extent possible; where not possible, alternative privacy by design safeguards should be used. Systems should not employ user experience and design decisions that obfuscate user choice or burden users with defaults that are privacy invasive.[24]

The Blueprint focused on predictable themes of AI privacy: user control, regulation around high-risk AI use, protection from unwarranted surveillance, and platform accountability. Part of the expectation of the Blueprint was that federal law already has built-in regulations that can extend to AI. For example, within the discussion of Data Privacy the Blueprint points to the Privacy Act of 1974 as providing protection for private information and storage of private information by the government.[25] It also pointed out that the National Institute of Standards and Technology (NIST) already had a structure to address privacy issues and risks. In fact, the NIST has its own AI guidance entitled AI Risk Management Framework, which focused on disclosure and design of AI systems.[26] Other federal and state laws are mentioned as facilitating privacy for individuals. For example, the Blueprint pointed out that the Department of Labor enforces the Labor-Management Reporting and Disclosure Act of 1959, which would have implications for AI surveillance of employees.[27] Moreover, states, such as

New York, have surveillance laws and restrictions for students which include a ban on biometric facial recognition surveillance for minors.[28]

Although the Trump administration has shifted U.S. policy on AI development, the Blueprint reiterated many of the themes that AI regulation and lawmakers will continue to prioritize. It focused on human accountability and control. It also had a focus on personal and civil rights of individuals and called for AI platforms to be accountable in their development and use of AI. It also has real concerns about black box AI development and criticized that approach to AI because of privacy and transparency issues. However, even during the Biden administration, it was aspirational and not enforceable. Many of the terms and approaches were ambiguous and not operationalized for legal compliance. There was also a focus on voluntary, industry self-regulation, which placed a high confidence on industry altruism.

Lawmakers are concerned about privacy and AI and have introduced several bills to try to regulate this important area. For example, in 2024, Senator Cathy McMorris Rodgers (D-WA) introduced the American Privacy Rights Act of 2024, which is modeled on the E.U.'s GDPR.[29] In the U.S. House of Representatives, James Comer (R-KY) and Jamie Raskin (D-MD) introduced the Federal AI Governance and Transparency Act, which focuses on federal transparency within AI systems.[30] As of this writing, Congress continues to investigate and analyze the issues of AI privacy, but with little movement in creating comprehensive legislation. In fact, creating a comprehensive approach to AI privacy may be unlikely because of gridlock, lobbying, and the nature that privacy laws in the U.S. are frequently sector specific.

Within AI, privacy consumer concerns have largely been a focus of the FTC rather than Congress. In 2024, the FTC announced that it was focusing on deception within AI that harmed consumers.[31] These investigations may lead to investigations over consumer data and privacy. Within healthcare, the role of HIPPA plays a major role in the way privacy is discussed within AI. In fact, the healthcare industry has been cautious of AI use because of HIPPA regulations and requirements. Systems that have Protected Health Information (PHI) run the risk of reidentification, which impacts data security and encryption. Systems also have to worry about data re-identification and encryption. These concerns force those in the healthcare industry to have serious conversations with AI developers. Healthcare has the potential to leverage AI, perhaps for the greatest benefit of society. For example, the ability to use AI for diagnostic radiology potentially could result in higher levels of accuracy and patient satisfaction. However, in order to leverage AI to its fullest potential requires massive amounts of patient data. Given the risks of AI and HIPPA noncompliance, privacy concerns continue.[32]

The takeaway of federal AI privacy protection is that true protection requires more that agency oversight or self-regulation. However, the lack of a comprehensive federal law on AI privacy, let alone AI in general, means that there are more questions than answers for users and platforms. The result is an uncertainty of standards, and while agencies and specific laws can regulate this dynamic field there are many areas of AI privacy that will be left unregulated. Biometric data use is largely regulated by states, which leaves many questions open about how AI could be used (or misused) in developing areas such as predictive policing, a type of forecasting of crime by AI. There are also questions about leveraging AI for consumer targeting and marketing. While there are laws about data gathering regulated by the FTC if it is unfair or deceptive, there are no real robust regulations about how this targeting can occur in terms of product recommendations and targeted advertising. This is something that E.U. law within the GDPR expressly addresses. For consumers, this means that they may be the target of AI more than they realize. All of this presents a larger legal and philosophical question, who is AI here to serve? People, businesses, or platforms? Identifying that priority is best done through national legislation, but it is evident that the law in the U.S. may be intentionally lagging behind technological development in order to encourage it.

The European Union's Approach to AI Privacy

The E.U.'s approach to privacy is rooted in human dignity and civil liberties. This is a significant difference from the U.S. which has a balance of privacy rights against values of freedom of speech and market innovation. Unlike the U.S., the E.U. and its member states focus on an individualistic, human-centered approach to privacy rights. That is why there are comprehensive E.U. privacy laws instead of sector-specific privacy protections, such as that found in HIPPA and FERPA in the U.S. U.S. privacy law was strongly influenced by Samuel Warren and Louis Brandeis' landmark 1890 *Harvard Law Review* article "The Right to Privacy," which articulated privacy rights through torts and pointed to the development of technology as a reason why privacy rights had to be protected.[33] In the U.S., technological change has influenced privacy protection and is one of the reasons why it is so sector specific. Contrast that with European history of totalitarianism, specifically the rise of Nazi Germany, which influenced post-World War II lawmakers to craft laws that focused on human dignity and individualized liberties. This is reflected in laws such as the European Convention on Human Rights which acknowledges "private and family life" and later laws like the Data Protection Directive and eventually the GDPR. These laws view privacy in the context with morality, which makes them more robust and less market driven in approach.

The process of lawmaking in the E.U. and U.S. also sets the two bodies apart. U.S. privacy law has evolved through case law, such as *Griswold v. Connecticut* and *Roe v. Wade*, whereas the E.U. has largely regulated privacy through charters and acts that regulate privacy in a more comprehensive way.[34] Moreover, the U.S. Constitution would likely to prevent many of the protections the E.U. provides, such as those found in the GDPR. E.U. limitation on access to information could run afoul of the Constitution's First Amendment. There would be also limitations placed on how the E.U. regulates privacy in the private sector since U.S. constitutional limits focus on state actors. Additionally, federalism in the U.S. would present a challenge to comprehensive privacy laws given that states have their own privacy regulations. Under the Commerce Clause, the U.S. federal government does have the authority to preempt state laws because of consumer protection. However, in the U.S. system, states can impose stricter laws, such as in the case with California's CCPA or CPRA. However, an attempt to standardize all laws in the U.S. like the E.U.'s GDPR or AI Act would have definite constitutional challenges by states. So, for those in the U.S. who look to the E.U. system of privacy regulations as a model, has limits in the U.S. Applying that system of regulation to the U.S. is not exactly legally possible given the legal parameters of the U.S. Constitution and the federal system of lawmaking.

That being said, there are ways that E.U. law does appear extra jurisdictionally, especially within the U.S. through the soft power of the economy. Global business presence often requires companies to comply with the strictest regulations so they can operate without having to compartmentalize services to specific countries. Because of that, there is the rise of the so-called Brussels Effect, which is when E.U. standards become de facto global standards because of the market power of the E.U.[35] Part of this effect is rooted in the E.U.'s requirement that certain standards, particularly privacy, have to be met in order to do business within the E.U. or when dealing with E.U. customers. There is an ongoing evolution of standards for AI, and there is some speculation that the E.U. AI privacy standards could become globalized. However, as the prior paragraph discusses, the way that it becomes a global standard will not be through formalized law. Instead, it will become a global standard because businesses make regulatory decisions based on marketplace access.

While not written with AI necessarily in mind, the GDPR is a significant law that impacts AI. The GDPR went into effect in May 2018 and represents the most comprehensive data privacy law in the world. It protects privacy as a human right and gives individuals certain rights relating to controlling their information. The principles of the GDPR are that personal data is processed in a transparent way for legitimate purposes. Individuals have certain rights to redress and correct information that is inaccurate, and, in some stances, have the right to have correct information removed upon petition, known as the "right of erasure" or "right to be forgotten.[36] Under Chapter 3 of the GDPR individuals have multiple rights including:

- Right to be informed (Articles 12–14): This encompasses how data is being used and collected. It requires transparency and privacy notices.[37]
- Right of Access (Article 15): Sometimes this is called the Data Subject Access Request (DSAR), which allows people to obtain access to their data and receive confirmation from the "controller" of the data to how it is being used.[38]
- Right to Rectification (Article 16): Individuals can correct or update personal data if inaccurate.[39]
- Right to Erasure (Article 17): Individuals have the right to request permanent deletion of personal data when no longer necessary. This is sometimes called the right to be forgotten and is rooted in the concept that the right to know information about a person is conditional upon relevance. This has a longstanding tradition in European law, particularly in France with the concept *le droit à l'oubli*. In the U.S., this right would directly violate the First Amendment freedom of the press as it would prevent the coverage of certain events.[40]
- Right to Restrict Processing (Article 18): In certain circumstances, such as contesting the accuracy of data or when the controller no longer needs it, an individual can request their data no longer be processed for any reason.[41]
- Right to Data Portability (Article 20): This right gives individuals the right to obtain data in a commonly used, machine-readable format upon request.[42]
- Right to Object (Article 21): Individuals can object to their personal data being used in processed for direct marketing or profiling, and when this request is made, the company must stop processing the data unless they can show "compelling legitimate grounds." That "override the interest, rights, and freedoms of the data subject."[43]
- Rights Related to Automated Decision-Making and Profiling (Article 22): Individuals have the right to not be subject to decisions made through automated processing if the decision "significantly affects" them. This article is anticipatory of AI decision-making. It provides a human "intervention" as well so an individual can "express his or her point of view and to contest the decision."[44]

These rights are also governed by clear consent laws by the user. This consent is also revocable under Article 7 of the GDPR. Remedies for violations of these articles are also significant. Individuals can file a complaint for violations under Article 77, and under Article 83, the penalties include "administrative fines up to 20,000,000 EUR, or in the case of an undertaking, up to 4% of the total worldwide annual turnover of the preceding financial year, whichever is higher."[45]

The GDPR's impact on AI is significant, especially in the way that AI can be designed and deployed in the E.U. One of the biggest issues is data access, which is essential for programming AI models. These legal requirements of the GDPR make it more difficult for AI to fully deploy its data in a way that leverages data for its full potential. This is compounded by the explainability and transparency requirements of the GDPR. Black box models of AI cannot be utilized in a way that makes the data and algorithms totally opaque. This means that AI platforms must have more explainable models, which can prove difficult in highly complex, non-linear thinking AI, like ChatGPT. All of this has a practical impact on AI design. Programmers are not just looking to create the most innovative AI platforms; they are also looking to create AI platforms that can pass the requirements of the GDPR. This may result in a weaker form of AI. For example, under the GDPR, designing a chatbot that stores copious amounts of personal data may be more useful but legally non-compliant. Certain dimensions of the GDPR present unique issues for AI that stores data that individuals may want removed under Article 17 or restricted under Article 18. Those rights create technical complexity for AI because deep learning models, such as LLMs or neural networks, look at patterns and develop new understandings over time. Removal of data is not as simple as just deletion because it is embedded in the system. There could be work arounds by creating synthetic data that does not duplicate the original data. There could also be certain attempts to create machine unlearning to forget data over time. Regardless of approach it signifies both the technical difficulty and expense of such regulations and shows that restrictive privacy laws may be an impediment to innovation and marketplace.

The E.U. also has a comprehensive AI Act that went into effect in 2024. The AI Act categorizes artificial intelligence under four risk levels: high risk, limited risk, minimal risk, and unacceptable risk. As the name indicates, unacceptable risk is illegal and represents systems that leverage AI for social scoring or manipulation.[46] High-risk AI has the most stringent regulations. These are systems that are used in high-stakes decision-making like recruitment, law enforcement, or healthcare. In these high-risk AI platforms, there must be a risk management system employed that includes an identification of foreseeable risks, an estimation and evaluation of these risks, and the creation and utilization of risk management measures to redress the risk.[47] These high-risk AI systems must also have human oversight that is proportionate to the risk, and this oversight must occur prior to the AI platform's introduction to the market.[48] The AI Act mandates data governance of these systems that take into consideration design, data collection, data preparation, assumptions of formulation, and mitigation of bias.[49] Transparency is also an issue within high-risk systems and the AI Act's Article 27 stipulates that deployers of high-risk AI must take certain transparency measures including:

a a description of the deployer's processes in which the high-risk AI system will be used in line with its intended purpose;
b a description of the period of time within which, and the frequency with which, each high-risk AI system is intended to be used;
c the categories of natural persons and groups likely to be affected by its use in the specific context;
d the specific risks of harm likely to have an impact on the categories of natural persons or groups of persons identified pursuant to point (c) of this paragraph, taking into account the information given by the provider pursuant to Article 13;
e a description of the implementation of human oversight measures, according to the instructions for use;
f the measures to be taken in the case of the materialization of those risks, including the arrangements for internal governance and complaint mechanisms.[50]

The lower-level risk AI does not have to adhere to these strict standards, but they do have some level of risk assessment and management.

The AI Act works together with the GDPR. For example, Article 5 of the AI Act prohibits the use of AI for manipulation, which intersects with the GDPR's requirements for transparency and disclosure of data use. Of particular concern is biometric data which the AI Act bans using for surveillance unless justified by law enforcement. The GDPR Article 9 also provides for clear consent requirements for use of this type of data. Both laws are concerned with the exploitive use of data without authorization or disclosure. The key difference between the two is the AI Act governs AI developers more explicitly whereas the GDPR provides protections for individuals' privacy. Both serve as safeguards for fundamental human rights and echo the themes of transparency and human control. However, gray areas will emerge under these laws, particularly around how data remains personal or not after it has been processed. Could traces of personal data within largely modified datasets still constitute personal data subject to regulation? Perhaps, but these types of nuanced questions have yet to be answered and will likely be the topic of lawsuits and privacy experts in the coming years.

What the E.U. laws show is that there will need to be a balance of rights and innovation. While the U.S. system favors innovation and the E.U.

favors privacy rights, both approaches signal the larger issue with striking the right balance. For AI to develop in a way that fosters both innovation and protection, there have to be mechanisms in place that provide some level of guidance for developers. Creating a global standard of AI is possible especially given the cross-national appeal of AI and economic pressures. It is conceivable that a standardized AI approach could emerge similar to the global treaties that govern copyright, such as the Berne Convention. However, even with those types of agreements national enforcement is an issue, and given that there is an AI race currently ongoing countries are leveraging their approach to AI to maximize their national competitive advantage. However, national interests make it challenging to create regulatory alignment.

Communicator's Guide to Privacy and AI

Given these different standards of privacy, what is the role of the communicator? Privacy concerns are perhaps the biggest issue for communicators navigating AI use. Many who work in highly regulated industries, such as healthcare, are more reluctant to even use the technology despite its potential for increased user experiences because of fears of non-compliance. In many ways the modern communicator will serve as an AI translator, helping users and others within their organizations to better understand the issues of privacy, transparency, and accountability. Because regulations, such as the AI Act and GDPR, provide for human appeals in decision-making it may be the communicator who finds themselves as the arbiter, or at least the explainer, of these issues. As transparency becomes more operationalized in terms of privacy, there may also be the rise of certain communications around the AI itself. These explanations require plain language discussions and overview of algorithms, data storage, and other complex technical issues. Opaque black box systems also require a fair amount of analysis and explanation to lay users of the technology. This means that communicators may find themselves operating in the nexus between the technical and layperson constituencies providing the essential tools for technological understandability.

AI privacy issues also present unique issues in reputation management. Data breaches are expensive both in terms of real and reputational costs. Privacy issues are rooted in understanding both what AI has and what it does in terms of data. Adverse results of data use, such as reidentification of previously de-identified data, will produce organizational crises. This provides ample opportunities for communicators who will likely find themselves navigating these organizational crises with the media and with those affected. There are already privacy concerns with the growth of big data and storage. Global commerce and the stringent rules of the E.U. mean that these crises of AI can have both consumer and regulatory impacts.

What is notable about U.S. and E.U. attempts to regulate privacy in AI is that much is still unresolved. The E.U.'s comprehensive AI regulations and the GDPR still do not anticipate every issue that can arise. The U.S. has taken a more market-driven approach to regulation that some may think is hands-off and more reliant on industry self-regulation. What both of these systems present are opportunities for industry, and communicators, to set ethical guidelines for AI use and practice. Because organizational reputations are often rooted in how an organization operates when no one is looking, it is perhaps the communicator who can fill this role as AI ethicist. Passive AI adoption and use is rife with problems, ethically, morally, and legally. Communicators are positioned to be the conscious of an organization and help it navigate the privacy issues that will inevitably be part of the day-to-day realities of the 2020s and beyond. Because consumers and users have a heightened awareness of privacy issues with social media, big data, and now AI, it will be incumbent for organizations to set their own standards that not only meet but exceed regulatory requirements regardless of jurisdiction.

What the privacy laws of AI show is that the field of AI regulation is in a state of flux. While foundational principles of privacy are established, the systems governing them are struggling with how to technologically apply those standards. The problem with AI privacy goes beyond the tension between human rights and innovation. Instead, the tension is how to write laws that have an evergreen quality that anticipate the future of a rapidly evolving technology. There seem to be some issues on the horizon that current regulations may not address. The national security aspect of privacy may bring in future development of AI. There may also be issues surrounding the issues of cross-border regulations of the technology. There will also be legal issues that arise that are a mixture of human and machine error. In addition, the way the technology works may be affected with black box AI being particularly criticized for its lack of transparency. Currently, lawmakers struggle with what values to best employ to regulate this industry. Global standards also may be difficult to reach given the traditions and ambitions of countries seeking to lead the world in AI development.

What communications should note is that their role is an essential one for many reasons. They are perhaps in the best position to meet legal standards of transparency. After all, that buzzword has been part of communication practice for decades, and it underscores the core values of communication practice. However, because much of the AI regulations have yet to be written and given the market factors that push back against regulation, it may be up to industry, rather than government, to fashion norms and best practices. The regulatory framework to protect AI privacy will likely constitute a floor of compliance, and reputation of AI platforms and companies that use the technology will be defined by their ethics. As a field that is rooted in ethical compliance and analysis, communicators are in the best position to navigate this space of uncertainty to produce new standards that benefit the industry, technology, and society writ large.

Discussion Questions

1 What are the major privacy concerns of AI? Which is the most important aspect of privacy that should be protected?
2 What system provides the best approach to AI regulation? Should the market or human rights dictate privacy laws? Can lawmakers strike a balance?
3 How workable is a comprehensive privacy law? What are the pitfalls of such an aspirational regulation?
4 What are the issues the E.U. and U.S. have not anticipated that will affect user privacy? Could there be ethical guidance that better addresses this concern?
5 Scenario: Suppose you are working in a global communications firm. The firm has decided to adopt a proprietary AI platform that creates chatbots for customer service questions from an online mail-order clothing business. The chatbots store the data of customers including past purchases, prior interactions with the chatbot, and addresses for shipping products. The user experience is improved with this chatbot service and memory. What are the potential privacy concerns? How do privacy regulations in the U.S. and E.U. differ in handling these types of technologies? Suppose a customer wants their information deleted. Are there any legal problems with that? Any technological problems? How would you advise the client on the pitfalls of such a system?

Notes

1 European Union, General Data Protection Regulation (GDPR), Regulation (EU) 2016/679 of the European Parliament and of the Council of 27 April 2016 on the Protection of Natural Persons with Regard to the Processing of Personal Data and on the Free Movement of Such Data and Repealing Directive 95/46/EC (General Data Protection Regulation, Official Journal of the European Union, L 119 (4 May 2016): 1-88, https://eur-lex.europa.eu/legal-content/EN/TXT/PDF/?uri=CELEX:32016R0679;
2 California Consumer Privacy Act of 2018, Cal. Civ. Code § 1798.100 et seq.
3 European Union, Regulation (EU) 2024/1689 of the European Parliament and of the Council of 13 June 2024 Laying Down Harmonised Rules on Artificial Intelligence and Amending Certain Union Legislative Acts (Artificial Intelligence Act), Official Journal of the European Union, L'2024/1689 (12 July 2024), https://eur-lex.europa.eu/legal-content/EN/TXT/PDF/?uri=OJ:L_202401689

4 Regulation (EU) 2016/679
5 Health Insurance Portability and Accountability Act of 1996, Pub. L. No. 104-191, 42 U.S.C. § 1320d et seq.; Family Educational Rights and Privacy Act of 1974, 20 U.S.C. § 1232g.
6 California Consumer Privacy Act of 2018
7 Regulation (EU) 2016/679
8 California Office of the Attorney General, "California Consumer Privacy Act (CCPA)," accessed December 13, 2024, https://oag.ca.gov/privacy/ccpa.
9 California Office of the Attorney General, "California Consumer Privacy Act (CCPA)."
10 California Consumer Privacy Act of 2018, Cal. Civ. Code § 1798.100 (a)(2).
11 Office of Governor Gavin Newsom, "California's Strong Economic Week," April 19, 2024, accessed December 13, 2024, https://www.gov.ca.gov/2024/04/19/californias-strong-economic-week/.
12 Jens Frankenreiter, "Cost-Based California Effects," *Yale Journal on Regulation* 39 (2022): 1098, accessed December 13, 2024, https://www.yalejreg.com/wp-content/uploads/09.-Frankenreiter-Article.-Final.pdf. There is some question as to the actual impact of the California Effect and the related concept of the E.U. Brussel's effect. In this article, Frankenreiter argues that empirically it seems that most of the companies with E.U. presence actually have a bifurgated E.U./U.S. presence with customers being treated differently. He argues that the same is potentially true for California. However, in the area of AI the California effect may actually be stronger given that so many tech companies are headquartered there, and they operate within the data supply chain.
13 Virginia Consumer Data Protection Act, Va. Code Ann. §§ 59.1-575 to 59.1-584 (2021).
14 Virginia Office of the Attorney General, "Virginia Consumer Data Protection Act Summary," February 2, 2023, accessed December 13, 2024, https://www.oag.state.va.us/consumer-protection/files/tips-and-info/Virginia-Consumer-Data-Protection-Act-Summary-2-2-23.pdf.
15 Colorado Privacy Act, Colo. Rev. Stat. § 6-1-1301 et seq. (2021).
16 "Biometric Battles: Rising AI Employment Litigation Trends," *Bloomberg Law Insights*, accessed December 13, 2024, https://pro.bloomberglaw.com/insights/privacy/biometric-battles-rising-ai-employment-litigation-trends/.
17 In re Clearview AI, Inc. Consumer Privacy Litigation, No. 1:21-cv-00135 (N.D. Ill. filed Jan. 14, 2021).
18 Chris Burt, "Clearview Settles BIPA Lawsuit, Plaintiffs Take 23% of Company," *Biometric Update*, June 2024, https://www.biometricupdate.com/202406/clearview-settles-bipa-lawsuit-plaintiffs-take-23-of-company.
19 National Conference of State Legislatures, "Artificial Intelligence 2024 Legislation," accessed December 13, 2024, https://www.ncsl.org/technology-and-communication/artificial-intelligence-2024-legislation.
20 California Assembly Bill 3204, 2024 Reg. Sess. (Cal. 2024).
21 New York Assembly Bill 3593, 2024 Reg. Sess. (N.Y. 2024).
22 Rhode Island House Bill 6286, 2024 Reg. Sess. (R.I. 2024).
23 Virginia Senate Joint Resolution 14, 2024 Reg. Sess. (Va. 2024).
24 The White House. "Blueprint for an AI Bill of Rights." *The White House*. Accessed December 14, 2024. https://bidenwhitehouse.archives.gov/ostp/ai-bill-of-rights/
25 5 U.S.C. § 552a (2020).
26 National Institute of Standards and Technology (NIST), *AI Risk Management Framework*, January 2023, accessed December 14, 2024, https://nvlpubs.nist.gov/nistpubs/ai/NIST.AI.600-1.pdf.

27 Labor-Management Reporting and Disclosure Act of 1959, Pub. L. No. 86-257, 73 Stat. 519 (1959).
28 New York State Assembly, *Amendment to Education Law*, enacted December 22, 2020, https://nyassembly.gov/leg/?default_fld=&leg_video=&bn=S05140&term=2019&Summary=Y&Text=Y.
29 American Privacy Rights Act of 2024, H.R. 8818, 118th Cong. (2024).
30 Federal AI Governance and Transparency Act, H.R. 7532, 118th Cong. (2024).
31 Federal Trade Commission, "FTC Announces Crackdown on Deceptive AI Claims and Schemes," *Federal Trade Commission*, September 2024, https://www.ftc.gov/news-events/news/press-releases/2024/09/ftc-announces-crackdown-deceptive-ai-claims-schemes.
32 Jacob Hansen et al., "Updating HIPAA Security to Respond to Artificial Intelligence." *Journal of AHIMA*. Accessed December 14, 2024. https://journal.ahima.org/page/updating-hipaa-security-to-respond-to-artificial-intelligence.
33 Samuel Warren and Louis Brandeis, "The Right to Privacy," *Harvard Law Review* 4, no. 5 (1890): 193–220.
34 Griswold v. Connecticut, 381 U.S. 479 (1965); Roe v. Wade, 410 U.S. 113 (1973), overruled by Dobbs v. Jackson Women's Health Organization, 597 U.S. 215 (2022).
35 Anu Bradford, "The Brussels Effect," *Northwestern University Law Review* 107, no. 1 (2012): 1–67; Anu Bradford, *The Brussels Effect: How the European Union Rules the World* (New York: Oxford University Press, 2020).
36 General Data Protection Regulation, art. 5, 2016 O.J. (L 119) 1 (EU).
37 General Data Protection Regulation, art. 12-14, 2016 O.J. (L 119) 1 (EU).
38 General Data Protection Regulation, art. 15, 2016 O.J. (L 119) 1 (EU).
39 General Data Protection Regulation, art. 16, 2016 O.J. (L 119) 1
40 General Data Protection Regulation, art. 17, 2016 O.J. (L 119) 1 (EU). Charles Arthur, "Explaining the Right to be Forgotten--the newest cultural shibboleth" *The Guardian*, May 14, 2014, https://www.theguardian.com/technology/2014/may/14/explainer-right-to-be-forgotten-the-newest-cultural-shibboleth. In France the right is often seen as a barrier to news coverage of French politicians' personal lives, particularly extramarital affairs.
41 General Data Protection Regulation, art. 18, 2016 O.J. (L 119) 1 (EU).
42 General Data Protection Regulation, art. 20, 2016 O.J. (L 119) 1 (EU).
43 General Data Protection Regulation, art. 21, 2016 O.J. (L 119) 1 (EU).
44 General Data Protection Regulation, art. 22, 2016 O.J. (L 119) 1 (EU).
45 General Data Protection Regulation, art. 83, 2016 O.J. (L 119) 1 (EU); General Data Protection Regulation, art. 87, 2016 O.J. (L 119) 1 (EU).
46 Regulation (EU) 2024/1689 of the European Parliament and of the Council of 20 June 2024 on Artificial Intelligence (AI Act), art. 5, 2024 O.J. (L 327) 1.
47 Regulation (EU) 2024/1689 of the European Parliament and of the Council of 20 June 2024 on Artificial Intelligence (AI Act), art. 9, 2024 O.J. (L 327) 1.
48 Regulation (EU) 2024/1689 of the European Parliament and of the Council of 20 June 2024 on Artificial Intelligence (AI Act), art. 14, 2024 O.J. (L 327) 1.
49 Regulation (EU) 2024/1689 of the European Parliament and of the Council of 20 June 2024 on Artificial Intelligence (AI Act), art. 10, 2024 O.J. (L 327) 1.
50 Regulation (EU) 2024/1689 of the European Parliament and of the Council of 20 June 2024 on Artificial Intelligence (AI Act), art. 27, 2024 O.J. (L 327) 1.

8

AI, ETHICS, AND INDUSTRY REGULATION

Can Big Tech Manage Itself?

Chapter Overview

This chapter examines the role of ethics in artificial intelligence (AI) and how ethical guidelines are addressing contemporary issues in the AI field. Specific attention is paid to the use of AI ethics in platform development, and how AI companies have created standards of care and practice within their AI use. The chapter also examines the ethical responsibilities of AI users, and how those users need to consider ethical decision-making in their use of the technology. This decision also examines the difference between trust and tolerance of AI within society, and how AI trust is earned through ethical compliance. The chapter concludes with an examination of the future of AI ethics, particularly the issue of overreliance on AI and the atrophying of human abilities in the wake of this transformative technology.

Keywords: Ethics, Ethics Policies, AI Decision-Making, Transparency, Bias, Trust

Ethics play an important role in artificial intelligence (AI) because it provides assurances that the systems will operate fairly, without bias, transparently, and for public good. As AI becomes more ubiquitous in society, the issues of fairness and the impact of AI technology on the society will become more important as AI becomes used in healthcare, criminal justice, education, employment, and in news. Ethics helps AI become responsible, and it addresses the underlying issues that the law may be too blunt or underdeveloped to address. While the law examines what is legal, ethics addresses what is just. Its role in decision-making, analysis, and predictions helps users and organizations make responsible decisions. Ethics also has the ability to address some of the broader philosophical issues of

DOI: 10.4324/9781003426561-8

technology in society such as algorithmic discrimination, human agency, autonomy of AI, privacy in data, disclosure of AI sources, and moral accountability of AI platforms.

As the previous chapters have shown, the main issues of AI center around human decision-making, fairness, discrimination, accountability, transparency, data protection, and agency. Ethics wrestles with the same issues but from a different perspective. Part of the ethical discussion of AI is centered on how AI can be integrated into human life, and how does it get leveraged to benefit society and not victimize it. There are also a lot of concerns around AI from an ethical standpoint. Communication professionals may question if it is ethical to even use AI as a tool because it seems to undermine the professional skills clients pay for. There is also a high level of distrust in AI by society, which presents questions around whether using AI is ethical without full disclosure to the public. In addition, the concerns about job displacement caused by AI present legitimate and long-term concerns that do not seem to be assuaged by laws or ethical codes.

In countries like the U.S. where laws are balancing market needs of AI development against certain protections for values such as privacy, AI ethics plays a major role. However, there are obvious questions as to how an industry, especially one that is growing exponentially into a multi-billion dollar one, can self-regulate. Can companies that are trying to leverage their own innovation to remain competitive actually regulate themselves in an effective manner? There are challenges, chief of which is there is no universal definition or expectation of what is ethical AI. To some, it may mean transparency, bias controls, and accountability. However, who operationalizes those terms? How does a company balance algorithm transparency with trade secrets? How can a black box AI system be easily explained to the public to promote understanding? The short answer is it can't. However, the more challenging aspect of AI ethics is that this is how most AI systems, particularly those in the U.S., will be regulated in the coming years. Political gridlock, challenges of well-defined regulations, and the fast-paced nature of AI development mean that ethics, not laws, are likely to be the governing structure of AI in the 2020s.

Communicators using AI also have ethical challenges. AI presents many opportunities for crafting well-constructed messages that appeal to the right audience. However, hyper-personalization, which AI does so well, presents ethical issues in data sharing. Mis- and disinformation proliferate through AI hallucinations. Crisis management through AI platforms leverages personal data and potentially presents privacy issues to create better communications. This means that communicators are uniquely positioned to be at the forefront of the AI ethics debate both in terms of being affected by ethical decisions and perhaps having to lead the industry, including those beyond communication, into establishing ethical guideposts.

This chapter examines the contemporary issues of AI ethics by examining the themes of ethical AI use. It discusses the challenges of self-regulation and shows how AI policies can be crafted to anticipate potential ethical challenges. Finally, the chapter concludes by looking at how AI ethics may result in a co-regulation partnership between the government and industry in the quest for creating a comprehensive way to manage this emergent and dynamic technology.

The Emergence of Self-Regulation in the AI Industry

As previous chapters demonstrate government regulations have many challenges. First, there is the challenge of the political process for regulation, and how lawmakers themselves have to catch up to the changing technology of AI. Second, there is the issue of jurisdictional challenges of AI regulation. This is evident in the myriad of state laws that currently exist or are under development, and also in the transnational tensions between the U.S. and E.U. systems of AI governance. Industry-led ethical standards allow for more tailored and targeted control of AI. Because industry ethics are presumably created by AI experts, the quality of norms and ethical regulations would be higher. There is also the residual benefit that industry ethical standards showcase responsible AI development, and in turn build public trust. By creating industry-led standards, there are also the benefits of encouraging innovation without stifling technological growth through legal exposure and litigation.

Key industry ethical guidelines currently exist. Major AI companies such as Google, OpenAI, Microsoft, Meta, and IBM all have AI ethical commitments. Most of these ethical stances say the same thing about responsible AI use. There is a commitment to responsibility, transparency, and human-centric design. There is also the inevitable commitment to social benefit of the technology as seen in Google's AI Principles which reads:

> As we consider potential development and uses of AI technologies, we will take into account a broad range of social and economic factors, and will proceed where we believe that the overall likely benefits substantially exceed the foreseeable risks and downsides.[1]

Meta reiterates a similar theme of responsibility in its five pillars of AI which include: privacy and security, fairness and inclusion, robustness and safety, transparency and control, and accountability and governance.[2] The emphasis on the human dimension of AI is important. Meta points out that users should know how AI is used and controlled in order for them to have confidence in the platform. These companies also commit to risk assessments and fairness testing to ensure ethical compliance and confidence in the systems.

However, ethical self-regulation has pitfalls, many of which are obvious. There is a lack of enforcement, an obvious conflict of interest, inconsistent standards, and limited accountability. Terms like transparency and public good are not operationalized, and even if they are, they may encompass the types of issues that present themselves with self-regulation. Historically self-regulation has not worked, sometimes with terrible results. The 2008 financial crisis was one such example where self-regulation by an industry led to an economic crisis. In fact, the repeal of the Glass-Steagall Act of 1933 that separated commercial banking from investment banking was a contributing factor to the Great Recession and cited as a reason why self-regulation in lieu of legal regulation does not present workable solutions.[3]

However, much of the discussion on industry self-regulation of AI is just talk. Frequently, it uses slogans and commitments that are ill-defined and not constructed to be enforced. Ethical industry standards can work, however, and there is a track record for this type of approach in other sectors. There could be, for example, clear industry soft-law guidelines that set forth a standardized criteria to operate. This could take the form of a certification for AI platforms that want to operate in certain markets. Such a standard would quell some issues of cross-jurisdictional issues on AI regulations, such as those found in the E.U. versus the U.S. This could also take the form of pre-certifications for AI platforms and AI risk assessments and reports that become standardized. There is some legal precedent for that style of reporting under the E.U.'s AI Act. It is also easy to envision an industry-wide AI Board that regulates this area of technology, similar to the voluntary trade associations that regulate the U.S. advertising industry on issues like deceptive practices.

However, there are those that are skeptical of this self-regulatory move, especially in the U.S. Ethics are expensive to enforce and develop, and with the competitive field of AI, it may be the case that the marketplace may impact how companies decide to implement ethics. Review boards and industry regulations also have the issue of independence and concerns over whether there is a conflict of interest between independent board reviewers and their fidelity to their employer. There is also the issue of the technology of AI itself, particularly around black box systems. Those types of AI have a very difficult time providing transparency, and even with the most robust review board and internal controls there is still a barrier to self-governance because the black box design does not allow a full knowledge of how the AI is working. For example, AI decision-making is a major ethical concern for the public. A derogatory decision, say for something like a loan, could prompt human oversight but also ethical inquiries into how that decision was made. Ultimately if the learning model operates as a black box, no one will be able to find that information out making the self-regulatory structure essentially meaningless.

So, the end question is what is self-regulation? Is it a genuine attempt at creating standards, or is it an attempt at window dressing to avoid more exacting laws and policies? If it is the latter then its utility is nonexistent. However, laws are not always the answer either. Sometimes they can be leveraged to keep competition out, as evidenced by regulatory capture theory.[4] There is also the issue of conflicting needs of the ethics within AI. Self-regulation allows for a more nuanced and flexible standard to help innovation thrive. Laws provide brightline rules with consequences that ensure compliance. AI platforms need both to operate effectively within the changing technological environment of the 2020s, yet striking that right balance presents and will continue to be a unique challenge.

Ethical Considerations in AI Use: Trust versus Tolerance

When discussing AI ethics, it is important to understand there are two major areas that are in some respects mutually exclusive. That is there are the ethics of AI platforms and the ethics of AI users. Industry self-regulation focuses on the platforms of AI themselves. The issue is the technology and the accountability of systems that can leverage their innovation to make real-world impact. In their ethical guidelines, IBM begins with a large question of what is AI ethics. It states:

> Examples of AI ethics issues include data responsibility and privacy, fairness, explainability, robustness, transparency, environmental sustainability, inclusion, moral agency, value alignment, accountability, trust, and technology misuse.[5]

IBM goes on to operationalize the core philosophies of their ethics as "respect for persons," which emphasizes individual agency in making important decisions. The company also points to beneficence, which is the obligation of AI companies to take an oath, similar to the Hippocratic Oath of physicians, to "do no harm." IBM also points to the issue of "fairness and equality" in their treatment of AI to five areas that support this mission found in The Belmont Report, which is a benchmark of ethical treatment of humans issued by the National Institute of Standards of Technology, a division within the U.S. Department of Commerce.[6] Published in 1979, the Belmont Report comes from a pre-AI, pre-internet world, but it has core values that have been infused in federal regulation and ethical codes. It was created by the National Commission for the Protection of Human Subject of Biomedical and Behavioral Research, which was a response to the infamous Tuskegee Syphilis Study in the 1940s in which African American men were lied to and denied medical treatment. It laid the foundation for research oversight, including the establishment of Institutional Review Boards (IRBs) in human research. In its Basic Ethical Principles, it states that there is the core principle of respect for persons. That respect includes two subparts. First, people have autonomy to make decisions for themselves. However, if a person has "diminished autonomy" they are "entitled to protection."[7] Another core principle is benefence, which requires people to be respected for their decisions and also "secure in their well-being." This requires "(1) do not harm and (2) maximize possible benefits and minimize possible harms."[8] The third principle is justice, which is imbued with a sense of fairness, and having "what is deserved."[9] This is encapsulated by the report's belief that:

> 1) to each person an equal share, (2) to each person according to individual need, (3) to each person according to individual effort, (4) to each person according to societal contribution, and (5) to each person according to merit.[10]

These principles are buttressed by actions like informed consent, ensuring people understand and comprehend decisions, and have a voluntariness that provides consent.[11]

Within self-regulation of AI, these principles can guide ethical action. That is why a company like IBM cites it as a guidepost for their own behavior. Rooted in it is the sense of accountability and transparency with people, and it attempts to eliminate any aspect of confusion or obfuscation of the truth when dealing with humans about significant choices. This includes concerns about privacy, AI job displacement, responsibility/liability, and bias.[12]

These themes are also reiterated in the stance on AI ethics by the United Nations Educational, Scientific and Cultural Organization (UNESCO). This group is dedicated to promoting peace and security though cooperation in education, science, culture, and communication. UNESCO has been focused on AI ethics, particularly the presence of ethical guardrails for organizations. In 2021, it created the Recommendation on the Ethics of Artificial Intelligence (Recommendation), which is applicable to all 194 member states of UNESCO. The Recommendation encompasses four core values of "human rights and human dignity," "living in peaceful just and interconnected societies," "ensuring diversity and inclusiveness," and "environment and ecosystem flourishing."[13]

Within these principles UNESCO also emphasizes there are rights within AI that should guide use and development. These rights are focused on a human-centric philosophy that is designed to protect individuals. They are: proportionality and do no harm, safety and security, right to privacy and data protection, multi-stakeholder and adaptive governance and collaboration, responsibility and accountability, transparency and explainability, human oversight and determination, sustainability, awareness and literacy, and fairness and nondiscrimination. These ten principles mirror many of the legal issues that lawmakers are trying to address, but their principles place the responsibility on the platform designers. The principles do not operationalize many of these terms. For example, transparency and explainability (T&E) are supposed to be "appropriate to the context" and there is recognition there are "tensions between T&E and other principles such as privacy, safety and security."[14] UNESCO also provides tools for implementation such as Readiness Assessment Methodology (RAM), which is a quantitative and qualitative assessment for AI ecosystems.[15]

While the UNESCO AI standards are a good approach in establishing a global ethical framework because they provide a unified set of standards, they are nonbinding. Their human-centric approach that emphasizes rights and dignities emphasizes universal standards of human agency and equitable outcomes. Yet those standards are not operationalized, and they do not have the particularity that a law does. There is also the potential that small AI businesses may have greater burdens in meeting these standards despite the fact that they may agree with the underlying philosophy.

Standards like the UNESCO AI Ethics Guidelines are an attempt at creating a standardized framework for AI use. It focuses on key surface-level issues such as bias, privacy and equitable access. However, what these guidelines fail to do is confront deeper, structural ethical issues that are part of AI's development and maintenance. For example, the issue of opaque black box technology means that users and developers will almost never fully understand AI decision-making. This structural dimension to AI presents a question about the fragmentary accountability of these systems, and while transparency and accountability are key parts of many ethical guideposts, they still have issues in implementation. Ethical solutions to these aspirations of explainable AI warrant legal regulations. However, even then there is the question can AI ever be ethical if the system itself is never fully understood or transparent to the creators?

There are also the economic pressures that affect ethical compliance. As AI develops, there is a more crowded marketplace for AI, and ethical compliance, while important, is expensive. There is also the issue of pace within ethics. Ethical adoption is slow, and it requires audits and tests to ensure compliance. In a business like AI, or any technologically driven business, speed to the marketplace provides competitive advantages. For example, OpenAI's ChatGPT had issues with hallucinations and misinformation when released, yet was placed on the marketplace anyway. That is how it gained market dominance within the AI field. Explainability within AI is probably one of the most expensive and slowest types of ethical compliance to deploy. Black box models are faster, and, in the current marketplace, more accurate than the alternative.

However, its ethical issues also causes hesitation to adoption by users. That is one of the most complex aspects of AI. Ethics may slow down the technological development, but it may actually speed up adoption of the technology. Adherence to ethical principles has the effect of increasing public acceptance and utilization of AI, which is a net benefit for the technology. However, the human dimension of trust is important when understanding the ethics of AI. Users will likely not trust a machine like they do an individual, no matter how anthropomorphic that machine is. AI trust is manufactured and symbolic as it is correlated to things like corporate credibility and brand reputation. Ethical AI does not create trust so much as it creates technological toleration. This toleration exists on a spectrum from low to high. The more forced the interaction is with AI the likelihood is that it will result in lower toleration. Forced or coerced interaction, such as a hiring screening, typically creates low trust because of the lack of power the user has in that situation. However, medium tolerance occurs where there is predictability and the ability to accept or reject the outcome of AI, such as with an algorithmic recommendation. People tend to "put up" with such realities because they have agency and the potential harm is minimized because it is ultimately up to the user, not the machine, to make a choice. The highest tolerance, or trust if it can rise to that level, is rare. People have to believe in the AI system's integrity and fairness. People at some level have to believe in the superiority of the platform and be willing to give their power over to the technology.

What ethical guidelines do is that they have to be designed to maximize trust as the final outcome. However, those designing ethical guidelines need to acknowledge that trust may never be accomplished and the best they may hope for is human tolerance. An ethical guideline that provides for human agency, including the ability to opt out of the AI system altogether, has the effect of increasing tolerance, i.e., trust of the system. So, when platforms are considering ethical guidelines, the primary focus should be human empowerment rather than technological solutions. That empowerment comes from agency, choice, oversight, transparency, fairness, and accountability. It has to consider what rights people have in relation to the technology. Those ethical guideposts should have the right to challenge decisions, opt outs, user power, rigorous transparency, and user consent that continues over time. This means ethics have to shift its focus from compliance to agency, and with that agency comes empowerment and ultimately trust in the new system. This may mean that those writing AI ethics have to shift focus from fairness and explainability to something akin to forcing the technology to bend toward human will. If users can leverage AI to their own wants and needs, including having the power to refuse it, then trust in AI may be achievable. This means that AI use goes from forced reliance to active participation and from control to collaboration to create an environment of authentic, human-centric use.

AI Ethics: Implementing the Technology

The ethical codes for AI technology and AI users present significant means of self-regulation. As the previous section demonstrates, AI ethics focuses on design, development, and deployment. Codes focus on the companies and developers, engineers, and programmers that create the AI. They are primarily concerned with outcomes and emphasizes fairness, transparency, and preemptive measures to mitigate harm. Ethical codes of use are separate in that they focus on how human beings should utilize the technology (or not). These guidelines focus not just on bad actors but responsible use within the broader context of work. However, it seems that these types of ethical guidelines are not a plentiful or robust. One study of business ethics of AI showed that there was a preoccupation with algorithmic bias, but an absence of guidelines around more nuanced issues such as fairness, accountability, sustainability, and transparency.[16] Other studies have found that ethical guidelines in these areas do not operationalize many terms, including ethics, and suffer from a lack of uniform values.[17]

Despite these policy issues, there are users that are more impacted from AI decision-makers. Within communication, the issue of AI ethics is particularly important because professionals leverage both generative and predictive AI to craft messages. The impact of these messages is significant for society because they are often communicating about high-impact topics such as health, politics, finance, and education. Considering the ethical values of transparency, accountability, and disclosure is essential to effective communication. For decades professional organizations within communications have articulated ethical standards that have an evergreen quality and attempt to be timeless in their values. These include the ethical codes of organizations such as Public Relations Society of America, Arthur Page Society, Society of Professional Journalists, and American Advertising Federation.[18] They have staying power because they approach ethics from broad, historically tested ethical principles. However, AI presents new ethical questions and unique circumstances that may not have a direct answer in current codes, and certainly not within the laws that have sometimes avoided tough AI decisions in favor of market-driven solutions. These types of ethical considerations presented by AI are essential for communicators who are in a unique position to leverage AI to create higher quality and more targeted communication that resonates with publics. Trust in media, marketing, brand messages, journalism, public relations, and advertising are impacted by the tools these sectors use. All of them have the ability to use predictive and generative AI in ways that transform their work, and this utilization requires there to be deliberative decision-making.

Unlike the ethical guidelines of technology that look at the structure of the AI as the major issue, communication AI ethics looks more at the human control. However, there are many questions about the ethics of using AI, and whether AI should be disclosed. Frequently, AI provides professional communication content. Should that creation be disclosed to the public? Is it unethical to not disclose AI as an author of a press release, blog, or news article? Does it even matter? One of the challenges this type of ethical question presents is that AI is becoming embedded in many of the technologies already used, so disclosing AI use in the future may be analogous to disclosing when the internet is used. It is more or less assumed that AI is part of the creation of contemporary content. That expectation is likely to continue going forward as generative AI becomes more sophisticated and commonplace within communication. There is also a complicated issue of whether AI disclosure should be context specific rather than universal. Persuasive content may warrant disclosure because of its impact as opposed to form letters or other non-persuasive communication. There is also the question of when such disclosures should even be given. Is real-time disclosure necessary or even possible? It is easy to imagine a real-time disclosure of AI when a customer interacts with a chatbot, but less workable to other forms of communication that are less instantaneous.[19]

These questions around disclosure have major implications. Disclosure of use of AI to write an intra-office email with instructions is vastly different than creating a deepfake advertisement for a new product. In this sense, disclosure becomes part of a discussion around the spectrum of human impact and personal expectations of transparency. As AI becomes more human like, there is the possibility that AI takes on roles of persuasion, such as brand ambassadors, product spokespersons, and even personal assistants. A synthetic brand representative can blur the line between human and non-human communication, leveraging deepfake technology to influence consumers. Personality replication is another issue that may present opportunities and risks for disclosure. Virtual simulations of deceased celebrities or influencers present issues around content, disclosure, and even identity theft. All of this is important because it uses AI for emotional manipulation and degradation of public trust when those anthropomorphic AI platforms persuade audiences. Also, unlike a celebrity who has an identity that is tied to the products or services they endorse, AI personas have no such reputation. These fake humans can simply be pulled and retooled for future use all while the public can develop trust, confidence, and empathy for them. It is difficult to argue that these types of scenarios do not warrant disclosure.

AI has the ability to curate reality for many of its users, and many ethical and legal questions center around discriminatory outputs. That is focusing on what AI says, but there is less attention paid to what it does not say. Programming AI to not discuss controversial subjects can also constitute an ethical omission. Silence is considered by some as a form of deception. It is also hard to identify because the issue is something that is not present. It requires an understanding of how AI is programmed, and what type of data it is populated with. It may require an audit for what is said and unsaid within the platform, and could even be covered in a terms of service contract with users. However, ethically silence is not synonymous with neutrality and choosing what not to include is a deliberate act that has implications for responsibility. Users are already seeing some disclosures around silence from AI systems that have programmed not to give responses on some types of queries. However, what is important is for those using AI in their own decision-making to understand what is being kept from them as an output, and recognizing again that human agency and decision-making cannot be delegated to AI.

The echo chamber of AI is another ethical issue. The ecosystem of AI technologies can facilitate reiteration of the same information that does not provide a full perspective on an issue. This is not quite disinformation or misinformation, as the information echo chamber is not about being wrong, it is about being unidimensional in perspective. This can lead to framing of certain information to please a user as well because the system prioritizes relevance and predicts the way a user may want to consume information. It is a subtle form of manipulation and can lead to a type of AI-user groupthink that is difficult to identify and overcome. Part of the challenge of this issue with the algorithmic engineered personalization of AI from sources like social media, content feeds, and news aggregation apps. It provides an increasingly narrow range of perspectives that all resonate with the user and are confirmatory to their preferences. Compounding the issue is that this type of system actually will produce a high level of user satisfaction and is likely to induce to use the technology more. The ethical issue for companies and users is what responsibilities do either have to go outside confirmatory belief systems and seek out new information. The downside of not seeking new information is the risk that users are making decisions based on bad information, even disinformation. The other downside of seeking out this "new" information is that it may challenge user beliefs, even offending them. The implications of this are also on a spectrum of impact. For example, the confirmatory content may present only recipes that a user would likely enjoy at the expense of new ideas for meals. On the end of the spectrum of confirmatory bias is that a user makes a high-stakes decision based on biased information that actually leads to their detriment. Consider, a user with high blood pressure who regularly engages in queries on big pharma conspiracy theories may be advised by AI not to get proper treatment for their otherwise treatable, but serious, condition. This presents questions about accountability. Should the AI platform anticipate these types of problems and proactively address them? Should users bear the sole responsibility of the decisions they make on biased, confirmatory information? There is no clear answer.[20]

There is also the question of how to use AI within message creation, especially if data allows for hyper-personalization. Tailored crisis messages can have a greater impact because user demographics, personality profiles, and historical behavior allow for better resonance. However, the lack of these items for certain groups can lead to unequal information access, and information asymmetry where the version of the truth is different and tailored for maximized information resonance. This leads to an issue where AI decides how much "truth" or which version of events an individual may have access to. It could create a type of disinformation that could be characterized as "personalized truth," which is diluted or inaccurate in exchange for message resonance. In crisis communication, this can produce great harm, and even perpetuate the crisis because of the disinformation it provides. Communicators could send bad communication unwittingly because of their overreliance of AI platforms. Because audience segmentation is one of the major benefits of AI that is utilized by the communication industry, there is a temptation to take AI outputs as a type of gospel. For example, AI communication with audiences who are highly educated could produce targeted messaging during a disease outbreak that creates a type of tiered system of truth – one for the scientifically savvy audience and one for the less informed or educated.

These ethical issues are not an issue because communicators are malicious or even uninformed. They exist because of the communication norms of the 2020s. Frequently, communicators are trying to break through noise and find the space to speak to audiences. There is also a maxim within communication to meet people "where they are," which emphasizes the ability to leverage insights of audiences to communicate with them effectively. There is also the sophistication of modern communication that does not utilize a one-size-fits-all approach and instead uses content optimization, audience segmentation, and predictive analysis to produce more effective messages. However, the ethical issue from a user is the tension between personalization and fairness. Equity of access to the truth is something that is essential for society, and AI as a tool can both facilitate and block good communication. This means that those trying to create AI user ethics need to look at the balance between fairness and effectiveness within communication. Is there ever a time where there can be information distributed that is segmented within society? Is there a type of informational inequality that AI facilitates and promotes without the knowledge of the user? How would a user even recognize this in an opaque AI system?

Some organizations have developed their own AI ethics to answer some of these types of questions. Most of them use similar themes of ethical approach including human oversight, agency and control, transparency of platform, fairness, and morality in outcome.[21] These themes embrace a larger ethical concept of power and humanness within this rapidly evolving field of AI. Perhaps the biggest takeaway is that ethical AI acknowledges human priorities and emphasizes human rights, agency, and well-being. The ethical use of AI has to acknowledge the power of the user, rather than the platform, to effectively control the excesses of the technology. The problem, however, is that without a full understanding of the technology many of these ethical guidelines are too surface to fully combat the real problems. Some of those guidelines are written to not fully engage with the challenges of AI because there is a need for perhaps symbolic compliance. There is also the tendency for policy writers to value the evergreen nature of guidelines at the expense of specificity. Good AI ethical guidelines should not try to create aspirational standards, but actionable ones that have accountability for those who are subject to them.

Future Trends in Industry Regulation

Many look to laws to inform themselves on how to act. However, legal compliance and ethical standards are not synonymous, and being legally compliant represents only a baseline for behavior. While laws have an enforceability that ethics frequently do not, they are not a replacement for ethical standards. Ethics also have several advantages over laws in handling unique situations, like the user of AI. Ethics are more context-specific, and have an adaptability that the law does not. Because ethics have the ability to set aspirations, they frequently have a futuristic quality that laws don't. Lawmakers often begin creating new standards from a reactive stance. For example, looking at AI issues in copyright, the U.S. Copyright Office created new standards on originality for AI-generated works. That is inherently reactive. Even the most forward-thinking law is usually only that is the fastest at reacting to a current situation. Ethical policies can address emergent issues, which within AI are even faster paced than most other technologies. Issues such as bias, discrimination, user content, explainability, transparency, human oversight, and access are all issues that ethics are uniquely able to address.[22] This is seen in both industry ethics for users, and ethics by platforms that create AI. However, there are real challenges to putting together comprehensive ethical guidelines.[23]

Constructing ethical guidelines presents challenges. One is that AI is complex and requires certain background knowledge to fully engage with emergent issues. The other is that there is no one group within an organization that has a monopoly on AI issues. Crafting a policy that is comprehensive and workable requires organizations to bring together multiple constituent groups such as communication, IT, management, legal, human resources, and even outside stakeholders to fully understand and address all of the issues and pitfalls that AI can provide. There is some merit in the idea of creating a permanent oversight board for AI ethics and even establishing an AI ethics officer. However, for smaller organizations that may not be practical or necessary. What is important, however, is that organizations prioritize AI ethics, as it will have an outsized impact on business and people in the coming years. There is also the question of what type of investment an organization needs to make to be ethically compliant. Software, reports, and personnel cost money, but an ethical breach is equally, if not more, expensive. Investing in ethics and the safeguards that are needed to create ethical use and outputs in AI is worth the cost.

In the future, there will be new ethical issues that present themselves that are not anticipated by current AI use. One thing that is on the horizon is the concept of AI personhood. The idea is that certain autonomous AI systems will have legal status, akin to a corporation. If AI becomes developed enough to be independent of human intervention new ethical policies will need to be put in place to ensure accountability. There is also the issue of deepfake and synthetic media. While there is a focus on misinformation, there is the larger question of when synthetic AI interactions need to be labeled as such. There is also the question of how anthropomorphic AI becomes capable at creating emotive and affective outputs that influence user behavior. That is already happening in the world of chatbots, but it creates a situation where ethical considerations must be taken into account when these systems can manipulate emotion in human users.[24]

One of the biggest fears of AI is the fact the technology can displace human workers. Inherent in that concern is another societal issue with even worse societal impact. How should users combat the fact that AI can erode critical thinking and facilitate human ability to do work, i.e., deskilling? Ethical considerations are important in answering this question because so much of what contemporary AI ethics focuses on is human oversight. When that oversight is done by humans who have cognitive atrophy because of over-reliance of AI, then what is the real benefit of the human dimension? This is seen already in phenomena like GPS navigation where human ability to read maps or figure out directions has been replaced with technology. AI ethics focuses on how humans need to oversee the technology and protect against it. However, a human who has developed their own cognitive knowledge and works with AI tools may lose their ability to oversee. For example, if public relations practitioners use AI to write press releases, then their ability to craft actual content on their own may be nonexistent because of a cognitive dependency. The same is true for other professions, such as doctors who may over-rely on AI for diagnostic analysis. This creates a bigger problem for society and humankind. It also signals that responsible AI use goes beyond just platform programming or operations. Ethical AI use also requires something of the user to ensure they retain the skills needed to control the technology. There is a risk of humans ceding control over AI ethics and accountability to the AI systems themselves in a type of ethical and moral outsourcing. This means that any ethical guidance also needs to put into place a mechanism for human reskilling and relearning if there is an erosion of cognitive capabilities and skills of AI. This may include training for people to recognize when there is an erosion of skills, and awareness training on blind obedience to AI outputs. This means that ethical guidelines not only have to place expectations on platforms but also take proactive measures to safeguard and promote human agency and abilities. Without those efforts, there is a serious risk that humans become a spectator within the rise of AI, and become subservient to decisions and machines they do not understand or control.

Discussion Questions

1 What is the most important ethical question affecting AI? How should ethical guides address this?
2 Who should write ethical guidance for AI? How would an organization put together the best working group to create an AI ethics policy?
3 Human agency is thought to be the most important aspect of monitoring AI. What does this mean, and how should AI ethics address human agency as the technology becomes more autonomous?
4 What is the biggest emergent issue in AI today, and how should organizations handle it? Do you think AI will change dramatically in the next

10 years enough to have autonomous AI systems? If that happens, then how do ethical policies need to work? Will those policies still be relevant?

5 Scenario: Suppose you are a communicator working on promoting a new healthcare service provider. Your communications use AI to both write content and email it to local residents. The AI is efficient both in writing and very insightful into what is the most effective message given the demographics of the area. Should your communications disclose that you are using AI? Suppose you create a chatbot system to help prospective patients. What are the ethics around those types of systems? Suppose the information gathered from the chatbots help your predictive AI craft messages. What are the ethics of that type of use? What are your obligations of disclosure?

Notes

1 Google, "Our AI Principles," *Google AI*, accessed December 14, 2024, https://ai.google/responsibility/principles/.
2 Meta, "Connect 2024: The responsible approach we're taking to generative AI," *Meta AI*, accessed December 14, 2024, https://ai.meta.com/responsible-ai/.
3 U.S. Congress, Banking Act of 1933 (Glass-Steagall Act), Pub. L. No. 73-66, 48 Stat. 162 (1933); U.S. Congress, Gramm-Leach-Bliley Act of 1999 (Financial Services Modernization Act), Pub. L. No. 106-102, 113 Stat. 1338 (1999).
4 Stigler, George J. "The Theory of Economic Regulation." *The Bell Journal of Economics and Management Science* 2, no. 1 (1971): 3–21.
5 IBM, "AI Ethics," *IBM Topics*, accessed December 14, 2024, https://www.ibm.com/topics/ai-ethics.
6 The National Commission for the Protection of Human Subjects of Biomedical and Behavioral Research, "Ethical Principles and Guidelines for the Protection of Human Subjects of Research" (The Belmont Report), April 18, 1979, https://www.hhs.gov/ohrp/regulations-and-policy/belmont-report/read-the-belmont-report/index.html#:~:text=Three%20basic%20principles%2C%20among%20those,of%20persons%2C%20beneficence%20and%20justice.
7 Ibid.
8 Ibid.
9 Ibid.
10 Ibid.
11 Ibid.
12 IBM, "AI Ethics."
13 UNESCO, "Recommendation on the Ethics of Artificial Intelligence," accessed December 14, 2024, https://www.unesco.org/en/artificial-intelligence/recommendation-ethics.
14 Ibid.
15 Ibid.
16 B. Attard-Frost, A. De los Ríos, and D. R. Walters, "The Ethics of AI Business Practices: A Review of 47 AI Ethics Guidelines," *AI Ethics* 3 (2023): 389–406.
17 A. S. Franzke, "An Exploratory Qualitative Analysis of AI Ethics Guidelines," *Journal of Information, Communication and Ethics in Society* 20, no. 4 (2022): 401–23.

18 *PRSA Code of Ethics*, Public Relations Society of America, accessed December 16, 2024, https://www.prsa.org/about/prsa-code-of-ethics; *AAF Club President Code of Conduct*, American Advertising Federation, accessed December 16, 2024, https://www.aaf.org/common/Uploaded%20files/Club%20Resources/Leadership%20Resources/AAF-Club-President-CodeOfConduct.pdf; *SPJ Code of Ethics*, Society of Professional Journalists, accessed December 16, 2024, https://www.spj.org/spj-code-of-ethics/; *Page Principles*, Page Society, accessed December 16, 2024, https://page.org/who-we-are/page-principles/.

19 Reid Blackman, "A Practical Guide to Building Ethical AI," *Harvard Business Review*, October 15, 2020, https://hbr.org/2020/10/a-practical-guide-to-building-ethical-ai; "Guiding Principles for Ethical and Responsible Artificial Intelligence," *Global Alliance for Public Relations and Communication Management*, accessed December 16, 2024, https://www.globalalliancepr.org/guiding-principles-for-ethical-and-responsible-artificial-intelligence; "Guidelines for the Secure and Ethical Use of Artificial Intelligence," *University of Iowa IT Security Office*, accessed December 16, 2024, https://itsecurity.uiowa.edu/guidelines-secure-and-ethical-use-artificial-intelligence; Public Relations Society of America (PRSA), "Ethical Use of Artificial Intelligence (AI) in Public Relations: Guidelines for Practitioners," accessed December 14, 2024. https://www.prsa.org/docs/default-source/about/ethics/ethicaluseofai.pdf?sfvrsn=5d02139f_2.

20 "Ethical AI: Artificial Intelligence for Social Progress," *Wall Street Journal* (video), accessed December 16, 2024, https://www.wsj.com/video/sponsored/ethical-ai-artificial-intelligence-for-social-progress/2EF75126-4DA7-44B9-AAAD-3197DF97237C. This is a video that is more informative about ethics within AI and human decision-making. It focuses on AI ethics within business in Canada. It focuses on some of the issues of AI ethics within transnational business. It focuses on redlines of ethics that have more risk-based approach ethics.

21 T. Hagendorff, "The Ethics of AI Ethics: An Evaluation of Guidelines," *Minds & Machines* 30 (2020): 99–120.

22 A. Jobin, M. Ienca, and E. Vayena, "The Global Landscape of AI Ethics Guidelines," *Nature Machine Intelligence* 1 (2019): 389–99. This study is dated but shows similar, but not exact, themes mentioned in the main text. This study from 2019 shows that the following themes were globally present in AI ethics: transparency, justice and fairness, non-maleficence, responsibility and privacy.

23 A. Kerr, M. Barry, and J. D. Kelleher, "Expectations of Artificial Intelligence and the Performativity of Ethics: Implications for Communication Governance," *Big Data & Society* 7, no. 1 (2020), https://doi.org/10.1177/2053951720915939.

24 Omar El Bahr, "The Ethics of Communication Between AI and Humans," *Forbes*, May 31, 2023, https://www.forbes.com/councils/forbescommunicationscouncil/2023/05/31/the-ethics-of-communication-between-ai-and-humans/.

9

THE FUTURE OF REGULATION OF AI IN THE 2020s

Chapter Overview

This chapter examines the future of AI policy and laws in the 2020s. Specifically, the chapter discusses the U.S. and E.U. approach to regulatory development, and the issues that such regulations play within geopolitical dominance in the AI race. The chapter goes on to analyze some of the competitive issues that AI laws create in terms of marketplace dominance of AI with a discussion of the U.S.-China AI competition. From this evaluation, the challenges of creating a globalized AI standard are presented along with suggestions for how communicators can create AI ethical guidelines that benefit industry, the public, and the profession.

Keywords: Future of AI, AI Regulations, AI Race, Global AI Standards

The development of AI continues to question longstanding norms and redefine human agency. Against that backdrop of warp-speed development, law and ethics struggle to keep up. Thinking about what the future of AI will be is a difficult task as it seems that society is already existing in a futuristic reality with chatbots, deepfakes, and AI decision-makers. However, the future of AI presents many challenges and opportunities, and lawmakers, corporations, non-profits, users, programmers, and individuals in general will need to better understand the technology to craft the rules that govern the technology. It is incumbent upon all of these constituency groups to note that AI is a tool, not an end unto itself, and that as a tool it needs to serve human values. That is the legacy that will be left to future generations who will no doubt see this technology evolve and grow in power, influence, and capability.

DOI: 10.4324/9781003426561-9

As the technology of AI continues to develop, there are several areas of law and ethics that will be the primary focus: privacy, liability, human oversight, and accuracy. However, as the technology evolves, there will be more nuanced issues that emerge. For example, AI has caused humankind to reexamine accountability as AI systems gain greater autonomy. Legally this could result in legal personhood for AI, but it also redefines the paradigm of blame. Centuries of legal precedent assign fault to a human wrongdoer, even if it's a product that does the wrong. Will AI be a product or service, will it have legal accountability as an agent, and will it have a type of human responsibility that shifts the boundaries of legal and ethical responsibility? That is a question that no doubt will be the subject of lawsuits and ethical discussion in the coming years.

Morality presents other questions about AI. The decision of AI to save a person when analyzing a medical report, or determining which people receive what information during a crisis poses unique existential questions. Whose morality is being promoted by AI? Can moral requirements be codified in law or ethical guidelines? Will the future require things like moral audits for AI systems, and then who determines what is compliant? In the current AI reality, this may seem like there is a simple answer because programmers or auditing teams can check to see what AI is producing. There can be clearly identified human oversight for AI system outputs. However, the questions and solutions become more complex as AI shifts into a more autonomous technology. The cognitive freedom of AI will evolve likely as it gains greater ability to be more personalized and predictive. It may even be able to anticipate human desires before they are articulated. Will this ability to think choose freely be constrained by law? How much ethical oversight can an organization have in an uncontrolled, anthropomorphic AI system? Time will tell.

U.S. Approach to AI Regulation: A Geopolitical Issue

More immediate legal and ethical issues will present themselves in the coming years. As the U.S. and E.U. regulate AI in their own way there is the issue of what will be the overriding AI approach. Part of this is a tension between human rights and market economy. As of this writing, the U.S. is the dominant country for the AI sector containing over 15,000 AI companies.[1,2] AI is also expected to grow from 1.5 billion parameters, values in an AI model that help it learn and make decisions, to over 100 billion in the next five years. That is incredible growth that will make AI more powerful and autonomous. U.S. lawmakers are concerned about the power and growth of AI, but they are also aware of the geopolitical issue of AI regulation. Enter AI politics. President Donald

Trump vowed to make the U.S. an AI superpower with a more deregulated approach.[3] He repealed President Joe Biden's Executive Order on AI because he and the Republican Party see it as a hindrance to AI development. The Republican Party's Platform in 2024 addressed AI regulation as a means to stifling innovation and likens it to cryptocurrency laws. It said:

> We will repeal Joe Biden's dangerous Executive Order that hinders AI Innovation and imposes Radical Leftwing ideas on the development of this technology. In its place, Republicans support AI Development rooted in Free Speech and Human Flourishing.[4]

The U.S. AI Safety Institute (AISI), which was created by the Biden administration in November 2023 and operates through the National Institute of Standards and Technology (NIST), is potentially going to be eliminated. The AISI was tasked with creating safety standards and security testing, but again the Trump administration may eliminate this institute because it is viewed by some as a bulwark against innovation. Its future is not certain, but some Republicans do support the AISI.[5]

All of these questions about U.S. regulation are rooted in the larger geopolitical issue of China's growth as an AI power. There are those who think that U.S. regulations should be kept to a minimum to allow the technology to be primarily a U.S.-centric force within the world. The 2022 CHIPS and Science Act, signed into law by President Biden, plays a role in U.S. AI development. That federal law provides funding for U.S. manufacturing of semiconductors, which are essential in the processing of large amounts of data and running complex algorithms.[6] President Trump's proactive approach to limiting Chinese access to U.S. technology, and his trade stances toward China will likely impact AI development. In 2025, President Trump signed an Executive Order that removed the Biden administration's AI policies stating that those regulations placed the United States at a competitive disadvantage globally in AI development. The order specifically rescinded President Biden's Executive Order 14110, Executive Order on Safe, Secure, and Trustworthy Development and Use of Artificial Intelligence, stating that the Biden order created too much government control over AI development. In the new order, President Trump directed that an AI Action Plan be developed by the White House AI and Crypto Czar and National Security Advisor that would position the U.S. as a global leader in the industry.[7] This approach by the Trump administration is in line with the U.S. position that regulatory oversight can harm competitive positioning of the U.S. in the global marketplace for AI. While there are critics of this approach, it is likely that the administration's position will be the norm in U.S. efforts to regulate AI in the foreseeable future.

There is also a question around how the U.S. may regulate open and closed-source AI models. Open model AI can be downloaded and changed by individuals for any purpose, but those models often are not as developed as closed model AI. In the most basic terms, open-source AI allows users to see and change the technology while closed source cannot. It is the difference between seeing a recipe and adding ingredients versus merely being able to consume the end product. China has been able to use open-sourced AI for its own purposes, and there are questions around whether U.S. regulations should encourage closed-source AI development. Of course, this presents a wide array of transparency and accountability issues, but new regulations could focus around this more technical issue of cross-border access given the risks associated with it.[8]

Of course, these geopolitical issues will be the focus of the President and Congress. The more granular issues of privacy, intellectual property, liability, and fairness will be worked on by federal agencies, state legislatures, and federal and state courts. The evolution of those laws and regulations will take more time as they will likely focus on narrow issues and address them with more specificity. Congressional and presidential regulation of AI will likely focus on those larger issues of national security, which will impact the developer side of AI. The user side of AI, notably intellectual property ownership and liability for outputs, will be developed on a case-by-case basis through lawsuits or by agency regulations that attempt to create guardrails for certain issues. In the coming years, it will also be likely that states create more working groups and AI oversight committees to examine contemporary issues, and it is also likely that AI law will develop more in the context of case law over certain issues like denial of a copyright registration, AI negligence, employment discrimination, and defamation.

There may also be some regulations that address job displacement by AI. The gig economy has already weakened job stability for some workers in specific sectors, like content creation. In the 2023 Hollywood Writer's Strike, one of the main points of contention was the role of AI in script writing and the job displacement it facilitates. The conflict between the Writers Guild of America (WGA) and the Alliance of Motion Picture and Television Producers (AMPTP) highlighted how AI may become a workplace issue and labor rights talking point in the coming years. It amplifies the issues of human ownership and the role AI plays in creative content development. This type of issue will likely continue in contracts, copyright disputes, and labor rights movements.[9]

The future of U.S. AI laws likely will focus on how to curb the dangerous excesses of the technology, while simultaneously encouraging growth. The issue of geopolitical dominance of AI by the U.S. will likely be a driving force behind any federal Congressional or Executive Order attempts at regulating the technology. While states and federal agencies may focus on issues that involve individual issues, particularly personal liability lawsuits, they will not provide the type of wholesale comprehensive laws that regulate AI. It is entirely possible given the Constitutional and political issues within the U.S. that such a law may never exist. Contemporary issues within AI also will cause AI regulations, particularly in the field of intellectual property, to rethink some of their core assumptions about property and creation. AI's transformative power continues to change core assumptions about how laws should work. Society will continue to demand human oversight and accountability for AI, but the doomsayers and naysayers of this technology are probably equally inaccurate as to the future realities of AI. In all likelihood, AI will continue to grow and have greater tolerance and use within society, but leveraging the technology to its full potential and potential displacement of humans remains to be seen.

E.U. and Global Trends in Regulating AI

The future of E.U. law and regulation of AI will likely continue on its path of a human rights-centric approach. Although the AI Act has become a benchmark for legal regulation of AI based on human rights, it still is dated and particularized to a technological reality that is evolving. The Brussel's Effect of E.U. law may normalize some of the transparency and data management laws globally, and even in the U.S., there be the presence of E.U. style rules either through company compliance or progressive state laws, such as those in California. However, the future issues the E.U. is likely to focus on remain in the realm of data privacy, liability, and human oversight of the technology. This will only heighten as AI becomes more autonomous and independent.

While the AI Act provides a basis for AI compliance and is innovative in the way it tiers AI platform risks, it presents some obstacles. First is the enforcement of the regulation of high-risk AI categories, such as biometric surveillance, predictive policing, and diagnostic AI within healthcare. Fines do exist for noncompliance, but the enforcement and monitoring of these systems within 27 E.U. member states will present logistical challenges. As progressive as the E.U. AI Act is it actually was written in an era with older concepts of AI. Generative AI systems, such as ChatGPT, were not fully considered or addressed in the law. So, the more nuanced issues of deepfakes, misinformation, content ownership, and infringement are areas the E.U. will likely focus on in the future. There potentially could be laws around AI labeling and watermarking that become more robust in future E.U. laws. Such systems could become normalized globally as standards as the fear and insidious nature of mis- and disinformation become global concerns.

Closed AI that leverages black box technology also creates problems for transparency and explanation requirements for AI. It also creates problems for assigning liability for actions. For example, suppose a self-driving car powered by AI hits a pedestrian instead of hitting the brakes. A black box AI model would not allow for the programmers or other investigators to fully understand why the system did that. It creates uncertainty and the inability to retool the platforms for better use.[10] This type of concern extends to other areas of AI use where decisions about law, healthcare, finances, and public safety. Not knowing how those systems make decisions creates obvious issues, but laws that mandate transparency can present unworkable solutions.

The E.U. has also struggled with figuring out how to assign liability. The E.U.'s Liability Directive is a start, but it does not anticipate all potential liabilities. Moreover, strict liability imposed on AI companies may provide a regulatory disincentive for them to have an E.U. presence. That may result in a marketplace reaction that is detrimental to the E.U. Privacy also presents a serious issue within regulation with the AI Act and General Data Protection Regulation (GDPR) creating perhaps the most comprehensive approach to AI privacy rights, but also a logistical obstacle at monitoring. Informed consent for users and issues about the modification of personal data for AI outputs will likely present new issues that are unresolved within the E.U. marketplace.

The specter of AI personhood is another issue that will likely affect both E.U. and U.S. systems. It presents logistical issues around accountability and liability in that if AI is the cause of a harm could it become the proverbial "empty chair" in a lawsuit. That means plaintiffs could not recover and presents issues around justice and human compensation for the bad acts of AI. In the future, it is possible that these issues of tiered risk and liability could create new solutions such as licensing or mandatory certification processes for AI platforms.

While the E.U.'s laws have an outsized impact in the global economy, creating a unified system of global governance of AI will prove difficult. National ambitions on AI dominance and the U.S. concerns over Chinese AI abilities would generally disfavor such an approach. It is important to note that while the U.S. and E.U. have a dominant force within AI regulation, there are other attempts to control AI. China, for example, is developing AI policies and some speculate that these may mirror some of the oversight and controls found in the E.U. It was among the first national to generate AI with the creation of the Cyberspace Administration of China's (CAC) Generative AI measures. However, these measures reflect the socialist values of China's government and are focused on political subversion.[11] However, these policies may also be more relaxed in areas, such as copyright.[12] Proposed laws seem to favor innovation over protection in a recognition to the global AI race between China and the U.S.[13] All of this means that the chances of a global AI standard is relatively slim because of the different regulatory approaches and values seen in the E.U., U.S., and China. The issues of national security, ideology, and state control are different in each system. There is also the issue that regulatory control is inversely related to competitive placement. In an era where there is an active AI race, this means that there is a greater fear of losing dominance than of bad actions of AI.

However, there could be some level of soft law agreements on how AI should work. This may come in the form of industry norms, or by the marketplace's own ethical guidelines. Examples like the OECD AI principles, which were adopted by multiple countries, may be a starting point for AI coalescing around some level of standards.[14] In fact, it seems that the general concerns about fairness, accountability, transparency, and human control are universal even though their specific operationalization are different. The developers of AI also bear responsibility for what they are willing to create and how the mechanisms of control are configured. Self-regulation, certification, industry norms, and trade conditions may actually present the most workable and likely global regulation of this transformative technology.

The Role of Future Regulations on Communication Practices

What does the future of AI regulation and ethics mean for communicators? In all likelihood, it means that they will be working in a field with much regulatory uncertainty in the 2020s. That will prove to be both positive and negative. The negative, of course, is that the rules of AI are not going to be solidified enough to have brightline guidance on what to do in certain circumstances. The positive is that communicators have the ability to set their own industry standards and have the opportunity to have a greater voice in the industry regulation of the field. Communicators often work in a field that is heavily impacted by issues like fairness, transparency, disclosure, and intellectual property ownership and control. Because of that, as an industry, communication is well situated to take on some of the novel AI issues that are likely to come about in the 2020s and beyond.

In the coming decade, there will be many issues that communicators will deal with as an industry, but some will rise to the surface faster. The first is AI authorship and the credit and ownership such content production creates. Communication is benefitted by the rapid generative text, images, and audio that generative AI can create. However, there will be restrictions on this use, potentially in the form of acknowledgment. Currently, within the communication field there is no universal requirement for disclosure, and as the technology becomes more embedded in daily operations, this type of disclosure may be unnecessary as it is assumed that AI plays a role in content development. This conflicts with some ethical standards of plagiarism and disclosure of source material, but there is no clear brightline rule of law or ethics that governs this. The end result may be based on societal expectations and technological norms.

Another issue communicators will face is deepfakes. Currently, the field is preoccupied with how deepfake technology helps facilitate a disinformation culture. That concern is warranted, and will likely continue. However, deepfake synthetic media have other purposes than to dupe viewers. They can be part of a communication strategy. For example, suppose a spokesperson uses deepfake technology to produce a message in another language for an audience who only speaks that language. That deepfake use could actually create greater accessibility to content increasing equity. However, there are many ethical issues with that approach. Do the viewers know it is a deepfake? Would the viewers have certain expectations of the organization because the language was used? Is the translation itself accurate? These are questions that warrant an industry discussion and proactive ethical guidance. However, it also demonstrates that the fear of AI can stifle more important, and potentially more relevant, issues.

Predictive AI is potentially more powerful within communication than generative AI. It can help communicators focus their work to specific audiences. It also can help with creating visibility through trend analysis and media monitoring. Predictive AI can also identify bias in terms of social media algorithms and other evaluations. However, communicators may not have a standardized approach to how these tools will be utilized, and those communicators with clients may have to take on the responsibility of educating them about AI systems. This raises issues within the field of privacy as well as targeted communications, which may be the most effective, could leverage private information. There are some regulations that could affect this market segmentation, such as the GDPR in the E.U. and CCPA in California, but again there may be more of an ethical consideration for this type of work. Communicators need to evaluate how data is collected, stored, and leveraged for outputs and have targeted discussions around disclosure of content gathering.

Communicators need to remember there is a human component to their job, and it is not just oversight of AI or communication outputs. Good communication has a human dimension that cannot be replicated by AI's synthetic understanding of emotion. Branding, reputation management, and crisis communication require authenticity that is facilitated through genuineness. As the previous chapters show, human oversight of AI is essential because AI does not bring the lived experience of humankind. It does not understand the nuance of situational understanding. It lacks genuine human emotion. That means that for those who are leveraging AI for their work, there must be an understanding that the technology of AI is not a replacement for but a tool of human beings. The human experience is one that embraces and instinctively knows the moral responsibility and accountability of action. It understands the concept of blame because humans have agency. Dignity as concept is predicated in the idea of human flourishing. Having tools, such as AI, make those high-stakes decisions for people can be a dehumanizing process. It is the reason why there is a difference between tolerating and embracing a new technology. The human dimension of AI is essential for limiting the exploitive nature of the platform. As a society, many have been taught about the biases of humankind, and the superiority of technology is taking these preconceived notions out of a decision. However, as the chapter on bias and discrimination shows, just results can come from biased decisions because human subjectivity is an irreplaceable part of decision-making. Only humans possess dignity and intrinsic worth, and only humans have the capacity for subjective experience, empathy, and deeper meaning. Without human oversight, AI decisions risk becoming reductionist. This is why AI must remain a tool – not a replacement for humankind.

Discussion Questions

1 What is the biggest concern about AI in the 2020s? Can the law or ethics combat this?
2 Why is human dignity so important in the discussion of AI?
3 What are the major geopolitical issues of the AI race in the 2020s? How do law and ethics impact this competition?
4 If you were identifying one overriding issue of AI, what would it be? How could a law address this? How could ethical guidelines direct action to prevent it?
5 Scenario: Suppose you are tasked with writing an ethical guideline for a company that uses generative and predictive AI. The company has a global presence that includes the U.S. and E.U. You want to write a guide that will be updated regularly but doesn't have to be rewritten

frequently. How would you construct this guidance? What issues would need to be revisited regularly? What universal principles would you use to guide your work in this area?

Notes

1 Statista, *Number of Artificial Intelligence (AI) Companies in Major Economies Worldwide in 2023* (2023), accessed December 16, 2024, https://www.statista.com/statistics/1413456/major-economies-ai-companies-worldwide/.
2 Alan Kennedy, "Ranked: Artificial Intelligence Startups, by Country," Visual Capitalist, September 13, 2023, accessed December 16, 2024, https://www.visualcapitalist.com/sp/global-ai-investment/.
3 C-SPAN, *Former President Trump Campaigns in Cedar Rapids, Iowa*, 2024, video, https://www.c-span.org/program/campaign-2024/former-president-trump-campaigns-in-cedar-rapids-iowa/635510.
4 Republican Party, *2024 Republican Party Platform*, The American Presidency Project, 2024, https://www.presidency.ucsb.edu/documents/2024-republican-party-platform.
5 Harry Booth and Tharin Pillay, "*What Donald Trump's Win Means for AI,*" Time, November 8, 2024, https://time.com/7174210/what-donald-trump-win-means-for-ai/.
6 CHIPS and Science Act, Public Law No. 117-167, 42 U.S.C. § 18901 (2022).
7 Executive Order Removing Barriers to American Leadership in Artificial Intelligence, January 23, 2025, https://www.whitehouse.gov/presidential-actions/2025/01/removing-barriers-to-american-leadership-in-artificial-intelligence/; Fact Sheet: President Donald J. Trump Takes Action to Enhance America's AI Leadership, January 23, 2025, https://www.whitehouse.gov/fact-sheets/2025/01/fact-sheet-president-donald-j-trump-takes-action-to-enhance-americas-ai-leadership/.
8 Harry Booth and Tharin Pillay, "What Donald Trump's Win Means for AI."
9 Jake Coyle, "In Hollywood writers' battle against AI, humans win (for now)?" *Associated Press*, September 27, 2023, https://apnews.com/article/hollywood-ai-strike-wga-artificial-intelligence-39ab72582c3a15f77510c9c30a45ffc8.
10 "AI's Mysterious 'Black Box' Problem, Explained," *University of Michigan-Dearborn News*, accessed December 16, 2024, https://umdearborn.edu/news/ais-mysterious-black-box-problem-explained.
11 Beatrice Nolan, "Beijing Appears to Be Demanding that Chinese AI Models Have 'Socialist Values'," *Business Insider,* July 22, 2024, https://www.businessinsider.com/china-government-ai-tech-chatbots-censorship-socialist-values-ccp-2024-7.
12 Zeyni Yang, "Four Things to Know about China's New AI Rules in 2024," *MIT Technology Review*, January 17, 2024, https://www.technologyreview.com/2024/01/17/1086704/china-ai-regulation-changes-2024/.
13 Johanna Costigan, "China's New Draft AI Law Priorities Industry Development, *Forbes*, March 22, 2024, https://www.forbes.com/sites/johannacostigan/2024/03/22/chinas-new-draft-ai-law-prioritizes-industry-development/.
14 Organisation for Economic Co-operation and Development (OECD), "AI Principles," accessed December 16, 2024, https://www.oecd.org/en/topics/sub-issues/ai-principles.html

BIBLIOGRAPHY

5 U.S.C. § 552a (2020).
15 U.S.C. §§ 1691 et seq. (Equal Credit Opportunity Act).
17 U.S.C. § 102(a)(1–8).
17 U.S.C. § 102(b).
17 U.S.C. § 107.
17 U.S.C. § 302.
17 U.S.C. § 507(b).
17 U.S. Code § 106 (1–6).
29 C.F.R. § 1607.16(R).
29 C.F.R. § 1607.4(D).
42 U.S.C. §§ 2000e et seq. (Title VII of the Civil Rights Act of 1964).
42 U.S.C. §§ 3601 et seq. (Fair Housing Act).
"AAF Club President Code of Conduct." *American Advertising Federation*. Accessed December 16, 2024. https://www.aaf.org/common/Uploaded%20files/Club%20Resources/Leadership%20Resources/AAF-Club-President-CodeOfConduct.pdf.
Abrams v. United States, 250 U.S. 616 (1919).
"AI Principles." *Google AI*. Accessed December 14, 2024. https://ai.google/responsibility/principles/.
American Law Institute. *Restatement (Second) of Torts* § 402A (1965).
Andy Warhol Foundation for the Visual Arts, Inc. v. Goldsmith, 598 U.S. 508 (2023).
Arendt, Hannah. *The Origins of Totalitarianism*. New York: Harcourt, Brace, 1951.
Arnstein v. Porter, 154 F.2d 464 (2d Cir. 1946).
Arthur, Charles. "Explaining the Right to be Forgotten—the newest cultrual shibboleth?" *The Guardian*, May 14, 2014. https://www.theguardian.com/technology/2014/may/14/explainer-right-to-be-forgotten-the-newest-cultural-shibboleth.
"Artificial Intelligence (AI) in Elections and Campaigns." *National Conference of State Legislatures*. Accessed November 22, 2024. https://www.ncsl.org/elections-and-campaigns/artificial-intelligence-ai-in-elections-and-campaigns.

Atari, Inc. v. North American Phillips Consumer Electronics Corp., 672 F.2d 607 (7th Cir. 1982).

Attard-Frost, B., A. De los Ríos, and D. R. Walters. "The Ethics of AI Business Practices: A Review of 47 AI Ethics Guidelines." *AI Ethics* 3 (2023): 389–406. https://doi.org/10.1007/s43681-022-00156-6.

Authors Guild v. Google Inc., 804 F.3d 202 (2d Cir. 2015).

Authors Guild v. OpenAI Inc., 23-CV-8292 (SHS) (S.D.N.Y. Apr. 1, 2024).

Bains, Chiraag. "The Legal Doctrine That Will Be Key to Preventing AI Discrimination." *Brookings Institution*. Accessed December 4, 2024. https://www.brookings.edu/articles/the-legal-doctrine-that-will-be-key-to-preventing-ai-discrimination/.

Baltimore Orioles, Inc. v. Major League Baseball Players Ass'n, 805 F.2d 663 (7th Cir. 1986).

Battle v. Microsoft Corporation, 2024 WL 4555687 (D. Md. July 7, 2023).

Bedayn, Jesse. *Class Action Lawsuit on AI-Related Discrimination Reaches Final Settlement*. Associated Press, November 20, 2024. https://apnews.com/article/artificial-intelligence-ai-lawsuit-discrimination-bias-1bc785c24a1b88bd425a-8fa367ab2b23.

Biden, Joseph R., Jr. *Executive Order on the Safe, Secure, and Trustworthy Development and Use of Artificial Intelligence*. October 30, 2023. https://www.federalregister.gov/documents/2023/11/01/2023-24283/safe-secure-and-trustworthy-development-and-use-of-artificial-intelligence

"Biometric Battles: Rising AI Employment Litigation Trends." *Bloomberg Law Insights*. Accessed December 13, 2024. https://pro.bloomberglaw.com/insights/privacy/biometric-battles-rising-ai-employment-litigation-trends/.

Blumenthal v. Drudge, 992 F. Supp. 44 (D.D.C. 1998).

Blyth v. Birmingham Waterworks Co. (1856) 11 Exch. 781, 156 ER 1047.

Booth, Harry, and Tharin Pillay. "What Donald Trump's Win Means for AI." *Time*, November 16, 2024. https://time.com/7174210/what-donald-trump-win-means-for-ai/.

Bond, Shannon. "Fake, Viral Images of an Explosion at the Pentagon Were Probably Created by AI." *NPR*, May 22, 2023. https://www.npr.org/2023/05/22/1177590231/fake-viral-images-of-an-explosion-at-the-pentagon-were-probably-created-by-ai.

Broussard, Meredith. *Artificial Unintelligence: How Computers Misunderstand the World*. Cambridge, MA: MIT Press, 2018.

Buchanan, Bruce G., and Edward H. Shortliffe, eds. *Rule-Based Expert Systems: The MYCIN Experiments of the Stanford Heuristic Programming Project*. Reading, MA: Addison-Wesley, 1984.

California Assembly Bill 3204, 2024 Reg. Sess. (Cal. 2024).

"California Consumer Privacy Act (CCPA)." *California Office of the Attorney General*. Accessed December 13, 2024. https://oag.ca.gov/privacy/ccpa.

California Consumer Privacy Act of 2018, Cal. Civ. Code §§ 1798.100–1798.199 (2020).

California Legislature. *California Consumer Privacy Act (CCPA) of 2018*. Cal. Civ. Code § 1798.100–1798.199.100 (2018). https://oag.ca.gov/privacy/ccpa.

California Legislature. "AB 2655: An Act to Amend Sections Related to Online Platforms and Deceptive Content." September 17, 2024. https://leginfo.legislature.ca.gov/faces/billTextClient.xhtml?bill_id=202320240AB2655.

California Legislature. "AB 2839: An Act to Prohibit Materially Deceptive Media in Political Advertisements." September 17, 2024. https://leginfo.legislature.ca.gov/faces/billNavClient.xhtml?bill_id=202320240AB2839.

California Office of the Attorney General. "California Consumer Privacy Act (CCPA)." Accessed December 13, 2024. https://oag.ca.gov/privacy/ccpa.

Campbell v. Acuff-Rose Music, Inc., 510 U.S. 569 (1994).

Canalas, Katie and Aaron Mok. "China's 'social credit' system ranks citizens and punishes them with throttled internet speeds and flight bans if the Communist Party deems them untrustworthy." *Business Insider*, November 28, 2022. https://www.businessinsider.com/china-social-credit-system-punishments-and-rewards-explained-2018-4.

Cartoon Network LP v. CSC Holdings, Inc., 536 F.3d 121 (2d Cir. 2008).

Cat Zakrzewski, "Federal regulators call AI discrimination a 'new civil rights frontier,'" *Washington Post*, April 25, 2023. https://www.washingtonpost.com/technology/2023/04/25/artificial-intelligence-bias-eeoc/.

Chaplinsky v. New Hampshire, 315 U.S. 568 (1942).

CHIPS and Science Act, Public Law No. 117-167, 42 U.S.C. § 18901 (2022).

"Clearview Settles BIPA Lawsuit, Plaintiffs Take 23% of Company." *Biometric Update*, June 2024. https://www.biometricupdate.com/202406/clearview-settles-bipa-lawsuit-plaintiffs-take-23-of-company.

Colorado General Assembly. *Colorado Artificial Intelligence Act (CAIA)*, Senate Bill 24-205. Enacted May 17, 2024. https://leg.colorado.gov/bills/sb24-205.

Colorado General Assembly. *Senate Bill 24-205: Concerning Consumer Protections for Interactions with Artificial Intelligence*. Enacted May 17, 2024. https://leg.colorado.gov/bills/sb24-205.

Colorado Revised Statutes, Title 6, Article 1: *Colorado Consumer Protection Act*. Available at: https://colorado.public.law/statutes/crs_title_6_article_1.

"Contribution Actions in All 50 States." *Matthiesen, Wickert & Lehrer, S.C.* Last modified March 2013. https://www.mwl-law.com/wp-content/uploads/2013/03/contribution-actions-in-all-50-states.pdf.

"Contributory Negligence." Law.com September 1, 2015. https://dictionary.law.com/Default.aspx?typed=contributory%20negligence&type=1

Costigan, Johanna. "China's New Draft AI Law Prioritizes Industry Development." *Forbes*, March 22, 2024. https://www.forbes.com/sites/johannacostigan/2024/03/22/chinas-new-draft-ai-law-prioritizes-industry-development/.

Council of the European Communities. *Council Directive 85/374/EEC on the Approximation of the Laws, Regulations and Administrative Provisions of the Member States Concerning Liability for Defective Products*, July 25, 1985, *Official Journal of the European Communities* L 210, 29–33. https://eur-lex.europa.eu/legal-content/EN/TXT/?uri=CELEX%3A31985L0374.

Coyle, Jake. In Hollywood writers' battle against AI, humans win (for now) Associated Press, September 25, 2023. https://apnews.com/article/hollywood-ai-strike-wga-artificial-intelligence-39ab72582c3a15f77510c9c30a45ffc8.

Crash Dummy Movie, LLC v. Mattel, Inc., 601 F.3d 1387 (Fed. Cir. 2010).

C-SPAN. *Former President Trump Campaigns in Cedar Rapids, Iowa*, 2024. Video. https://www.c-span.org/program/campaign-2024/former-president-trump-campaigns-in-cedar-rapids-iowa/635510.

Curtis Publishing Co. v. Butts, 388 U.S. 130 (1967).

Cybersecurity and Infrastructure Security Agency. *Consolidated Risk in Focus: Generative AI and Elections*. May 2024. https://www.cisa.gov/sites/default/files/2024-05/Consolidated_Risk_in_Focus_Gen_AI_ElectionsV2_508c.pdf.

Dal Bó, Ernesto. "Regulatory Capture: A Review." *Oxford Review of Economic Policy* 22, no. 2 (2006): 203–225.

Daniel, Lars. "Hurricane Helena Deepfakes Flooding Social Media, Hurt Real People." *Forbes*, October 4, 2024. https://www.forbes.com/sites/larsdaniel/2024/10/04/hurricane-helena-deepfakes-flooding-social-media-hurt-real-people/.

Dastin, Jeffrey. "Insight: Amazon Scraps Secret AI Recruiting Tool That Showed Bias Against Women." *Reuters*, October 10, 2018. https://www.reuters.com/article/world/insight-amazon-scraps-secret-ai-recruiting-tool-that-showed-bias-against-women-idUSKCN1MK0AG/.

Delzer, Erielle. "Bogus Videos from the Hurricanes Are Going Viral. Here's How to Spot Old and Fabricated Footage Online." *CBS News*, October 15, 2024. https://www.cbsnews.com/news/hurricane-viral-video-how-to-spot-old-fabricated-ai-footage/.

Department of Homeland Security. *Artificial Intelligence Roles and Responsibilities Framework in Critical Infrastructure*. November 14, 2024. https://www.dhs.gov/sites/default/files/2024-11/24_1114_dhs_ai-roles-and-responsibilities-framework-508.

Dobbs, Dan B., Paul T. Hayden, and Ellen M. Bublick. *The Law of Torts*. 2nd ed. St. Paul, MN: West Academic Publishing, 2011.

Doe v. MySpace, Inc., 528 F.3d 413 (5th Cir. 2008).

Donoghue v. Stevenson, [1932] AC 562 (HL).

EEOC v. iTutorGroup, Inc., Civil Action No. 1:22-cv-02565 (E.D.N.Y. 2022).

Egbert v. Lippmann, 104 U.S. 333 (1881).

El Bahr, Omar. "The Ethics of Communication Between AI and Humans." *Forbes*, May 31, 2023. https://www.forbes.com/councils/forbescommunicationscouncil/2023/05/31/the-ethics-of-communication-between-ai-and-humans/.

Ellery, Simon. "Fake Photos of Pope Francis in a Puffer Jacket Go Viral, Highlighting the Power and Peril of AI." *CBS News*, March 28, 2023. https://www.cbsnews.com/news/pope-francis-puffer-jacket-fake-photos-deepfake-power-peril-of-ai/.

Etzioni, Amitai. "The Capture Theory of Regulations—Revisited." *Society* 46 (2009): 319–323.

European Commission. "Code of Practice on Disinformation." *Digital Strategy*. Last modified June 2022. https://digital-strategy.ec.europa.eu/en/policies/code-practice-disinformation.

European Commission. *Proposal for a Directive of the European Parliament and of the Council on Adapting Non-Contractual Civil Liability Rules to Artificial Intelligence (AI Liability Directive)*. COM(2022) 496 final, September 28, 2022. Accessed December 10, 2024. https://eur-lex.europa.eu/legal-content/EN/TXT/?uri=CELEX%3A52022PC0496.

European Group on Tort Law. *Principles of European Tort Law*, Art. 4:103, "Duty to Protect Others from Damage." Accessed December 8, 2024. http://www.egtl.org/PETLEnglish.html.

European Parliamentary Research Service. *Briefing: AI Liability Directive—Digital and Product Liability Rules for the AI Era*, EPRS_BRI(2023)739342, June 2023. Accessed December 10, 2024. https://commission.europa.eu/business-economy-euro/doing-business-eu/contract-rules/digital-contracts/liability-rules-artificial-intelligence_en.

European Union. *Charter of Fundamental Rights of the European Union*. 2012/C 326/02. October 26, 2012. https://eur-lex.europa.eu/legal-content/EN/TXT/?uri=CELEX:12012P/TXT.

European Union, Regulation (EU) 2024/1689 of the European Parliament and of the Council of 13 June 2024 Laying Down Harmonised Rules on Artificial Intelligence and Amending Certain Union Legislative Acts (Artificial Intelligence

Act), Official Journal of the European Union, L'2024/1689 (12 July 2024), https://eur-lex.europa.eu/legal-content/EN/TXT/PDF/?uri=OJ:L_202401689

European Union, General Data Protection Regulation (GDPR). Regulation (EU) 2016/679 of the European Parliament and of the Council of 27 April 2016 on the Protection of Natural Persons with Regard to the Processing of Personal Data and on the Free Movement of Such Data and Repealing Directive 95/46/EC (General Data Protection Regulation, Official Journal of the European Union, L 119 (4 May 2016): 1–88. https://eur-lex.europa.eu/legal-content/EN/TXT/PDF/?uri=CELEX:32016R0679.

Executive Order Removing Barriers to American Leadership in Artificial Intelligence. January 23, 2025. https://www.whitehouse.gov/presidential-actions/2025/01/removing-barriers-to-american-leadership-in-artificial-intelligence/.

Fact Sheet: President Donald J. Trump Takes Action to Enhance America's AI Leadership. January 23, 2025. https://www.whitehouse.gov/fact-sheets/2025/01/fact-sheet-president-donald-j-trump-takes-action-to-enhance-americas-ai-leadership/.

Faguy, Ana. "New DeSantis Ad Superimposes Fighter Jets in AI-Altered Video of Speech." *Forbes*, May 25, 2023. https://www.forbes.com/sites/anafaguy/2023/05/25/new-desantis-ad-superimposes-fighter-jets-in-ai-altered-video-of-speech/.

Fair Housing Council of San Fernando Valley v. Roommates.com, LLC, 521 F.3d 1157 (9th Cir. 2008) (en banc).

Federal Communications Commission. *FCC Proposes Disclosure of AI-Generated Content in Political Ads*. October 19, 2023. https://www.fcc.gov/document/fcc-proposes-disclosure-ai-generated-content-political-ads.

Federal Election Commission. *Commission Approves Notification of Disposition of Interpretive Rule on Artificial Intelligence in Campaign Ads*. September 2024. https://www.fec.gov/updates/commission-approves-notification-of-disposition-interpretive-rule-on-artificial-intelligence-in-campaign-ads/.

Federal Emergency Management Agency (FEMA). "Hurricane Rumor Response." *U.S. Department of Homeland Security*. Accessed November 19, 2024. https://www.fema.gov/disaster/recover/rumor/hurricane-rumor-response.

Federal Trade Commission. *Big Data: A Tool for Inclusion or Exclusion? Understanding the Issues*. Washington, DC: Federal Trade Commission, January 2016. https://www.ftc.gov/system/files/documents/reports/big-data-tool-inclusion-or-exclusion-understanding-issues/160106big-data-rpt.pdf.

Federal Trade Commission. "Using Artificial Intelligence and Algorithms." *FTC Business Blog*, April 8, 2020. https://www.ftc.gov/business-guidance/blog/2020/04/using-artificial-intelligence-algorithms.

Federal Trade Commission. "Aiming for Truth, Fairness, and Equity in Your Company's Use of AI." *FTC Business Blog*, April 19, 2021. https://www.ftc.gov/business-guidance/blog/2021/04/aiming-truth-fairness-equity-your-companys-use-ai.

Federal Trade Commission. "Keep Your AI Claims in Check." *FTC Business Blog*, February 27, 2023. https://www.ftc.gov/business-guidance/blog/2023/02/keep-your-ai-claims-check.

Federal Trade Commission. "Luring the Test of AI and Engineering Consumer Trust." *FTC Consumer Alerts*, May 3, 2023. https://www.ftc.gov/consumer-alerts/2023/05/luring-test-ai-and-engineering-consumer-trust.

Federal Trade Commission. *Operation AI Comply: Detecting AI-Infused Frauds and Deceptions*. September 2024. https://consumer.ftc.gov/consumer-alerts/2024/09/operation-ai-comply-detecting-ai-infused-frauds-and-deceptions.

Feist Publications, Inc. v. Rural Telephone Service Co., 499 U.S. 340 (1991).
Finley, Ben. *Deepfake of Principle's Voice Is the Latest Case of AI Being Used for Harassment*. Associated Press. April 30, 2024. https://apnews.com/article/ai-maryland-principal-voice-recording-663d5bc0714a3af221392cc6f1af985e.
Fish, Morris J. "An Eye for an Eye: Proportionality as a Moral Principle of Punishment." *Oxford Journal of Legal Studies* 28, no. 1 (2008): 57–71.
Folke, Carl, Stephen Carpenter, Marten Schetter, Terry Chapin, Johan Rockström. "Resilience Thinking: Integrating Resilience, Adaptability, and Transformability." *Ecology and Society* 15, no. 4 (2010). https://www.jstor.org/stable/26268226.
Forbes Advisor Business Team. "Best AI Tools of 2024." *Forbes*. Accessed November 12, 2024. https://www.forbes.com/advisor/business/ai-tools/.
Force v. Facebook, Inc., 934 F.3d 53 (2d Cir. 2019).
Fourth Estate Public Benefit Corp. v. Wall-Street.com, 586 U.S. 96 (2019).
Frankenreiter, Jens. "Cost-Based California Effects." *Yale Journal on Regulation* 39 (2022): 1098.
Franzke, A. S. "An Exploratory Qualitative Analysis of AI Ethics Guidelines." *Journal of Information, Communication and Ethics in Society* 20, no. 4 (2022): 401–23.
General Data Protection Regulation (GDPR), Regulation (EU) 2016/679 of the European Parliament and of the Council of 27 April 2016 on the Protection of Natural Persons with Regard to the Processing of Personal Data and on the Free Movement of Such Data. *Official Journal of the European Union L* 119 (2016): 1–88.
Gertz v. Robert Welch, Inc., 418 U.S. 323 (1974).
Getty Images (US), Inc. v. Stability AI, Inc., No. 1:23-cv-00135 (D. Del. filed Feb. 3, 2023).
Goldwater v. Ginzburg, 414 F.2d 324 (2d Cir. 1969).
Gonzalez v. Google LLC, 598 U.S. 617 (2023).
Google. *AI Principles: Responsible AI Practices*. Accessed December 10, 2024. https://ai.google/responsibility/principles/.
Governor's Office. "Governor Newsom Signs Bills to Combat Deepfake Election Content." September 17, 2024. https://www.gov.ca.gov/2024/09/17/governor-newsom-signs-bills-to-combat-deepfake-election-content/.
Graham v. John Deere Co., 383 U.S. 1 (1966).
Graver Tank & Mfg. Co. v. Linde Air Prods. Co., 339 U.S. 605 (1950).
Gray, Anthony. "The Historical Development of the Fault Basis of Liability in the Law of Torts." In *The Impact of Law's History: What's Past is Prologue*, edited by Sarah McKibbin, Jeremy Patrick, and Marcus K. Harmes, 105–130. Cham: Palgrave Macmillan, 2022.
Hafiz Gaffar and Saleh Albarashdi. "Copyright Protection for AI-Generated Works: Exploring Originality and Ownership in a Digital Landscape." *Asian Journal of International Law*, 15(1): 23–46 (2025).
Hagendorff, T. "The Ethics of AI Ethics: An Evaluation of Guidelines." *Minds & Machines* 30 (2020): 99–120.
Harper & Row Publishers, Inc. v. Nation Enterprises, 471 U.S. 539 (1985).
Heaven v. Pender, (1883) 11 QBD 503 (CA).
Health Insurance Portability and Accountability Act of 1996, Pub. L. No. 104–191, 42 U.S.C. § 1320d et seq.
Henderson v. Source for Public Data, L.P., 53 F.4th 110 (4th Cir. 2022).
hiQ Labs v. LinkedIn Corp., 31 F.4th 1180 (9th Cir. 2022).
Hustler Magazine, Inc. v. Falwell, 485 U.S. 46 (1988).
IBM. "AI Ethics." *IBM Topics*. Accessed December 14, 2024. https://www.ibm.com/topics/ai-ethics.

IBM. "Deep Learning." *IBM*. Accessed November 14, 2024. https://www.ibm.com/topics/deep-learning.

IBM. "Natural Language Processing (NLP)." *IBM*. Accessed November 14, 2024. https://www.ibm.com/topics/natural-language-processing.

IBM Cloud Education. "What is Artificial Intelligence (AI)?" *IBM*. Accessed November 12, 2024. https://www.ibm.com/cloud/learn/what-is-artificial-intelligence.

Illinois General Assembly. *House Bill 5322: Illinois Commercial Algorithmic Impact Assessments Act*. Accessed December 6, 2024. https://legiscan.com/IL/text/HB5322/id/2921992.

Ingram, David. "Elon Musk's X Boosts Election Conspiracy Theories as AI Trends Accelerate." *NBC News*, October 26, 2024. https://www.nbcnews.com/tech/misinformation/elon-musk-x-boosts-election-conspiracy-theories-ai-trends-twitter-rcna176941.

In re Clearview AI, Inc. Consumer Privacy Litigation, No. 1:21-cv-00135 (N.D. Ill. filed Jan. 14, 2021).

Jobin, A., M. Ienca, and E. Vayena. "The Global Landscape of AI Ethics Guidelines." *Nature Machine Intelligence* 1 (2019): 389–99.

Jones v. Dirty World Entertainment Recordings LLC, 755 F.3d 398 (6th Cir. 2014).

Kelly, Jack. "How Companies Are Hiring and Firing with AI." *Forbes*, November 4, 2023. https://www.forbes.com/sites/jackkelly/2023/11/04/how-companies-are-hiring-and-firing-with-ai/.

Kelly, Jack. "Workers Who Use Artificial Intelligence Are More Likely to Fear That AI May Replace Them." *Forbes*, January 8, 2024. https://www.forbes.com/sites/jackkelly/2024/01/08/workers-who-use-artificial-intelligence-are-more-likely-to-fear-that-ai-may-replace-them/.

Kennedy, Alan. "Ranked: Artificial Intelligence Startups, by Country." Visual Capitalist, May 13, 2023. Accessed December 16, 2024. https://www.visualcapitalist.com/sp/global-ai-investment/.

Kerr, A., M. Barry, and J. D. Kelleher. "Expectations of Artificial Intelligence and the Performativity of Ethics: Implications for Communication Governance." *Big Data & Society* 7, no. 1 (2020). https://journals.sagepub.com/doi/epub/10.1177/2053951720915939.

Kimzey v. Yelp, Inc., 836 F.3d 1263 (9th Cir. 2016).

Kohls v. Bonta, No. 2:24-cv-02527 JAM-CKD, Order Granting Plaintiff's Motion for Preliminary Injunction, 752 F.Supp. 3d 1187 (E.D. Cal., October 2, 2024).

Kuklychev, Yevgeny. "DeSantis War Room Deepfake Attack on Trump Lays Bare AI Threat to Elections." *Newsweek*, June 8, 2023. https://www.newsweek.com/desantis-war-room-deepfake-attack-trump-lays-bare-ai-threat-elections-1805303.

MacPherson v. Buick Motor Co., 217 N.Y. 382, 111 N.E. 1050 (1916).

McCarthy, John, Marvin Minsky, Nathaniel Rochester, and Claude Shannon. *A Proposal for the Dartmouth Summer Research Project on Artificial Intelligence*. Hanover, NH, 1955. http://jmc.stanford.edu/articles/dartmouth/dartmouth.pdf.

McCreary County v. American Civil Liberties Union, 545 U.S. 844 (2005).

McDermott, John. "R1 a Rule Based Configurer of Computer Systems." *Artificial Intelligence* 19, no. 2 (1982): 39–88.

Meta. "Connect 2024: The responsible approach we're taking to generative AI." *Meta AI*. Accessed December 14, 2024. https://ai.meta.com/responsible-ai/.

Microsoft. *Responsible AI Principles*. Accessed December 10, 2024. https://www.microsoft.com/en-us/ai/responsible-ai.

Midway Mfg. Co. v. Arctic Int'l, Inc., 704 F.2d 1009 (7th Cir. 1983).

Milkovich v. Lorain Journal Co., 497 U.S. 1 (1990).
Mill, John Stuart. *On Liberty*. London: John W. Parker and Son, 1859.
Miller, Katherine. "AI's Ostensible Emergent Abilities Are a Mirage." *Stanford Institute for Human-Centered Artificial Intelligence (HAI)*, May 8, 2023. https://hai.stanford.edu/news/ais-ostensible-emergent-abilities-are-mirage.
Milton, John. *Areopagitica: A Speech for the Liberty of Unlicensed Printing*. London, 1644.
Mobley v. Workday, 2024 WL 3409146 (N.D. Cal. July 12, 2024).
Musk, Elon (@elonmusk). "Excited to announce our new project!" *X*, November 22, 2024.
Naruto v. Slater, 888 F.3d 418 (9th Cir. 2018).
National Association of Attorneys General. *54 Attorneys General Call on Congress to Study AI and Its Harmful Effects on Children*. Press Release, September 5, 2023. https://www.naag.org/press-releases/54-attorneys-general-call-on-congress-to-study-ai-and-its-harmful-effects-on-children/.
National Commission for the Protection of Human Subjects of Biomedical and Behavioral Research. "Ethical Principles and Guidelines for the Protection of Human Subjects of Research." *The Belmont Report*. April 18, 1979. https://www.hhs.gov/ohrp/regulations-and-policy/belmont-report/read-the-belmont-report/index.html.
National Conference of State Legislatures. "Artificial Intelligence 2024 Legislation." Last modified September 9, 2024. Accessed November 18, 2024. https://www.ncsl.org/technology-and-communication/artificial-intelligence-2024-legislation.
Newton v. Diamond, 388 F.3d 1189 (9th Cir. 2004).
New York City Council. *Int. No. 1894-A, Local Law 144 of 2021: Automated Employment Decision Tools Bias Audits*. Enacted July 5, 2023.
New York Times Co. v. Sullivan, 376 U.S. 254 (1964).
Nilsson, Nils J. *The Quest for Artificial Intelligence: A History of Ideas and Achievements*. Cambridge: Cambridge University Press, 2009.
Nolan, Beatrice. "Beijing Appears to Be Demanding that Chinese AI Models Have 'Socialist Values'." *Business Insider*, July 22, 2024. https://www.businessinsider.com/china-government-ai-tech-chatbots-censorship-socialist-values-ccp-2024-7.
Obermeyer, Zaid, Brian Powers, Christine Vogeili, and Sendhil Mullainathan. "Dissecting racial bias in an algorithm used to manage the health of populations." *Science* 366, no. 6464 (2019): 1–82.
Office of Governor Gavin Newsom. "California's Strong Economic Week." April 19, 2024. Accessed December 13, 2024. https://www.gov.ca.gov/2024/04/19/californias-strong-economic-week/.
OpenAI. *AI Safety and Responsibility*. Accessed December 10, 2024. https://openai.com/safety/.
Organisation for Economic Co-operation and Development (OECD). "AI Principles." Accessed December 16, 2024. https://www.oecd.org/en/topics/sub-issues/ai-principles.html
Oxford English Dictionary. "Artificial Intelligence." Accessed November 12, 2024. https://www.oed.com/dictionary/artificial-intelligence_n?tab=meaning_and_use#38531565.
Palsgraf v. Long Island Railroad Co., 248 N.Y. 339 (1928).
Petrella v. Metro-Goldwyn-Mayer, Inc., 572 U.S. 663 (2014).
Pew Research Center. "What the Data Says About Americans' Views of Artificial Intelligence." November 21, 2023. https://www.pewresearch.org/short-reads/2023/11/21/what-the-data-says-about-americans-views-of-artificial-intelligence/.

Phillips, Timothy. *This is Why We Can't Have Nice Things: Mapping the Relationship Between Online Trolling and Mainstream Culture*. Cambridge, MA: MIT Press, 2015.

Pranshu Verma, Will Oremus, and Zakrzewski, Cat. "AI didn't sway the election, but it deepened the partisan divide." *Washington Post*, November 9, 2024. https://www.washingtonpost.com/technology/2024/11/09/ai-deepfakes-us-election/.

PRSA Code of Ethics. *Public Relations Society of America*. Accessed December 16, 2024. https://www.prsa.org/about/prsa-code-of-ethics.

Poritz, Isiah. OpenAI Fails to Escape First Defamation Suit from Radio Host. *Bloomberg Law*, November 19, 2024. https://news.bloomberglaw.com/ip-law/openai-fails-to-escape-first-defamation-suit-from-radio-host.

Public Relations Society of America. "The Ethical Use of Artificial Intelligence." Accessed December 1, 2024, https://www.prsa.org/docs/default-source/about/ethics/ethicaluseofai.pdf?sfvrsn=5d02139f_2.

Pulliam-Moore, Charles. "Blade Runner 2049 Studio Sues Elon Musk over Copyright Infringement." *The Verge*, October 21, 2024. https://www.theverge.com/2024/10/21/24276092/alcon-entertainment-blade-runner-2049-tesla-musk-warner-bros-discovery-copyright.

Randall v. Sorrell, 548 U.S. 230 (2006).

Reno v. American Civil Liberties Union, 521 U.S. 844 (1997).

Republican Party. *2024 Republican Party Platform*. The American Presidency Project, 2024. https://www.presidency.ucsb.edu/documents/2024-republican-party-platform.

Roose, Kevin. "Can AI Be Blamed for a Teen's Suicide?" *New York Times*, October 23, 2024. https://www.nytimes.com/2024/10/23/technology/characterai-lawsuit-teen-suicide.html.

Roth v. United States, 354 U.S. 476 (1957).

Rudy, Melissa. "Elon Musk Wants People to Submit Medical Scans to His Grok AI Chatbot." *Fox News*, October 2024. https://www.foxnews.com/health/elon-musk-wants-people-submit-medical-scans-grok-ai-chatbot.

Rumelhart, David E., Geoffrey E. Hinton, and Ronald J. Williams. "Learning Representations by Back-Propagating Errors." *Nature* 323, no. 6088 (1986): 533–6.

Rylands v. Fletcher [1868] UKHL 1, (1868) LR 3 HL 330.

Sawyer, R. Keith. *Explaining Creativity: The Science of Human Innovation*. Oxford: Oxford University Press, 2012.

Sheldon v. Metro-Goldwyn Pictures Corp., 81 F.2d 49 (2d Cir. 1936).

Shepardson, David. "FCC Finalizes $6 Million Fine Over AI-Generated Biden Robocalls." *Reuters*, September 26, 2024. https://www.reuters.com/world/us/fcc-finalizes-6-million-fine-over-ai-generated-biden-robocalls-2024-09-26/.

Sid & Marty Krofft Television Prods., Inc. v. McDonald's Corp., 562 F.2d 1157 (9th Cir. 1977).

Silverman v. CBS Inc., 870 F.2d 40 (2d Cir. 1989).

Sony Corp. of America v. Universal City Studios, Inc., 464 U.S. 417 (1984).

St. Amant v. Thompson, 390 U.S. 727 (1968).

Statista. "Number of Artificial Intelligence (AI) Companies in Major Economies Worldwide in 2023." 2023. Accessed December 16, 2024. https://www.statista.com/statistics/1413456/major-economies-ai-companies-worldwide/.

Statista. "Artificial Intelligence – Worldwide." Accessed November 12, 2024. https://www.statista.com/outlook/tmo/artificial-intelligence/worldwide.

Stern Electronics, Inc. v. Kaufman, 669 F.2d 852 (2d Cir. 1982).

Stigler, George J. "The Theory of Economic Regulation." *The Bell Journal of Economics and Management Science* 2, no. 1 (1971): 3–21.

Swenson, Ali and Will Weissert. *New Hampshire Officials Investigate AI-Generated Robocall Claiming to Be Biden, Meant to Suppress Voter Turnout.* Associated Press, January 22, 2024. https://apnews.com/article/new-hampshire-primary-biden-ai-deepfake-robocall-f3469ceb6dd613079092287994663db5.

Thaler v. Perlmutter, No. 1:22-cv-01564 (D.D.C. Aug. 18, 2023).

The White House. "Blueprint for an AI Bill of Rights." Accessed November 14, 2024. https://www.whitehouse.gov/ostp/ai-bill-of-rights/.

Three Boys Music Corp. v. Bolton, 212 F.3d 477 (9th Cir. 2000).

Triesman, Rachel. "Katy Perry's own mom feel for her Met Gala AI photo. Do you know what to look for?" *NPR*, May 7, 2024. https://www.npr.org/2024/05/07/1249570785/katy-perry-met-gala-deepfake.

Turing, Alan M. "Computing Machinery and Intelligence." *Mind* 59, no. 236 (1950): 433–60.

Twitter, Inc. v. Taamneh, 598 U.S. 471 (2023).

UNESCO. "Recommendation on the Ethics of Artificial Intelligence." Accessed December 14, 2024. https://www.unesco.org/en/artificial-intelligence/recommendation-ethics.

UNESCO. "Recommendation on the Ethics of Artificial Intelligence Monitoring and Evaluation Framework (RAM)." Accessed December 14, 2024. https://www.unesco.org/ethics-ai/en/ram?hub=32618.

United States v. Alvarez, 567 U.S. 709 (2012).

University of Michigan-Dearborn News. "AI's Mysterious 'Black Box' Problem, Explained." Accessed December 16, 2024. https://umdearborn.edu/news/ais-mysterious-black-box-problem-explained.

Urantia Found. v. Kristen Maaherra, 114 F.3d 955 (9th Cir. 1997).

U.S. Code, 20 U.S.C. § 1232g (Family Educational Rights and Privacy Act of 1974).

U.S. Code, 42 U.S.C. § 1320d et seq. (Health Insurance Portability and Accountability Act of 1996).

U.S. Code, 47 U.S.C. § 230, "Protection for Private Blocking and Screening of Offensive Material." Accessed November 21, 2024. https://www.law.cornell.edu/uscode/text/47/230.

U.S. Congress. *Banking Act of 1933 (Glass-Steagall Act)*, Pub. L. No. 73-66, 48 Stat. 162 (1933).

U.S. Congress. *Gramm-Leach-Bliley Act of 1999 (Financial Services Modernization Act)*, Pub. L. No. 106-102, 113 Stat. 1338 (1999).

U.S. Congress. *Protect Elections from Deceptive AI Act*, S. 2770, 118th Cong., 1st sess., introduced September 12, 2023. https://www.congress.gov/bill/118th-congress/senate-bill/2770.

U.S. Congress. *AI Transparency in Elections Act of 2024*, S. 3875, 118th Cong., 2nd sess., introduced March 6, 2024. https://www.congress.gov/bill/118th-congress/senate-bill/3875.

U.S. Congress. *AI Transparency in Elections Act of 2024*, H.R. 8668, 118th Cong., 2nd sess., introduced April 10, 2024. https://www.congress.gov/bill/118th-congress/house-bill/8668.

U.S. Congress. *Candidate Voice Fraud Prohibition Act*, H.R. 4611, 118th Cong., 1st sess., introduced June 12, 2024. https://www.congress.gov/bill/118th-congress/house-bill/4611.

U.S. Congress. *Federal Artificial Intelligence Risk Management Act of 2024*, H.R. 6936, 118th Cong., 2nd sess., introduced February 14, 2024. https://www.congress.gov/bill/118th-congress/house-bill/6936.

U.S. Congress. *Securing Elections from AI Deception Act*, H.R. 8858, 118th Cong., 2nd sess., introduced March 22, 2024. https://www.congress.gov/bill/118th-congress/house-bill/8858.

U.S. Copyright Office. *Registration Decision Regarding Zarya of the Dawn*. February 21, 2023. https://www.copyright.gov/docs/zarya-of-the-dawn.pdf.

U.S. Copyright Office. *Copyright Registration Guidance: Works Containing Material Generated by Artificial Intelligence*. March 16, 2023. https://www.copyright.gov/ai/ai_policy_guidance.pdf.

U.S. Copyright Office. "Copyright Registration Guidance: Works Containing Material Generated by Artificial Intelligence." *Federal Register* 88, no. 51 (2023): 16190–3.

U.S. Copyright Office. *Compendium of U.S. Copyright Office Practices*, 3rd ed. Washington, DC: U.S. Copyright Office, 2021. Accessed November 25, 2024. https://www.copyright.gov/comp3/docs/compendium.pdf.

U.S. Department of Commerce, National Institute of Standards and Technology. *AI Risk Management Framework*. January 2023. Accessed December 14, 2024. https://nvlpubs.nist.gov/nistpubs/ai/NIST.AI.600-1.pdf.

U.S. Department of Justice. "Justice Department Secures Groundbreaking Settlement Agreement with Meta Platforms (Formerly Known as Facebook) to Resolve Allegations of Discriminatory Advertising." June 21, 2022. Accessed December 4, 2024. https://www.justice.gov/opa/pr/justice-department-secures-groundbreaking-settlement-agreement-meta-platforms-formerly-known.

U.S. Equal Employment Opportunity Commission. "EEOC Launches Initiative on Artificial Intelligence and Algorithmic Fairness." Accessed December 4, 2024. https://www.eeoc.gov/newsroom/eeoc-launches-initiative-artificial-intelligence-and-algorithmic-fairness.

U.S. Equal Employment Opportunity Commission. "iTutorGroup to Pay $365,000 to Settle EEOC Discriminatory Hiring Suit." Accessed December 4, 2024. https://www.eeoc.gov/newsroom/itutorgroup-pay-365000-settle-eeoc-discriminatory-hiring-suit.

U.S. Equal Employment Opportunity Commission. *Select Issues in Assessing Adverse Impact: Software, Algorithms, and Artificial Intelligence*. Accessed December 4, 2024. https://www.eeoc.gov/laws/guidance/select-issues-assessing-adverse-impact-software-algorithms-and-artificial.

U.S. House of Representatives. "Artificial Intelligence Task Force Report." December 2024. https://www.speaker.gov/wp-content/uploads/2024/12/AI-Task-Force-Report-FINAL.pdf.

Vadukul, Alex. "Coca-Cola's Holiday Ads Were Created with A.I." *New York Times*, November 20, 2024. https://www.nytimes.com/2024/11/20/style/coca-cola-holiday-ads-ai.html.

Virginia Consumer Data Protection Act, Va. Code Ann. §§ 59.1-575 to 59.1-584 (2021).

Virginia Office of the Attorney General. "Virginia Consumer Data Protection Act Summary." February 2, 2023. Accessed December 13, 2024. https://www.oag.state.va.us/consumer-protection/files/tips-and-info/Virginia-Consumer-Data-Protection-Act-Summary-2-2-23.pdf.

Wall Street Journal. "Ethical AI: Artificial Intelligence for Social Progress." *Wall Street Journal* (video). Accessed December 16, 2024. https://www.wsj.com/video/sponsored/ethical-ai-artificial-intelligence-for-social-progress/2EF75126-4DA7-44B9-AAAD-3197DF97237C.

Warner-Jenkinson Co. v. Hilton Davis Chem. Co., 520 U.S. 17 (1997).

Warren, Elizabeth. "Corporate Capture of the Rulemaking Process." *The Regulatory Review*, June 14, 2016.

Washington Legislature. *Washington Law Against Discrimination (WLAD)*, RCW Title 49, Chapter 49.60. Accessed December 6, 2024. https://apps.leg.wa.gov/RCW/default.aspx?cite=49.60.

Watson v. Fort Worth Bank & Trust, 487 U.S. 977 (1988).

Weizenbaum, Joseph. "ELIZA—A Computer Program for the Study of Natural Language Communication Between Man and Machine." *Communications of the ACM* 9, no. 1 (1966): 36–45.

Wes Davis. "AI generated art cannot be copyrighted, rules a U.S. Federal Judge, The Verge, August 18, 2023, https://www.theverge.com/2023/8/19/23838458/ai-generated-art-no-copyright-district-court.

White House. *Blueprint for an AI Bill of Rights*. Accessed December 14, 2024. https://bidenwhitehouse.archives.gov/ostp/ai-bill-of-rights/.

White House Office of Science and Technology Policy. *Blueprint for an AI Bill of Rights*. Accessed November 29, 2024. https://www.whitehouse.gov/ostp/ai-bill-of-rights/#human.

Williams Electronics, Inc. v. Arctic International, Inc., 685 F.2d 870 (3d Cir. 1982).

Williams v. Gaye, 895 F.3d 1106 (9th Cir. 2018).

Wright, Lucas, Roxana Muenster, Briana Becchione, Tianyao Qu, Pika Cai, Alen Smith, Comm 2350 Student Investigators, Jacob Metcalf, Nathan Matias. "Null Compliance: NYC Local Law 144 and the challenges of algorithm accountability." *Proceedings of the 2023 ACM Conference on Fairness, Accountability, and Transparency (FAccT)*, December 2023. https://dl.acm.org/doi/10.1145/3630106.3658998

Wu, Timothy. *The Attention Merchants: The Epic Scramble to Get Inside Our Heads*. New York: Knopf, 2016.

Yang, Zeyni. "Four Things to Know About China's New AI Rules in 2024." *MIT Technology Review*, January 17, 2024. https://www.technologyreview.com/2024/01/17/1086704/china-ai-regulation-changes-2024/.

Zeran v. America Online, Inc., 129 F.3d 327 (4th Cir. 1997).

INDEX